SAINT JOSEPH
BALTIMORE CATECHISM

THE TRUTHS OF OUR CATHOLIC FAITH
CLEARLY EXPLAINED AND ILLUSTRATED
With Bible Readings, Study Helps
and Mass Prayers

*Includes the very latest Questions and Answers
added by the Episcopal Committee of the
Confraternity of Christian Doctrine*

•

OFFICIAL REVISED EDITION

No. 2

Explained by

REV. BENNET KELLEY, C.P.

CATHOLIC BOOK PUBLISHING CO.
NEW YORK

This Edition of the
BALTIMORE CATECHISM
is dedicated to
SAINT JOSEPH
the Foster Father of
JESUS
the First Teacher of these truths.

— ACKNOWLEDGMENT —

We wish to thank the Religious of the following Congregations who have reviewed advance copies of this new St. Joseph's Catechism and offered many valuable suggestions: Brothers of the Christian Schools, Sisters of Charity, Sisters of Christian Charity, Sisters of the Cross and Passion, Dominican Sisters, Felician Sisters, Sisters of St. Joseph, Sisters of St. Joseph of Newark, Sisters of Mercy, Mission Helpers of the Sacred Heart, Oblate Sisters of Providence, Religious of the Sacred Heart.

(T-242)

NIHIL OBSTAT: Richard Kugelman, C.P., S.T.L., S.S.L.   *Censor Deputatus*

IMPRIMI POTEST: Canisius Hazlett, C.P.   *Provincial*

NIHIL OBSTAT: Eugene F. Richard, M.S.   *Censor Deputatus*

IMPRIMATUR: ✠ Francis Cardinal Spellman   *Archbishop of New York*

PREFACE

This Catechism aims at combining the old with the new. Of the old, it retains the text of the Revised Baltimore Catechism, Number Two. This is still the standard text for the middle and upper grades of grammar school in most dioceses.

But there is much that is new. In addition to the recent Supplement added to the Official Text by the Episcopal Committee, there are abundant explanations given to help the children understand the difficult parts of each lesson. It is usually the practice to have the children memorize the answers in the text, but this is of comparatively little value if the children do not understand well what they are memorizing. The explanatory material has been adapted to the age and general intelligence of children in the upper grades of grammar school.

Pictures have been used profusely throughout to aid the children both in understanding each lesson and in the memory work involved, since pictures always help the memory process.

To give life to the formulas in which the doctrine is expressed, Sacred Scripture has been used extensively, since in the Scriptures we find presented to us by the Holy Spirit the living figure of Our Lord Jesus Christ, who is the Heart and Center of the Catechism, besides being its invisible Author.

To help the children use what they have learned in their relationship with God, constant use has been made of the Sacred Liturgy. The Catholic Faith can be better understood only when it is lived and expressed.

The primary law of Christ, His new law of charity, is the keynote of the whole Catechism.

It is hoped that with the aid of this New St. Joseph Edition of the Baltimore Catechism the teacher will find it easier to present to the children not only the verbal expression of the teachings of our Faith, but the person of Our Lord Jesus Christ Himself, who is "the way, and the truth, and the life" (John 14, 6).

FATHER BENNET, C.P.

CONTENTS

PRAYERS FOR EVERY DAY

PART ONE: The Creed

PART TWO: The Commandments

PART THREE: The Sacraments and Prayer

PRAYERS FOR EVERY DAY

The Sign of the Cross. In the name of the Father, and of the Son, and of the Holy Spirit. Amen.

The Lord's Prayer. Our Father who art in heaven, hallowed be Thy name; Thy kingdom come; Thy will be done on earth as it is in heaven. Give us this day our daily bread; and forgive us our trespasses as we forgive those who trespass against us; and lead us not into temptation, but deliver us from evil. Amen.

The Hail Mary. Hail Mary, full of grace! The Lord is with thee; blessed art thou among women, and blessed is the fruit of thy womb, Jesus. Holy Mary, Mother of God, pray for us sinners, now and at the hour of our death. Amen.

Glory Be to the Father. Glory be to the Father, and to the Son, and to the Holy Spirit. As it was in the beginning, is now, and ever shall be, world without end. Amen.

The Apostles' Creed. I believe in God, the Father Almighty, Creator of heaven and earth; and in Jesus Christ, His only Son, Our Lord; who was conceived by the Holy Spirit, born of the Virgin Mary, suffered under Pontius Pilate, was crucified, died, and was buried. He descended into hell; the third day He arose again from the dead; He ascended into heaven, sitteth at the right hand of God, the Father Almighty; from thence He shall come to judge the living and the dead. I believe in the Holy Spirit, the Holy Catholic Church, the communion of saints, the forgiveness of sins, the resurrection of the body, and life everlasting. Amen.

The Confiteor. I confess to Almighty God, to blessed Mary ever Virgin, to blessed Michael the Archangel, to blessed John the Baptist, to the holy Apostles Peter and Paul, and to all the saints, that I have sinned exceedingly in thought, word and deed, through my fault, through my fault, through my most grievous fault. Therefore, I beseech blessed Mary ever Virgin, blessed Michael the Archangel, blessed John the Baptist, the holy Apostles Peter and Paul, and all the saints, to pray to the Lord our God for me.

May Almighty God have mercy on me, forgive me my sins, and bring me to everlasting life. Amen.

May the Almighty and merciful Lord grant me pardon, absolution, and remission of all my sins. Amen.

An Act of Faith. O my God, i firmly believe that Thou art one God in three Divine Persons, Father, Son, and Holy Spirit; I believe that Thy divine Son became man, and died for our sins, and that He will come to judge the living and the dead. I believe these and all the truths which the Holy Catholic Church teaches, because Thou hast revealed them, who canst neither deceive nor be deceived.

An Act of Hope. O my God, relying on Thy almighty power and infinite mercy and promises, I hope to obtain pardon of my sins, the help of Thy grace, and life everlasting, through the merits of Jesus Christ, my Lord and Redeemer.

An Act of Love. O my God, I love Thee above all things, with my whole heart and soul, because Thou art all-good and worthy of all love. I love my neighbor as myself for the love of Thee. I forgive all who have injured me, and ask pardon of all whom I have injured. (3 years)

An Act of Contrition. O my God, I am heartily sorry for having offended Thee, and I detest all my sins, because of Thy just punishments, but most of all because they offend Thee, my God, who art all-good and deserving of all my love. I firmly resolve, with the help of Thy grace, to sin no more and to avoid the near occasions of sin. (3 years)

Morning Offering. O my God, I offer Thee all my prayers, works, and sufferings, in union with the Sacred Heart of Jesus, for the intentions for which He pleads and offers Himself in the Holy Sacrifice of the Mass, in thanksgiving for Thy favors, in reparation for my offenses, and in humble supplication for my temporal and eternal welfare, for the conversion of sinners, and for the relief of the poor souls in purgatory.

I wish to gain all the indulgences attached to the prayers I shall say and to the good works I shall perform this day.

Another Morning Offering. O Jesus, through the Immaculate Heart of Mary, I offer Thee my prayers, works, joys and sufferings of this day for all the intentions of Thy Sacred Heart, in union with the Holy Sacrifice of the Mass throughout the world, in reparation for my sins, for the intentions of all our Associates, and in particular for all the intentions of this month *(mention intention if known)*.

The Angelus

℣. The angel of the Lord declared unto Mary.

℟. And she conceived of the Holy Ghost.

Hail Mary, full of grace! The Lord is with thee; blessed art thou among women, and blessed is the fruit of thy womb, Jesus. Holy Mary, Mother of God, pray for us sinners, now and at the hour of our death. Amen.

℣. Behold the handmaid of the Lord.

℟. Be it done unto me according to thy word. Hail Mary, etc.

℣. And the Word was made flesh.
℟. And dwelt among us. Hail Mary, etc.
℣. Pray for us, O holy Mother of God.
℟. That we may be made worthy of the promises of Christ.

Let us Pray. Pour forth, we beseech Thee, O Lord, Thy grace into our hearts, that we to whom the Incarnation of Christ, Thy Son, was made known by the message of an angel, may by His passion and cross be brought to the glory of His resurrection, through the same Christ Our Lord. Amen.

Regina Coeli. (*Said during Eastertide instead of the Angelus*)
Queen of heaven, rejoice, Alleluia.
For He whom thou didst deserve to bear, Alleluia.
Hath risen as He said, Alleluia.
Pray for us to God, Alleluia.
℣. Rejoice and be glad, O Virgin Mary! Alleluia.
℟. Because Our Lord is truly risen, Alleluia.

Let us Pray. O God, who by the resurrection of Thy Son, Our Lord Jesus Christ, hast vouchsafed to make glad the whole world, grant, we beseech Thee, that, through the intercession of the Virgin Mary, His Mother, we may attain the joys of eternal life. Through the same Christ Our Lord. Amen.

Hail, Holy Queen. Hail, Holy Queen, Mother of mercy, hail, our life, our sweetness, and our hope! To thee do we cry, poor banished children of Eve! To thee do we send up our sighs, mourning and weeping in this vale of tears! Turn then, most gracious advocate, thine eyes of mercy toward us; and after this, our exile, show unto us the blessed fruit of thy womb, Jesus! O clement, O loving, O sweet Virgin Mary!

The Blessing before Meals. ✠ Bless us, O Lord, and these Thy gifts, which we are about to receive from Thy bounty, through Christ Our Lord. Amen.

Grace after Meals. ✠ We give Thee thanks for all Thy benefits, O Almighty God, who livest and reignest forever. Amen.
    May the souls of the faithful departed, through the mercy of God, rest in peace. Amen.

Ejaculations. My Jesus, mercy. Most Sacred Heart of Jesus, have mercy on us. Mother of mercy pray for us. Jesus, Mary and Joseph, bless us now and at the hour of our death.

PART 1. THE CREED

JESUS SAID:

I SPEAK WHAT I HAVE SEEN WITH THE FATHER.

(ST. JOHN 8:38 1:18)

I HAVE COME A LIGHT INTO THE WORLD THAT WHOEVER BELIEVES IN ME MAY NOT REMAIN IN THE DARKNESS.

(ST. JOHN 12:46)

THE CREED IS WHAT WE BELIEVE:

It is what God teaches us through His Son, Our Lord Jesus Christ, who has come into the world to teach us all truth. We must try to live by all He teaches us through His Church.

LESSON 1 — The Purpose of Man's Existence

A baby studies his fingers and toes to see what they are made of. As he gets a little older, his mind wants to know the answer to three questions about himself: *Who made me? What for? Who will show me how?* This lesson answers those three questions, which are so important that our whole lives depend on the way they are answered.

BOY and GIRL: Who made us?

CHRIST: God made you.

BOY and GIRL: What for?

CHRIST: To know Him, to love Him, and to serve Him in this world, and to be happy with Him forever in heaven.

BOY and GIRL: What does "serve" mean?

CHRIST: To work for someone and try to please him because you love him.

BOY and GIRL: Who will show us how?

CHRIST: I will show You through My Church.

1. Who made us?

God made us.

2. Who is God?

God is the Supreme Being, infinitely perfect, who made all things and keeps them in existence.

3. Why did God make us?

God made us to show forth His goodness and to share with us His everlasting happiness in heaven.

4. What must we do to gain the happiness of heaven?

To gain the happiness of heaven we must know, love, and serve God in this world.

5. From whom do we learn to know, love, and serve God?

We learn to know, love, and serve God from Jesus Christ, the Son of God, who teaches us through the Catholic Church.

Note: For meanings of words in each Lesson, see Dictionary and Index on page **244.**

6. Where do we find the chief truths taught by Jesus Christ through the Catholic Church?

We find the chief truths taught by Jesus Christ through the Catholic Church in the Apostles' Creed.

7. Say the Apostles' Creed.

I believe in God, the Father Almighty, Creator of heaven and earth; and in Jesus Christ, His only Son, Our Lord; who was conceived by the Holy Spirit, born of the Virgin Mary, suffered under Pontius Pilate, was crucified, died, and was buried. He descended into hell; the third day He arose again from the dead; He ascended into heaven, sitteth at the right hand of God, the Father Almighty; from thence He shall come to judge the living and the dead. I believe in the Holy Spirit, the Holy Catholic Church, the communion of saints, the forgiveness of sins, the resurrection of the body, and life everlasting. Amen.

Many false teachers will tell the child that he is made in order to find happiness in wealth, pleasure, fame, or power. In reality, most people act as if they were made for these things rather than to love God. Listening to these false teachers and imitating their actions will only lead to unhappiness and the loss of heaven.

"For wide is the gate and broad is the way that leads to destruction, and many there are who enter that way. How narrow the gate and close the way that leads to life! And few there are who find it" (Matt. 7, 13-14).

DISCUSSION QUESTIONS:

1. Suppose a great astronomer does not know why God made him and a little child does. Which of the two is better off? Why?

2. To get to heaven we have to know, love, and serve God. Which of these three things is most important? Why?

3. Is there anything on earth that we have to do that is more important than loving God?

4. What makes people unhappy?

5. Did God have to make us?

6. If we make something, we own it. God made us. Does He own us?

7. If a girl loves a radio more than her Rosary beads, is she going full speed toward heaven?

8. Suppose a boy spends five hours a day playing ball and only five minutes praying, is he doing all he can to love God?

9. Is it important to try to find out the meaning of the truths in the Apostles' Creed? Why?

10. Can we love God if we do not know Him?

TRUE OR FALSE: *(Also change each false statement to a true one.)*

1. God made the stars.

2. Once God makes things, He forgets about them.

3. God does not care whether we are happy or not.

4. We cannot be perfectly happy here on earth.

5. If we really love God, we will want to serve Him.

6. It does not matter whether or not we serve God, as long as we do not hurt anyone else.

7. In order to love God we have to know everything about Him.

8. Jesus Christ uses others to help Him teach us about God.

9. We do not have to believe everything that Jesus has taught, as long as we believe most of it.

10. The Apostles' Creed does not contain all the teachings of the Church — only the most important ones.

FILL IN THE BLANKS:

1. God is the Supreme . . . ., infinitely perfect, who made all things and keeps them in . . . .

2. God made us to show forth His . . . .

3. To gain the happiness of heaven, we must . . . ., ..., and . . . . God.

4. Jesus Christ teaches us through the . . . .

5. The chief truths taught by the Church are found in the . . . .

READ FROM THE BIBLE:

The purpose of Life — Ps. 48; Matt. 6, 19-33; 20, 25-28; 22, 36-40; John 17, 3; Phil. 3, 17-22: 1 John 2, 15-17.

Christ, our Teacher — John 1, 1-18; 7, 16-30; 8, 12-20.

Christ teaches through the Church — Luke 10, 16; Acts 5, 12-42.

(Note: At the end of each lesson, readings will be suggested from the Bible. These are not .given to "prove" the teachings of the catechism. We "prove" things from the teaching of the Church. See Q. 23F. The Bible was given by God to the Church to help in the explanation of its teachings. Reading the passages suggested will give a deeper insight into the meaning of each lesson. Be sure to read the passages quoted in the body of each lesson also.)

CLASS PROJECT:

Each of the following items can help us to get to heaven. Some of them are nearly always a help but others are often a hindrance since we like them so much we often use them to please ourselves at a time when something else would please God more.

Prayer book, TV set, clothes, Rosary, baseball glove, ice skates, Communion, miraculous medal, electric train, scapular, dog, statue of St. Joseph, Sacred Heart badge, party, money, holy water, bathing suit, gun, holy picture, amusement park, jewelry, crucifix, Bible, camera, church, ice cream.

Make two columns and put each item in its proper column. It would be well to have a project book in which to keep all class projects.

I. Things that are usually a help to get to heaven.	II. Things that are often a hindrance.
. . . .	. . . .
. . . .	. . . .
. . . .	. . . .
. . . .	. . . .
. . . .	. . . .
. . . .	. . . .

Now see if you can add at least five items to each list.

PRAYER:

O God, You have prepared invisible good for those who love You. Pour Your love into our hearts that, loving You in all things and above all things, we may receive Your promises which surpass every desire. Through Christ Our Lord. Amen.

(Missal: Collect for Fifth Sunday after Pentecost)

LESSON 2 — God and His Perfections

"I believe in God, the Father Almighty, Creator of heaven and earth . . ."

A. WHAT IS GOD?

8. What do we mean when we say that God is the Supreme Being?

When we say that God is the Supreme Being we mean that He is above all creatures, the self-existing and infinitely perfect Spirit.

Supreme means "highest." *Self-existing* is explained in Question 10, *infinitely perfect* in Question 11 and *spirit* in Question 9.

9. What is a spirit?

A spirit is a being that has understanding and free will but no body, and will never die.

God is a spirit. A body has to be in a certain definite place, but a spirit does not. A spirit is more real than a body since a body can be destroyed, but a spirit cannot. God is the most real Being there is. But to picture God we usually draw a kind elderly man.

10. What do we mean when we say that God is self-existing?

When we say that God is self-existing we mean that He does not owe His existence to any other being.

God is self-existing. This means that He can live without help. We need help to live.

We need food.　　We need air.　　We need clothing.　　We need shelter.

We need other people to help us, especially our mothers and fathers.

Mother and father　　　　　Policeman　　　　Scientist

If we do not get enough air, food and drink, and help from others, we shall die. But God does not need anything or anyone to help Him. He can exist without help. That is what we mean when we say that God is self-existing.

11. What do we mean when we say that God is infinitely perfect?

When we say that God is infinitely perfect we mean that He has all perfections without limit.

Perfections are good qualities which something has. For example, advertisements for automobiles may list the perfections of the automobiles, their size, beauty, speed, power, comfort, and so forth.

B. WHAT ARE GOD'S PERFECTIONS?

12. What are some of the perfections of God?

Some of the perfections of God are: God is eternal, all-good, all-knowing, all-present, and almighty.

God also has good qualities or perfections. Perhaps we can better understand them by comparing them with the perfections of man.

MAN: Man has intelligence.	GOD: God has intelligence.
Man has strength.	God has power.
Man has goodness.	God has goodness.
But man also has limitations	*God has no limitations*
Man is limited in knowledge.	God knows all things.
Man is limited in strength.	God can do all things.
Man is limited in goodness.	God is all-good.
Man is limited in time.	God is eternal.

13. What do we mean when we say that God is eternal?

When we say that God is eternal we mean that He always was and always will be, and that He always remains the same.

14. What do we mean when we say that God is all-good?

When we say that God is all-good we mean that He is infinitely lovable in Himself, and that from His fatherly love every good comes to us.

15. What do we mean when we say that God is all-knowing?

When we say that God is all-knowing we mean that He knows all things, past, present, and future, even our most secret thoughts, words and actions.

16. What do we mean when we say that God is all-present?

When we say that God is all-present we mean that He is everywhere.

17. If God is everywhere, why do we not see Him?

Although God is everywhere, we do not see Him because He is a spirit and cannot be seen with our eyes.

18. Does God see us?

God sees us and watches over us with loving care.

19. What is God's loving care for us called?

God's loving care for us is called Divine Providence.

20. What do we mean when we say that God is almighty?

When we say that God is almighty we mean that He can do all things.

21. Is God all-wise, all-holy, all-merciful, and all-just?

Yes, God is all-wise, all-holy, all-merciful, and all-just.

C. HOW DO WE KNOW ABOUT GOD?

We know about God through reason and revelation.

22. Can we know by our natural reason that there is a God?

We can know by our natural reason that there is a God, for natural reason tells us that the world we see about us could have been made only by a self-existing Being, all-wise and almighty.

We study the world with our mind, our reason, to see what its Maker is like. If we study a picture, we can learn something about the artist: his artistic ability, his eyesight, etc. If we study the world, we can see God's power and intelligence.

23. Can we know God in any other way than by our natural reason?

Besides knowing God by our natural reason, we can also know Him from supernatural revelation, that is, from the truths found in Sacred Scripture and in Tradition, which God Himself has revealed to us.

Supernatural means "above the natural." These truths are above our natural power to think out for ourselves. God had to tell us or we would not know them.

23 A.* What do we mean when we say that God has revealed these truths to us?

When we say that God has revealed these truths to us we mean that He has made them known to certain persons, to be announced to their fellow men as the word of God.

These persons chosen and sent by God are called "witnesses" to Him. The prophets and Apostles were the chief witnesses. Our Lord

---

* The Questions and Answers shown in italics are known as the "Supplement" to the Official Revised Baltimore Catechism No. 2.

said to the Apostles, "You shall be witnesses for Me. . . even to the very ends of the earth" (Acts 1, 8).

The *Holy Bible* is like a letter, and *Tradition* is like messengers which God sends to teach us about Himself.

23 B. What is the Bible?

The Bible is the written word of God, committed to His Church for the instruction and sanctification of mankind.

23 C. What do we mean when we say that the entire Bible is inspired?

When we say that the entire Bible is inspired we mean that its principal author is God, though it was written by men whom God enlightened and moved to write all those things, and only those things, that He wished to be written.

The men who wrote the Bible were inspired by the Holy Spirit.

Inspiration is a force that God puts into a man so that he can write what God wants him to write. Just as electricity gives light and power, so does inspiration give God's light and power, the light and power that come from the Holy Spirit.

This enables a writer to write just what God wants Him to, though he uses his own language, his own style and his own writing skill. The power of inspiration keeps the writer from making a mistake. There are no errors or mistakes in the Bible. All that is there is truth.

God used many men to write the Bible, just as we use many pens or pencils to write. When we think of the human authors of the Bible, there are many books that make up the Bible. But when we think of the divine Author, God, the Bible is one book.

Sometimes we know who the human author of a book is and sometimes we don't. For example, we know that the Acts of the Apostles were written by St. Luke, but we don't know who wrote the Book of Job. But we always know the main author —God.

23 D. How is the Bible divided?

The Bible is divided into the Old Testament, written before the coming of Jesus Christ, and the New Testament, written after His ascension into heaven.

Land of the Bible

BOOKS OF THE OLD TESTAMENT

Genesis	Tobias	Daniel
Exodus	Judith	Osee
Leviticus	Esther	Joel
Numbers	Job	Amos
Deuteronomy	Psalms	Abdia
Josue	Proverbs	Jona
Judges	Ecclesiastes	Michea
Ruth	Canticle of	Nahum
1 Kings	Canticles	Habacuc
2 Kings	Wisdom	Sophonia
3 Kings	Sirach	Aggai
4 Kings	Isaia	Zacharia
1 Paralipomenon	Jeremia	Malachia
2 Paralipomenon	Lamentations	1 Machabees
1 Esdras	Baruch	2 Machabees
2 Esdras	Ezechiel	

BOOKS OF THE NEW TESTAMENT

St. Matthew
St. Mark
St. Luke
St. John
The Acts of the Apostles

The Epistles

Paul to the Romans
1 Corinthians
2 Corinthians
Galatians
Ephesians
Philippians
Colossians
1 Thessalonians

2 Thessalonians
1 Timothy
2 Timothy
Titus
Philemon
To the Hebrews
St. James
1 St. Peter
2 St. Peter
1 St. John
2 St. John
3 St. John
St. Jude
The Apocalypse of
St. John the Apostle

The hero of the Bible is Our Lord Jesus Christ. Pope Benedict XV said, "Every single page of either Testament seems to center round Christ " (Encyclical on the Bible). The Old Testament, written before the coming of Christ, shows man's need for God's special help and his desire for a Redeemer.

The books of the New Testament, written after Christ's time on earth, give us His life and His teachings. They center round His Passion and death, the great acts of His love for us.

23 E. Are all the passages of the Bible to be understood according to our modern manner of expression?

No; some of the passages of the Bible are not to be understood according to our modern manner of expression, since they contain certain figures of speech, parables, and literary forms used by the people of ancient times but not employed in the present.

For example, the parable of the Good Samaritan was not something that really happened, but a story Our Lord told to show us how to love one another. The Church tells us what parts of the Bible really happened and what parts teach lessons.

23 F. How can we know the true meaning of the Bible?

We can know the true meaning of the Bible from the teaching authority of the Catholic Church, which has received from Jesus Christ the right and the duty to teach and to explain all that God has revealed.

Parts of the Bible are difficult to understand. St. Peter says this of the Epistles of St. Paul: "Our most dear brother Paul also, according to the wisdom given him, has written to you . . . In these epistles there are certain things difficult to understand, which the unlearned and the unstable distort, just as they do the rest of the Scriptures also, to their own destruction " (2 Peter 3, 15-16). The Church helps us to understand the Bible and to be sure of what God meant in each part of it.

23 G. Are Catholics encouraged by the Church to read the Bible?

Yes; Catholics are encouraged by the Church to read the Bible, especially the Gospels, which tell about the earthly life of Jesus Christ, the Son of God made man.

It is good to read a little bit of the Gospels every day. Special indulgences are granted for the reading of the Bible. The Bible is rich food and even a little can be very nourishing to our soul. Read it slowly and carefully. Think of what you read. Ask the Holy Spirit to help you and He will make the parts that are hard at first clearer as time goes on.

23 H. What is the chief message of the New Testament?

The chief message of the New Testament is the joyful announcement of our salvation through Jesus Christ.

"These things are written that you may believe that Jesus is the Christ, the Son of God, and that believing, you may have life in His name" (John 20, 31).

23 I. *What is Divine Tradition?*

Divine Tradition is the unwritten word of God — that is, truths revealed by God, though not written in the Bible, and given to the Church through word of mouth by Jesus Christ or by the apostles under the inspiration of the Holy Spirit.

23 J. *Has Divine Tradition ever been committed to writing?*

Divine Tradition has been committed to writing, especially by saintly writers called Fathers, who lived in the early centuries but were not inspired, as were those who wrote the Bible.

Among the many holy men who have been called Fathers of the Church, these are the eight most important.

Those who wrote in Greek:	Those who wrote in Latin:
St. Athanasius	St. Ambrose
St. Basil the Great	St. Augustine
St. Gregory Nazianzen	St. Jerome
St. John Chrysostom	St. Gregory the Great

23 K. *Has Divine Tradition the same force as the Bible?*

Yes; Divine Tradition has the same force as the Bible, since it too contains God's revelation to men.

23 L. *By what kind of act do we believe the doctrines contained in the Bible and in Divine Tradition?*

We believe the doctrines contained in the Bible and Divine Tradition by an act of divine faith, which means that we accept them on the authority of God, who can neither deceive nor be deceived.

DISCUSSION QUESTIONS:

1. Could there be two Supreme Beings? Why not?
2. Does God have a long white beard?
3. Is an angel a spirit? Is a soul a spirit?
4. Does God need to eat food to stay alive?
5. Does God know what we are thinking right now?
6. If God could be mean, what perfection would He lack?
7. Why does God not have to study?
8. Suppose someone told you there was no God. How could you show him he was wrong?
9. What is another name for Sacred Scripture?
10. How can we increase our knowledge about God?

TRUE OR FALSE: *(Also change each false statement to a true one.)*

1. God needs to make things in order to keep Himself happy.
2. God is good only to those who are good to Him.
3. God is in this room right now.
4. God cannot stop people from committing sin.
5. By studying a flower, we can get a little idea of God's beauty.

FILL IN THE BLANKS:

1. God is the Supreme .... above all ....
2. A spirit has understanding and ....
3. Some of the perfections of God are ...., ...,
.........., ..., and ....
4. When we say God is all-good we mean ....
....
5. We cannot see God because He is a ....
6. God's care of us is called ....
7. God can do all things because He is ....
8. God will always exist because He is ....
9. We can know some things about God by natural ....
10. God tells us things about Himself in ....
and ....

READ FROM THE BIBLE:

The perfections of God — Ps. 28; 32; 45; 102; 135; 138; 143; 144.
God can be known by reason — Rom. 1, 18-23.
The Bible is inspired by God — 2 Tim. 3, 14-17.
Divine truth comes also through Tradition — 2 Thess. 2, 14.

CLASS PROJECT:

How to find a quotation from the Bible — Take for example, Matt. 10, 25. The name of the book is given first, Matthew. Look in the contents to find out on what page the book St. Matthew starts. The first number (10) given after the name of the book is the chapter number. The second number (25) is that of the verse. Now see if you can find this passage. Then look for the passages quoted in the next ten lessons.

Tomorrow let each one bring to school some object or picture which makes him think of one or more of the following; God's power, His wisdom, His greatness, His goodness, His beauty, His care of us, His unchangeableness, His eternity.

PRAYER:

O God, You show Your almighty power chiefly by sparing and having mercy: increase Your mercy toward us so that, running to the things You have so promised, we may be made sharers in the goods of heaven. *(Missal: Collect for Tenth Sunday after Pentecost)*

LESSON 3 — The Unity and Trinity of God

"Now it came to pass when all the people had been baptized, Jesus also having been baptized and being in prayer, that heaven was opened, and the Holy Spirit descended upon Him in bodily form as a dove, and a voice came from heaven, 'Thou art My beloved Son, in Thee I am well pleased'" (Luke 3, 21-22).

A. UNITY OF GOD

In God there is one NATURE.

24. Is there only one God?

Yes, there is only one God.

B. TRINITY OF GOD

In God there are three PERSONS.

25. How many Persons are there in God?

In God there are three divine Persons — the Father, the Son, and the Holy Spirit.

A NATURE is WHAT someone or something is.

A PERSON is WHO someone is.

- 22 -

THE BLESSED TRINITY does NOT mean:

1 God in 3 Gods	
1 Nature in 3 Natures	**BUT:** 1 NATURE
1 Person in 3 Persons	in 3 PERSONS

26. Is the Father God?

The Father is God and the first Person of the Blessed Trinity.

27. Is the Son God?

The Son is God and the second Person of the Blessed Trinity.

The Son is also called the Word, or Image of the Father.

28. Is the Holy Spirit God?

The Holy Spirit is God and the third Person of the Blessed Trinity.

The Holy Spirit is also called: the Spirit, the Holy Ghost, the Spirit of the Father, the Spirit of Jesus, the Advocate, etc.

29. What do we mean by the Blessed Trinity?

By the Blessed Trinity we mean one and the same God in three divine Persons.

30. Are the three divine Persons really distinct from one another?

The three divine Persons are really distinct from one another.

This means: The Father is not the Son.
         The Son is not the Holy Spirit   *(See diagram*
         The Father is not the Hloy Spirit.   *opposite page)*

31. Are the three divine Persons perfectly equal to one another?

The three divine Persons are perfectly equal to one another, because all are one and the same God.

The Father is all-powerful.	The Father is eternal.
The Son is all-powerful.	The Son is eternal.
The Holy Spirit is all-powerful.	The Holy Spirit is eternal.
The Father knows all things.	The Father is everywhere.
The Son knows all things.	The Son is everywhere.
The Holy Spirit knows all things.	The Holy Spirit is everywhere.

32. How are the three divine Persons, though really distinct from one another, one and the same God?

The three divine Persons, though really distinct from one another, are one and the same God because all have one and the same divine nature.

If we wanted to show this, we would have to put the three circles one on top of the other, since all three have the same nature.

33. Can we fully understand how the three divine Persons, though really distinct from one another, are one and the same God?

We cannot fully understand how the three divine Persons, though really distinct from one another, are one and the same God because this is a supernatural mystery.

34. What is a supernatural mystery?

A supernatural mystery is a truth which we cannot fully understand, but which we firmly believe because we have God's word for it.

There are two kinds of mysteries, natural and supernatural. A NATURAL mystery is something hidden or unknown here on earth. For example: the nature of electricity, what is at the bottom of the ocean, what is in the center of the earth, what is beyond the last star, how old the earth is, and so forth.

A SUPERNATURAL mystery is something about God or our soul that we could not find out for ourselves, but which God has made known to us. We can know some things about supernatural mysteries from what God has told us, but not everything about them. For example: the truths contained in the Apostles' Creed.

DISCUSSION QUESTIONS:

1. Does God have the same number of natures as you do?
2. In what ways do a father, mother, and child resemble the Blessed Trinity?
3. In what way are they different?
4. What is the difference between saying "three persons" and "three gods"?

5. Is the Father older than the Son?
6. Is the Holy Ghost everywhere?
7. Can the Holy Ghost do all that the Father can do?
8. Can we love the Father if we do not love the Son?
9. Can we know all about the Blessed Trinity? Why not?
10. What is a supernatural mystery?

TRUE OR FALSE: *(Also change each false statement to a true one.)*

1. There are three natures in God.
2. In the Father there are three Persons.
3. The Holy Ghost has the same nature as the Father.
4. The Holy Ghost is not the same Person as the Son.
5. The Father is equal to the Holy Ghost.
6. The Father made the Holy Ghost.
7. The Holy Ghost always was.
8. A mystery is a truth about which we can know nothing.
9. If we study hard we can learn all about the Blessed Trinity.
10. By study and prayer it is possible to learn much about the mysteries of our faith.

FILL IN THE BLANKS:

1. In the Blessed Trinity there are three divine . . . . in one divine . . . .

2. The three divine Persons are: . . . ., ..., and . . . .

3. The three divine Persons are perfectly . . . . to one another and really . . . . from one another.

4. We cannot understand exactly how there are three Persons in God because it is a . . . .

5. Even though we cannot understand exactly how there are three Persons in God, we believe that there are because . . . .

READ FROM THE BIBLE:

Read over the Epistle and Gospel for the Mass of Trinity Sunday.

CLASS PROJECT:

Tonight let each boy in the class try to add to the list of natural mysteries given on page 24. Ask your mother or father or find out from some book. And let each girl add to the list of supernatural mysteries given on the same page.

PRAYER:

Glory be to the Father, and to the Son, and to the Holy Ghost. As it was in the beginning, is now, and ever shall be, world without end. Amen.

LESSON 4 — Creation and the Angels

"God saw that all He had made was very good" (Genesis 1, 31).

35. What do we mean when we say that God is the Creator of heaven and earth?

When we say that God is the Creator of heaven and earth we mean that He made all things from nothing by His almighty power.

36. Which are the chief creatures of God?

The chief creatures of God are angels and men.

A. THE ANGELS

37. What are angels?

Angels are created spirits, without bodies, having understanding and free will.

But to picture them we have to draw bodies or heads with wings.

38. What gifts did God bestow on the angels when He created them?

When God created the angels He bestowed on them great wisdom, power and holiness.

Angels are like men in some things but different in others.

MEN	Soul and Body	ANGELS	Spirit but no Body
The human mind knows things only by study and experience.		Angels have brilliant intelligences and do not have to study.	
Human power is very limited.		Angelic power is far greater.	

- 26 -

39. Did all the angels remain faithful to God?

Not all the angels remained faithful to God; some of them sinned.

"And there was a battle in heaven; Michael and his angels battled with the dragon, and the dragon fought and his angels. And they did not prevail, neither was their place found any more in heaven. And that great dragon was cast down, the ancient serpent, he who is called the devil and Satan, who leads astray the whole world; and he was cast down to the earth and with him his angels were cast down" (Apocalypse 12, 7-9).

B. THE GOOD ANGELS

40. What happened to the angels who remained faithful to God?

The angels who remained faithful to God entered into the eternal happiness of heaven, and these are called good angels.

41. What do the good angels do in heaven?

In heaven the good angels see, love, and adore God.

42. How do the good angels help us?

The good angels help us by praying for us, by acting as messengers from God to us, and by serving as our guardian angels.

43. How do our guardian angels help us?

Our guardian angels help us by praying for us, by protecting us from harm, and by inspiring us to do good.

The Angel Raphael was a good angel sent by God to protect and help Tobias. (Read Tobias, chapters 5-12)

C. THE BAD ANGELS

44. What happened to the angels who did not remain faithful to God?

The angels who did not remain faithful to God were cast into hell, and these are called bad angels, or devils.

45. What is the chief way in which the bad angels try to harm us?

The chief way in which the bad angels try to harm us is by tempting us to sin.

The devil even tried to get Our Blessed Lord to sin. He never succeeded. (Read Matthew 4, 1-11; Luke 4, 1-13)

46. Do all temptations come from the bad angels?

Some temptations come from the bad angels; but other temptations come from ourselves and from the persons and things about us.

47. Can we always resist temptations?

We can always resist temptations, because no temptation can force us into sin, and because God will always help us if we ask Him.

DISCUSSION QUESTIONS:

1. Can anyone but God make something out of nothing? Why not?
2. Is a man more important than a horse? than a mountain? than the sun?
3. If an angel is a spirit and God is a spirit, what is the difference between God and an angel? (See the explanation of Question 12.)
4. Are angels wiser than men?
5. Can you name any of the good angels?
6. Are the good angels perfectly happy in heaven?
7. Do our guardian angels sleep at night? Why not?
8. Why can't we see our guardian angels?
9. Can the devils make us commit sin?
10. Are bad thoughts sins or temptations?

TRUE OR FALSE: *(Also change each false statement to a true one.)*

1. Before creation only God existed.
2. There is only one devil.
3. Angels do not have wings.
4. Angels are stronger than men.
5. Some of the angels refused to serve God.
6. The devils have horns and fiery tails.
7. Men are more intelligent than devils.
8. God allows the devils to tempt us.
9. It is a sin to be tempted.
10. Our guardian angels leave us in time of temptation.

FILL IN THE BLANKS:

1. God made all things out of .... by His ....
2. The chief creatures of God are .... and ....
3. Some of the angels committed .... by refusing to
....
4. The leader of the bad angels is called ....
5. The leader of the good angels is called ....
6. When some of the angels refused to serve God, there was a great .... in heaven.
7. We are helped on earth by our .... angels.
8. The bad angels are called ....
9. The devils try to .... us to sin.
10. Temptations also come from .... and from
....

CLASS PROJECT FROM THE BIBLE:

Divide the class into four groups. Let each group read together the account of a particular good or bad angel as given in the Bible or your Bible History. Then let a spokesman for each group report to the class in general on that angel.

Good Angels:

GROUP I. Read the Book of Tobias, chapters 5 to 12.

What did the angel look like? Did Tobias know he was an angel? Why did the angel go with Tobias? How did he help him? When did he finally make himself known as an angel? What was the reaction of Tobias and his father when they found out that Raphael was an angel? What did Raphael say about the type of food he ate? What did he tell them to do before he disappeared?

GROUP II. Read Luke 1, 11-38 and 2, 8-14.

Where did the angel appear to Zachary? What was Zachary's reaction? What did the angel tell Zachary? Did Zachary believe him? Did the angel tell Zachary his name and what he did? Was it the same angel who appeared to Mary? How did he greet Mary? What was her reaction? What did he tell her? When the angel appeared to the shepherds at the birth of Christ, what was their reaction? What did the angel tell them? Then what did they see?

Bad Angels:

GROUP III. Read Genesis 3, 1-6.

Do you think the devil is an animal? Why is he called a serpent? Look at the picture of the battle in heaven on page 27, and it might help. What did he say to Eve? What was her answer? Did the devil tell her to obey God? Did he tell the truth about what God had said? Did Eve give in to the temptation? Why do you think she did? Did Adam commit sin, too? Why do you think he did? Was the devil smarter than they were?

GROUP IV. Read the temptation of Christ in Matthew 4, 1-11.

Where was Jesus tempted? Did the Holy Spirit want Jesus to be tempted by the devil? Did the devil try to get Our Lord to work miracles just to help Himself? Did Our Lord ever work miracles to show off or for selfish reasons? What did the devil promise Our Lord if He would worship him? Did he succeed in fooling Our Lord? The Gospel says the devil tried many other temptations; did he ever succeed? What temptations does the devil give us like those he gave Our Lord? Can they ever get too strong? How can we overcome them?

PRAYER:

Angel of God, my guardian dear
To whom His love commits me here,
Ever this day be at my side,
To light and guard, to rule and guide. Amen.

CREATION

A. CREATION

48. What is man?

Man is a creature composed of body and soul, and made to the image and likeness of God.

49. Is this likeness to God in the body or in the soul?

This likeness to God is chiefly in the soul.

The likeness to the Blessed Trinity is found chiefly in man's soul, but there is a resemblance in the body too—not, however, in the body of one man alone, but in man and woman united in marriage and the child which is the normal fruit of the marriage.

"God created man in His image. In the image of God He created him. Male and female He created them. Then God blessed them and said to them, 'Be fruitful and multiply'" (Gen. 1, 27-28).

However, the image is found chiefly in man's soul, since that is a spirit just as God is a spirit.

50. How is the soul like God?

The soul is like God because it is a spirit having understanding and free will, and is destined to live forever.

51. Who were the first man and woman?

The first man and woman were Adam and Eve, the first parents of the whole human race.

51 A. *Is it possible that there are intelligent beings created by God on other planets of the universe?*

Yes; it is possible that there are intelligent beings created by God on other planets of the universe, because God's power is unlimited.

52. What was the chief gift bestowed on Adam and Eve by God?

The chief gift bestowed on Adam and Eve by God was sanctifying grace, which made them children of God and gave them the right to heaven.

Grace will be explained in Lesson 9.

53. What other gifts were bestowed on Adam and Eve by God?

The other gifts bestowed on Adam and Eve by God were happiness in the Garden of Paradise, great knowledge, control of the passions by reason, and freedom from suffering and death.

God's Gifts

Great knowledge: Adam and Eve had knowledge poured into their minds by God. They did not have to study or go to school.

Control of the passions by reason: Passions are emotions in the soul, such as anger, fear, hatred, desire, joy, sorrow, etc. Adam and Eve would not become angry unless they wanted to. They would never be afraid of anything unless they wanted to. They would never cry unless they wanted to.

Freedom from suffering and death: There would be no sickness, weakness, weariness, or bodily discomfort. They would not have to go to the dentist, take castor oil, or go to the hospital. When they finished their time on earth they would go to heaven without dying.

B. THE FALL

54. What commandment did God give Adam and Eve?

God gave Adam and Eve the commandment not to eat of the fruit of a certain tree that grew in the Garden of Paradise.

It was not a real fruit, but a symbol of some pleasure God forbade them, to test their love for Him.

55. Did Adam and Eve obey the commandment of God?

Adam and Eve did not obey the commandment of God, but ate of the forbidden fruit.

C. THE PUNISHMENT

56. What happened to Adam and Eve on account of their sin?

On account of their sin Adam and Eve lost sanctifying grace, the right to heaven, and their special gifts; they became subject to death, to suffering, and to a strong inclination to evil, and they were driven from the Garden of Paradise.

1. GOD'S COMMAND: — Do not eat of the tree of good and evil, lest you die.

2. THE DEVIL'S TEMPTATION: — If you eat this fruit, you shall be as gods.

God loved Adam and Eve and wanted to keep them trom harm.

The devil, symbolized by the serpent, said: "Don't love God, love yourselves. Be your own gods and do your own will. What God says is too difficult."

3. THE FALL

4. THE PUNISHMENT

Adam and Eve disobeyed God and did their own will.

The gate to heaven was closed. Adam and Eve lost their gifts and the friendship of God.

57. What has happened to us on account of the sin of Adam?

On account of the sin of Adam, we, his descendants, come into the world deprived of sanctifying grace and inherit his punishment, as we would have inherited his gifts had he been obedient to God.

58. What is this sin in us called?

This sin in us is called original sin.

59. Why is this sin called original?

This sin is called original because it comes down to us through our origin, or descent, from Adam.

60. What are the chief punishments of Adam which we inherit through original sin?

The chief punishments of Adam which we inherit through original sin are: death, suffering, ignorance, and a strong inclination to sin.

61. Is God unjust in punishing us on account of the sin of Adam?

God is not unjust in punishing us on account of the sin of Adam, because original sin does not take away from us anything to which we have a strict right as human beings, but only the free gifts which God in His goodness would have bestowed on us if Adam had not sinned.

GOD'S GIFTS TO US:

1. Grace.
2. Great knowledge.
3. Control of passions by reason.
4. Freedom from sickness and death.

THE DEVIL'S GIFTS TO US:

1. Original sin.
2. Ignorance.
3. A strong inclination to sin.
4. Suffering and death.

62. Was any human person ever preserved from original sin?

The Blessed Virgin Mary was preserved from original sin in view of the merits of her Divine Son; and this privilege is called her Immaculate Conception.

THE IMMACULATE CONCEPTION

Our Lady's words to Bernadette at Lourdes, "I am the Immaculate Conception."

Our Lady is so different from us. We have sin, but she did not. But she feels sorry for us. The healing waters of Lourdes are a sign of her love for us and her desire to help us in our troubles.

THE IMMACULATE CONCEPTION — In Prophecy

1. GOD'S PROMISE OF A REDEEMER

God did not abandon man after the sin of Adam and Eve, as we shall see in Question 77. He promised that the devil's victory over Adam and Eve would be turned into a defeat. He promised to send a Redeemer who would at the same time come from mankind, so that through this Redeemer man could truly conquer the devil. And as the devil had conquered through a woman, so would God conquer through a woman. One day there would come a woman who would be completely the devil's enemy, over whom he would have no power at all. Through her

God's Words in Garden of Eden.
(Genesis 3, 15)

seed, or child, she would crush his head. That is why we see so many pictures of Mary with a snake under her feet. She is the woman promised by God to be the devil's terrible enemy.

The World in Slavery to the Devil.

2. MAN'S NEED OF A REDEEMER

Meanwhile, the human race was under the power of the devil. Everyone born into the world had original sin on his soul and was therefore a slave of the devil. Even those who did die without mortal sin on their souls could not enter heaven, but had to wait in what we call Limbo (called Abraham's bosom by Christ in Luke 16,22, and a prison by St. Peter in 1 Peter 3,19) until after the death of Christ. (See Question 95.) Men could not understand why there was sickness and suffering on earth and did not know what happened after death. God did not send the Redeemer right away, so that men would see from all these things what a terrible thing sin was and how much they needed a Redeemer.

THE IMMACULATE CONCEPTION — The Fulfillment

3. BEGINNING OF REDEMPTION

When the fullness of time had come, God prepared to send His Son into the world as the Redeemer. He had already planned the kind of Mother He wanted for His Son, so He created her soul and united it to her body in the womb of her mother, St. Ann. But Mary's soul, unlike all other souls which had come into this world after Adam and Eve, had no original sin on it. It was immaculate.

Mary Immaculate — the Sinless One in a Sinful Race.

God looked into the future and saw the day on which His Son would die on the Cross. He accepted in advance the Precious Blood of His Son as the price of Mary's redemption. He used the Precious Blood to redeem her ahead of time by preserving her from all sin. This privilege which God granted to Mary of being conceived and born without original sin is called her *Immaculate Conception.*

4. PREPARING FOR WARFARE AGAINST THE DEVIL

As a result of her Immaculate Conception, Mary came into this world full of grace and was never under Satan's power. She was the only one (except for Christ) whose soul was always turned perfectly toward God's will. Her Immaculate Heart was always full of perfect love for Him. She was completely the devil's enemy and prepared for the warfare with him which was to result in his complete defeat. By her surrender to God's will, she was ready to reverse the defeat mankind had suffered through Eve's refusal of God's will.

Mary and Her Seed *versus* the Devil and His Seed.

Because of her love of God she became the Mother of Christ and joined Him in the battle with the devil which will be described in Lesson 8.

DISCUSSION QUESTIONS:

1. Does God have eyes?
2. In what way does the soul resemble the Blessed Trinity?
3. In what way do bodies resemble the Blessed Trinity?
4. Why does man's soul resemble God more than his body does?
5. Is it easier for us to commit sin than it was for Adam? Why?
6. Before they sinned, would Adam and Eve become sorrowful if they did not want to? Why not?
7. Did Eve ask God's help when the devil tempted her?
8. What harm came to us from the sin of Adam and Eve?
9. Why do many statues of Our Lady have a snake at the base?
10. Was Our Lady redeemed by Christ?

TRUE OR FALSE: *(Also change each false statement to a true one.)*

1. If we trace our ancestry back far enough, we are all related.
2. God's greatest gift to man was freedom from suffering.
3. Death came into the world as a result of original sin.
4. If Adam and Eve had not sinned, babies would not possess such strong desires to have their own way.
5. Mary did not need to have Christ redeem her.

FILL IN THE BLANKS:

1. God's chief gift to Adam and Eve was ....
2. Other gifts which God gave them were: ....
................., ..., ...
................., and ....
3. God gave Adam and Eve a command to test their ....
....
4. The sin we inherit from Adam and Eve is called ....
5. Death came into the world as a .... for sin.
6. Every child born today has an inclination to ....
7. Original sin makes us slaves of ....
8. The Immaculate Conception means that Mary was ....
....
9. Christ redeemed Mary by His ....
10. Mary's Immaculate Conception made her the enemy of ....

READ FROM THE BIBLE:

God as Creator — Gen. 1 and 2; Ps. 8; 18; 103; Prov. 8.
The Fall — Gen. 3; Rom. 5, 12-19; 7, 13-25.

CLASS PROJECT:

Be on the watch to notice how many things you have to do that you find hard, which you would have found easy to do if Adam and Eve had not sinned. Write them down and bring them in tomorrow.

PRAYER:

O Mary, conceived without sin, pray for us who have recourse to thee.

LESSON 6 — Actual Sin

"Behold this Heart which has loved men so much, which has heaped on them so many benefits. In exchange for this infinite love it finds ingratitude; instead it meets with forgetfulness, indifference, outrages" (Words of the Sacred Heart to St. Margaret Mary, complaining of man's sins).

63. Is original sin the only kind of sin?

Original sin is not the only kind of sin; there is another kind, called actual sin, which we ourselves commit.

64. What is actual sin?

Actual sin is any willful thought, desire, word, action, or omission forbidden by the law of God.

Road Directions

Help us to get where we are going and to avoid danger.

Disregarding Directions

Means accidents and tragedy.

Laws of God

HONOR THY FATHER AND MOTHER

Help us to get where we are going and to avoid danger.

Breaking God's Laws

Means the tragedy of sin.

65. How many kinds of actual sin are there?

There are two kinds of actual sin: mortal sin and venial sin.

A. MORTAL SIN

66. What is mortal sin?

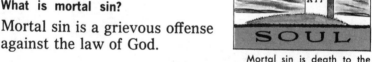

Mortal sin is a grievous offense against the law of God.

Mortal sin is death to the life of grace in the soul.

67. Why is this sin called mortal?

This sin is called mortal, or deadly, because it deprives the sinner of sanctifying grace, the supernatural life of the soul.

68. Besides depriving the sinner of sanctifying grace, what else does mortal sin do to the soul?

Besides depriving the sinner of sanctifying grace, mortal sin makes the soul an enemy of God, takes away the merit of all its good actions, deprives it of the right to everlasting happiness in heaven, and makes it deserving of everlasting punishment in hell.

"Every sin must be said to renew in a certain way the Passion
of Our Lord, 'crucifying again to
themselves the Son of God and
making Him a mockery'" (Heb.
6, 6).—Words of Pope Pius XI in
his encyclical on Reparation to the
Sacred Heart. This applies only to
deliberate sin — sin committed on
purpose.

69. What three things are necessary to make a sin mortal?

To make a sin mortal these three things are necessary:

first, the thought, desire, word, action or omission
must be seriously wrong or considered seriously
wrong;

second, the sinner must be mindful of the serious
wrong;

third, the sinner must fully consent to it.

Briefly, the conditions are:

1. Serious matter
2. Sufficient reflection
3. Full consent of the will

B. VENIAL SIN

70. What is venial sin?

Venial sin is a less serious offense against the law of
God, which does not deprive the soul of sanctifying
grace, and which can be pardoned even without sacramental confession.

Venial sin is a disease in the
life of grace in the soul. It is less
serious than mortal sin, but much
more serious than a sickness, or
even the death, of the body.

71. How can a sin be venial?

A sin can be venial in two ways:

first, when the evil done is not seriously wrong;

second, when the evil done is seriously wrong, but
the sinner sincerely believes it is only slightly
wrong, or does not give full consent to it.

72. How does venial sin harm us?

Venial sin harms us by making us less fervent in the service of God, by weakening our power to resist mortal sin, and by making us deserving of God's punishments in this life or in purgatory.

73. How can we keep from committing sin?

We can keep from committing sin by praying and by receiving the sacraments; by remembering that God is always with us; by recalling that our bodies are temples of the Holy Spirit; by keeping occupied with work or play; by promptly resisting the sources of sin within us; by avoiding the near occasions of sin.

Pray	Receive sacraments frequently	Remember God is always with us	Remember our bodies are temples of the Holy Ghost	Keep busy with work or play	Resist temptations	Avoid near occasions of sin

C. CAPITAL SINS

74. What are the chief sources of actual sin?

The chief sources of actual sin are: pride, covetousness, lust, anger, gluttony, envy, and sloth, and these are commonly called capital sins.

THE TREE OF SIN

The capital sins are the chief roots of sin. They are inclinations in our will to go against God's will in different ways.

75. Why are these called capital sins?

They are called capital sins, not because they, in themselves, are the greatest sins, but because they are the chief reasons why men commit sin.

D. OCCASIONS OF SIN

76. What are the near occasions of sin?

The near occasions of sin are all persons, places, or things that may easily lead us into sin.

PERSONS	PLACES	THINGS

We are strictly obliged to avoid all near occasions of sin. Otherwise it shows God we are willing to hurt Him to please ourselves. "He who loves danger will perish in it" (Sirach 3, 25).

DISCUSSION QUESTIONS:

1. Does God give us laws to put chains on us and keep us from having fun? Why does He give us laws anyway?

2. Is an actual sin which we ourselves commit worse than the original sin with which we are born? Why?

3. Which is worse: to burn to death or to commit a mortal sin? Why?

4. Do you think anyone with even one mortal sin on his soul really loves God? Even if he thinks he does?

5. Did our sins have anything to do with Our Lord's dying on the Cross?

6. Suppose you think stealing a dime from your mother is a mortal sin and you do it. Is that a mortal sin for you?

7. Suppose you do something that is really a mortal sin, but you do not know it. Is that a mortal sin for you if you find out later on about it?

8. Suppose you do something that is really a mortal sin, but you think it is a venial sin. What kind of sin is it for you?

9. Suppose you did something you thought was not a sin and then found out that it was a mortal sin. Was it a mortal sin for you?

10. Can we keep out of sin if we do not pray and go to Communion often?

TRUE OR FALSE:

1. Laws are made to be broken.

2. To desire willfully what is forbidden by God is a sin, even if we do not do anything about it.

3. To think deliberately about something we are not supposed to think about is a sin.

4. God does not care whether we commit sin or not.

5. Every bad thought is a mortal sin.

6. No one can make us commit sin.

7. It is worse to commit a deliberate venial sin than to have the measles.

8. With a venial sin on your soul you cannot go to Communion.

9. With a venial sin on your soul it is better to stay away from Communion.

10. It is a sin to refuse to avoid a near occasion of sin.

FILL IN THE BLANKS:

1. The five ways of committing an actual sin are by . . . . ,
. . . . , ... , ... , ...

2. The two kinds of actual sin are . . . . and . . . .

3. Mortal sin is . . . . in the life of grace in the soul.

4. Venial sin is . . . . in the life of grace in the soul.

5. The three things necessary to make a sin mortal are: . . . .
. . . . , ... , ... , and . . . .

6. If we die with a venial sin on our soul we go to . . . .

7. If we die with a mortal sin on our soul we go to . . . .

8. Name several ways of keeping out of sin . . . .
. . . .
. . . .

9. The seven capital sins are: ...., ...,

............, ..., ..., ...,

....

10. If certain persons we associate with are constantly making it hard for us in one way or another to keep out of sin, then they are

for us. ....

READ FROM THE BIBLE:

The evil of sin — Gen. 4, 1-16; 11, 1-9; Ps. 35; Is. 5; Matt. 21, 33-34; John 8, 21-59.

Our attitude toward sin — Rom. 6, 12-23, 1 Pet. 4, 1-6.

The story of Joseph — Gen. 37; 39-50.

Avoiding occasions of sin — Matt. 5, 27-30.

CLASS PROJECT:

Tonight read the comic section of the paper very carefully. Then when everyone else has finished reading it, take a colored pencil and mark a large X over every sin you see committed there. Write on a separate sheet of paper the name of the sin and bring both to class tomorrow for Sister to correct.

Tell if the sin is a thought, a desire, a word, an action, or an omission.

Tell if it is mortal or venial. (Perhaps Sister can help you on this.)

Watch especially for the following sins: superstition, uncharitable speech, boastful or bragging speech, disobedience, murder, fighting, quarreling, "getting even," immodesty in dress (especially in women), vanity, stealing, damaging property, lying, and the seven capital sins: pride, covetousness, lust, anger, gluttony, envy and sloth.

PRAYER:

(In reparation for sins of the tongue)

The Divine Praises: Blessed be God. Blessed be His Holy Name. Blessed be Jesus Christ, true God and true Man. Blessed be the Name of Jesus. Blessed be His Most Sacred Heart. Blessed be His Most Precious Blood. Blessed be Jesus in the Most Holy Sacrament of the Altar. Blessed be the great Mother of God, Mary most Holy. Blessed be her Holy and Immaculate Conception. Blessed be her Glorious Assumption. Blessed be the Name of Mary, Virgin and Mother. Blessed be St. Joseph, her most chaste spouse. Blessed be God in His Angels and in His Saints.

An indulgence of 3 years. An indulgence of 5 years, if said publicly. A plenary indulgence under the usual conditions, if said daily for a month. (No. 696.)

"I believe ... in Jesus Christ, His only Son, Our Lord; who was conceived by the Holy Spirit, born of the Virgin Mary ..."

77. Did God abandon man after Adam fell into sin?

God did not abandon man after Adam fell into sin, but promised to send into the world a Savior to free man from his sins and to reopen to him the gates of heaven.

This has been explained on page 36.

78. Who is the Savior of all men?

The Savior of all men is Jesus Christ.

This is the Greek symbol for Christ.
In Greek X is a Ch, P is an R.
So we have CHR, the first three letters of Christ.

79. What is the chief teaching of the Catholic Church about Jesus Christ?

The chief teaching of the Catholic Church about Jesus Christ is that He is God made man.

80. Why is Jesus Christ God?

Jesus Christ is God because He is the only Son of God, having the same divine nature as His Father.

81. Why is Jesus Christ man?

Jesus Christ is man because He is the Son of the Blessed Virgin Mary and has a body and soul like ours.

Mary is like the garden in which grew the flower, which is Christ.

82. Is Jesus Christ more than one Person?

No, Jesus Christ is only one Person; and that Person is the second Person of the Blessed Trinity.

83. How many natures has Jesus Christ?

Jesus Christ has two natures: the nature of God and the nature of man.

Remember from Question 25: A nature is WHAT someone is.
A person is WHO someone is.

One Person   Two Natures

84. Was the Son of God always man?

The Son of God was not always man, but became man at the time of the Incarnation.

85. What is meant by the Incarnation?

By the Incarnation is meant that the Son of God, retaining His divine nature, took to Himself a human nature, that is, a body and soul like ours.

Briefly, the Incarnation means THE SON OF GOD BECAME MAN. Sacred Scripture says, "The Word (that is, the Son of God) was made flesh, and dwelt (the Greek word means 'pitched his tent') among us" (John 1, 14). Jesus Christ is true God and true man, one with the Father and Holy Spirit and one with us.

86. How was the Son of God made man?

The Son of God was conceived and made man by the power of the Holy Spirit in the womb of the Blessed Virgin Mary.

87. When was the Son of God conceived and made man?

The Son of God was conceived and made man on Annunciation Day, the day on which the Angel Gabriel announced to the Blessed Virgin Mary that she was to be the Mother of God.

St. Thomas tells us that in sending His Son into the world, God wanted to contract a certain spiritual marriage between Him and human nature. Therefore, He sent the angel to ask Mary's consent in place of the whole human race. This is brought out in the prayer: the Angelus.

THE ANGELUS

1. God sent the Angel to ask for Mary's hand in marriage.

2. Mary said, "Yes."

3. God sent the Holy Spirit to make her the Mother of His Son.

"The angel of the Lord declared unto Mary."

"Behold the handmaid of the Lord."

"And the Word was made flesh."

88. Is St. Joseph the father of Jesus Christ?

Jesus Christ had no human father, but St. Joseph was the spouse of the Blessed Virgin Mary and the guardian, or foster father, of Christ.

Joseph was not the father of Christ in the flesh, as our human fathers are. He was, though, really Mary's husband and did have a father's rights over Christ, the Son of God.

St. Francis de Sales gives this comparison:

1. If a farmer owns a garden, he has the right to what it produces. If a dove drops a seed into the garden and a flower grows, does the farmer not own the flower?

2. St. Joseph is the farmer and the garden is Mary. St. Joseph, as Mary's husband, would have rights over the fruit, that is, Mary's Child. The Holy Spirit, the dove, dropped a seed into Mary in a spiritual manner. The flower that grew from her was Christ. Did not Joseph have a father's rights over Christ, even though it was not he who planted the seed? Certainly he did, and Christ Himself recognized St. Joseph's rights by obeying him as a father.

89. When was Christ born?

Christ was born of the Blessed Virgin Mary on Christmas Day, in Bethlehem, more than nineteen hundred years ago.

89 A. How many years did Jesus Christ live on earth?

Jesus Christ lived on earth about thirty-three years.

89 B. How did Jesus Christ spend His life on earth?

Jesus Christ spent His childhood, youth and early manhood in the home of His mother Mary and His foster father Joseph, working as a carpenter in the village of Nazareth in Palestine; He spent His last years in the work of His public ministry.

89 C. What work did Jesus Christ perform in the course of His public ministry?

In the course of His public ministry Jesus Christ gave us an example of great virtue, preached the message of salvation, proved the truth of His message through miracles and prophecies, and established the Church with its sacrifice and sacraments for the salvation of men until the end of time.

He showed that He was a witness sent by the Father to lead men to heaven. "I am the way, and the truth, and the life. No one comes to the Father, but through Me" (John 14, 6).

DISCUSSION QUESTIONS:

1. When God did not abandon man after Adam's sin, what perfection or quality mentioned in Lesson 2 was He showing?
2. Did God's promise to send a Savior have any reference to our Blessed Mother?
3. Who is Jesus Christ?
4. Which Person of the Blessed Trinity is He: the Father? the Son? the Holy Spirit? or all three?
5. How many persons are there in Christ?
6. Did Christ come from heaven, from earth, or from both places?
7. Did God force Mary to become the Mother of Christ?
8. What was the difference between Mary's way of acting toward God and Eve's way of acting?
9. If Mary had said "no" to the angel, would she have become the Mother of God?
10. Why should we thank Mary for what she did for us?

TRUE OR FALSE: *(Also change each false statement to a true one.)*

1. Jesus Christ always existed.
2. Jesus is the same Person as the Father.
3. There are two Persons in Christ.
4. There are three natures in Christ.
5. The one Person who is Christ was always God.
6. When Christ became man He lost His divine nature.
7. To say "The Word was made flesh" is the same as to say, "The Son of God became man."
8. Mary became a mother by the power of the Holy Spirit.
9. St. Joseph had a father's love for Christ.
10. Mary was the only human parent of Christ.

FILL IN THE BLANKS:

1. After Adam sinned, God in His mercy promised to send . . . .
2. The Savior of the world is . . . .
3. Jesus Christ is the Son of . . . . and the Son of . . . .
4. He was always the Son of . . . . , but He was not always the Son of . . . .
5. Jesus Christ is the . . . . Person of the Blessed Trinity.
6. He has two natures: . . . . and . . . .
7. To say "The Word was made flesh" is to express the mystery called the . . . .
8. Christ was conceived in the womb of . . . .
9. This was done by the power of . . . .
10. The day on which this took place is called . . . .

READ FROM THE BIBLE:

Old Testament types of Our Lady — Books of Judith and Esther. The Incarnation — Ps. 2; Luke 1-2; Matt. 1-2; John 1, 1-14; Gal. 4, 1-7; Col. 1, 15-20.

CLASS PROJECT:

The following are some symbols of Christ:

IHS — The first three letters in Greek (JES) of the name Jesus.

XP — The first two letters in Greek of the name Christ.

AW — The first and last letters of the Greek alphabet (alpha and omega), symbolizing Christ, the beginning and end of all things.

A lamb is a symbol of Christ, the Lamb of God.

A fish symbolizes Christ, Savior. The five letters (I-CH-TH-Y-S) of the Greek word for fish stand for "Jesus Christ, Son of God, Savior."

And, of course, a cross is a symbol of Christ.

Pay a visit to the church between now and tomorrow morning. See how many of these or other symbols of Christ you can find.

PRAYER: Say "The Angelus," on page 6.

LESSON 8 — The Redemption

"I believe . . . in Jesus Christ . . . who suffered under Pontius Pilate, was crucified, died and was buried. He descended into hell; the third day He arose again from the dead; He ascended into heaven, sitteth at the right hand of God, the Father Almighty; from thence He shall come to judge the living and the dead . . ."

A. GOD'S COMMAND: "My Son is to die on the Cross to show men I love them" (See John 3, 16; 10, 18).

B. TEMPTATION: The devil said to Mary, and then to Christ, "God's will is too hard. Do what you want instead."

C. VICTORY: Mary, "Behold the handmaid of the Lord" (Luke 1, 38).

Christ, "Father, Thy will be done" (Matt. 26, 42).

D. REWARD: "Jesus has . . . entered . . . into heaven itself to appear now before the face of God on our behalf" (Hebrews 9, 24).

This victory reverses the defeat of Adam and Eve. (See page 33.)

90. What is meant by the Redemption?

By the Redemption is meant that Jesus Christ, as the Redeemer of the whole human race, offered His sufferings and death to God as a fitting sacrifice in satisfaction for the sins of men, and regained for them the right to be children of God and heirs of heaven.

Briefly, the Redemption means CHRIST DIED FOR OUR SINS.

It was His loving obedience to His Father, even to the extreme point of dying on the Cross, which redeemed us. The disobedience of Adam, and of all others who have listened to the devil and sinned, or will sin, had offended the Father deeply, because He loves us. But the act of love of Christ, dying on the Cross, was more pleasing to the Father than our sins were displeasing to Him.

Because He was pleased, the Father accepted the sacrifice of His Son. He took Him to heaven as a sign that He will take all others there who will share in the sacrifice of His Son.

The one who shared most in this was Mary. She reversed Eve's action. Eve refused God's will and brought death into the world. Mary accepted God's will and brought the Redeemer into the world, who won eternal life for us.

91. What were the chief sufferings of Christ?

The chief sufferings of Christ were His bitter agony of soul, His bloody sweat, His cruel scourging, His crowning with thorns, His crucifixion, and His death on the cross.

92. When did Christ die?

Christ died on Good Friday.

93. Where did Christ die?

Christ died on Golgotha, a place outside the city of Jerusalem.

94. What do we learn from the sufferings and death of Christ?

From the sufferings and death of Christ we learn God's love for man and the evil of sin, for which God, who is all-just, demands such great satisfaction.

There are three things we learn from the sufferings and death of Christ:

I. GOD'S LOVE FOR MAN. St. John tells us, "In this we have come to know His love, that He laid down His life for us" (1 John 3, 16).

II. THE EVIL OF SIN. "He bore our sins in His body upon the tree, that we, having died to sin, might live to justice" (1 Peter 2, 24). We cannot see the harm sin does to our soul, but studying the crucifix will help us to realize it. Our sins did that to Him.

III. THE NEED OF SATISFACTION. God could have forgiven sin without requiring any satisfaction. But He did even better. If He forgave us without any satisfaction, His justice would not have been satisfied and we would always feel guilty. So He made it possible for us to make satisfaction for our sins.

He did this —

FIRST: by sending His Son, whose loving obedience even to the death of the Cross pleased Him more than sin displeased Him.

SECONDLY: by making it possible for us to share in that satisfaction through (A) Baptism and (B) the Holy Sacrifice of the Mass.

A. By *Baptism*, which makes us members of the Mystical Body of Christ. Then Christ, the head of the Body, can satisfy for us. It is like apologizing with your tongue for something you did wrong with your hands.

The flame shows our love ascending to God.

B. By *the Holy Sacrifice of the Mass*, which offers to God all our actions, especially our sufferings, in union with those of Christ.

Our own actions, even our best ones, and our own sufferings, even the worst ones we endure, could never of *themselves* please God as much as we have hurt Him by sin. But when our actions, our sufferings, our love are all united with the actions, the sufferings and the love of Christ (symbolized by the flame in this picture), and offered up with Him in the Mass, then we can please God more than we have hurt Him by sin.

In other words, we can make full satisfaction for our sins through Christ.

95. What do we mean when we say in the Apostles' Creed that Christ descended into hell?

When we say that Christ descended into hell we mean that, after He died, the soul of Christ descended into a place or state of rest, called limbo, where the souls of the just were waiting for Him.

The word "hell" simply means *the place of the dead*. Usually it refers to the place of the damned souls, but here in the Apostles' Creed it has its first meaning of the place of the dead. However, Christ did not go to all the dead, but only to the good souls, such as Abraham, Moses, David, St. Ann, St. John the Baptist, St. Joseph, and many others who had died before He did.

96. Why did Christ go to limbo?

Christ went to limbo to announce to the souls waiting there the joyful news that He had reopened heaven to mankind.

97. Where was Christ's body while His soul was in limbo?

While His soul was in limbo, Christ's body was in the holy sepulchre.

98. When did Christ rise from the dead?

Christ rose from the dead, glorious and immortal, on Easter Sunday, the third day after His death.

99. Why did Christ rise from the dead?

Christ rose from the dead to show that He is true God and to to teach us that we, too, shall rise from the dead.

Christ did not rise by the power of His HUMAN nature, but by the power of His DIVINE nature, which He shares with the Father and the Holy Spirit. That is why we often find it said in Scripture that the Father raised Him from the dead. This He did to show how pleased He was with the sacrifice of His Son, and that He was accepting that sacrifice, as we shall see on page 170, in connection with the sacrifice of the Mass.

100. Will all men rise from the dead?

All men will rise from the dead, but only those who have been faithful to Christ will share in His glory.

101. When did Christ ascend into heaven?

Christ ascended, body and soul, into heaven on Ascension Day, forty days after His Resurrection.

The Resurrection and Ascension are not so much two different mysteries as two aspects of one and the same mystery of Christ's glorification.

102. Why did Christ remain on earth forty days after his Resurrection?

Christ remained on earth forty days after His Resurrection to prove that He had truly risen from the dead and to complete the instruction of the apostles.

103. What do we mean when we say that Christ sits at the right hand of God, the Father Almighty?

When we say that Christ sits at the right hand of God, the Father Almighty, we mean that Our Lord as God is equal to the Father, and that as man He shares above all the saints in the glory of His Father and exercises for all eternity the supreme authority of a king over all creatures.

It does not mean that Christ in heaven is sitting down doing nothing, but that He has the throne of authority. He is King over all men. The authority of all rulers on earth comes from Him. The feast of Christ the King is the last Sunday in October.

104. What do we mean when we say that Christ will come from thence to judge the living and the dead?

When we say that Christ will come from thence to judge the living and the dead, we mean that on the last day Our Lord will come to pronounce a sentence of eternal reward or of eternal punishment on everyone who has ever lived in this world.

This day will be a fearful day for the enemies of Christ and His Church — even for those within the Church who are in mortal sin.

But for those who love Christ, it will be a glorious day. It is the day for which the Church is constantly waiting and praying. It will be the day on which Christ will come and take us all, both the living and the dead, to be with Him body and soul forever in heaven.

DISCUSSION QUESTIONS:

1. Did God plan the death of his Son?
2. Was He mean to do this? Why not?
3. Which was the more important in redeeming us: Christ's bodily pain or the love of His Sacred Heart? Why?
4. Does Christ love us more than His Father does? Give a reason for your answer.
5. Could we make full satisfaction for our own sins if Christ had not died on the Cross for us? Why not?
6. How do we make the satisfaction of Christ our own?
7. Where did Christ's soul go immediately after death? What for?
8. Did Christ rise from the dead or did the Father raise Him?
9. Is Christ King of this country?
10. Is the second coming of Christ something to fear?

TRUE OR FALSE: *(Also change each false statement to a true one.)*

1. God did not want His Son to die on the Cross.
2. Our Blessed Mother did not want Him to die on the Cross.
3. God could have forgiven us even if Christ had not died on the Cross.
4. Christ suffered so much to show the greatness of His love.
5. The devil tried to prevent Christ from doing His Father's will.
6. Our Lady willingly offered up her Son for men's sins.
7. Christ could not stop the soldiers from nailing Him to the Cross.
8. When Christ descended into hell, He released all the souls condemned to the hell of fire.
9. The Father raised Christ's body from the dead and took Him to heaven to show He was pleased with His Son's sacrifice.
10. The Father has made all men subjects of Christ the King and Mary the Queen.

FILL IN THE BLANKS:

1. Christ undid the harm done to the human race by another man named ....

2. Mary undid the harm done to the human race by another woman named ....

3. Christ redeemed us by His sufferings and death, which were the outward expression of the .... of His Sacred Heart.

4. The five chief sufferings of Christ, which we think of in the five sorrowful mysteries of the Rosary, are ...., ..., ..., ..., ...

5. The three things we learn from the sufferings and death of Christ are ...., ..., and ....

6. We share in the satisfaction of Christ chiefly by ...., and ....

7. When we say that Christ descended into hell, we do not mean that He went to see all the dead, but only those in ....

8. Christ rose from the dead to show .... and to teach. ....

9. The Father raised His Son from the dead to show ....
....

10. Christ rose from the dead by the power of His ....
nature.

READ FROM THE BIBLE:

It is hard to single out passages from the Bible to explain this lesson, since the whole Bible treats of it. The central theme of the Bible is that Jesus, the Son of God, is the Christ, or Redeemer. The Old Testament is filled with types and prophecies of the coming Redemption. The New Testament gives the historical account of the Redemption and explains it for us. The following passages are suggested:

1. The first promise of redemption — Gen. 3, 15. See page 36.

2. The account of Noe — Gen. 6; 7; and 8. See 1 Pet. 3, 18-22.

3. Abraham's sacrifice of Isaac — Gen. 22. This is a symbol of the Father sacrificing His Son for us on the Cross, then raising Him from the dead. See Heb. 11, 17-19.

4. Moses and the Israelites in the desert — Ex. 1-20; 32-34; Num. 13-14; Deut. 1-4; 34; Jos. 1-11. Moses was a type of Christ who rescues us from the Egyptian slavery of Satan, brings us through the the Red Sea by Baptism in which our enemy, original sin, is drowned, leads us through the desert of this world to the promised land of heaven, meanwhile giving us to drink of the rock which is Himself (see 1 Cor. 10, 1-11) of the living waters of the Holy Spirit (see John 7, 37-39). He feeds us with the manna of the Eucharist (John 6, 32-33), and heals the bites of the poisonous serpents of our own sins by the true brazen serpent of the Cross, the blood of which is poured out on us in the Sacrament of Penance (John 3, 14-15).

The enemies of the Israelites, mentioned throughout the Old Testament, were a symbol of the enemies of our soul, especially sin. God often told the Hebrews to kill every one of their enemies, even the women, children and cattle, to show us that we must completely kill every trace of sin in us to reach heaven.

5. Some prophecies of the Passion — Ps. 21; 68; Is. 53.

6. The accounts of the Redemption itself — Matt. 26-28; Mark 14-16; Luke 22-24; John 18-21. See Acts, Ch. 1, for the Ascension.

7. For our share in the Redemption, see especially Matt. 16, 21-28; Rom. 6, 1-11; 1 Pet. 2, 21-25.

Note. To read all this will take some time, but it will be time well spent, as this is the most important lesson in the catechism.

CLASS PROJECT:

I. Make the Stations of the Cross. Then write a reflection on each Station that fits one your age. Page 252 may give you some ideas.

II. Read the hymn "Exultet" at the beginning of the Easter Vigil Service from your Missal. How many effects and symbols of the Redemption can you find there?

PRAYER:

Holy Mother pierce me through.
In my heart each wound renew
Of my Savior crucified.   *(From the hymn "Stabat Mater")*

LESSON 9 — The Holy Spirit and Grace

". . . I believe in the Holy Spirit . . ."

God's Gifts to Adam

The Devil's Gifts to Us

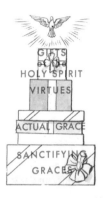
Christ's Gifts to Us

"Where the offense has abounded, grace has abounded yet more" (Romans 5, 20).

Christ, seated at the right hand of the Father, pours down His gifts on us, gifts greater than those lost by Adam, gifts which overcome for us the evil gifts of the devil. (See Lesson 5.)

A. THE HOLY SPIRIT

105. Who is the Holy Spirit?

The Holy Spirit is God and the third Person of the Blessed Trinity.

The Holy Spirit, symbolized by a dove, comes from the Father and the Son like love from the heart. He is the mutual Love of the Father and the Son.

106. From whom does the Holy Spirit proceed?

The Holy Spirit proceeds from the Father ond the Son.

107. Is the Holy Spirit equal to the Father and the Son?

The Holy Spirit is equal to the Father and the Son, because He is God.

108. What does the Holy Spirit do for the salvation of mankind?

The Holy Spirit dwells in the Church as the source of its life and sanctifies souls through the gift of grace.

As we shall see in Lesson 11, the Church is the Mystical Body of Christ. He is the Head and we are the members.

The Holy Spirit is the soul of the Church. He dwells in it to give it life. The life-blood of grace which flows through every living member of the Mystical Body of Christ comes from the Holy Spirit.

Mystical Body of Christ

B. GRACE

109. What is grace?

Grace is a supernatural gift of God bestowed on us through the merits of Jesus Christ for our salvation.

110. How many kinds of grace are there?

There are two kinds of grace: sanctifying grace and actual grace.

This means that these are the two chief kinds of grace. Any gift of God can be called a grace, but these are the two most important.

111. What is sanctifying grace?

Sanctifying grace is that grace which confers on our souls a new life, that is, a sharing in the life of God Himself.

CHRIST IN US

Briefly, GRACE IS LIFE — divine life in our soul. By it, Christ lives in us and we in Him. As St. Paul says, "It is now no longer I that live, but Christ lives in me" (Gal. 2, 20). Or as Christ Himself says, "Abide in Me, and I in you" (John 15, 4).

Grace will be more fully treated in the Section on the Sacraments, especially pages 146 and 147.

Grace is Divine Life in Our Soul

112. What are the chief effects of sanctifying grace?

The chief effects of sanctifying are:

first, it makes us holy and pleasing to God;
second, it makes us adopted children of God;
third, it makes us temples of the Holy Ghost;
fourth, it gives us the right to heaven.

EFFECTS OF GRACE

| Makes us Children of God | Makes us Temples of the Holy Ghost | Gives us the Right to Heaven, Our Home |

113. What is actual grace?

Actual grace is a supernatural help of God which enlightens our mind and strengthens our will to do good and to avoid evil.

Actual graces are special HELPS God gives us, like a lift to get a car out of the mud or a red light to warn of danger.

God gives us many actual graces each day. They last as long as we need them and then go. They are really actions of God to help us.

But sanctifying grace is permanent and, unless we lose it by sin, it will last until it becomes the life of glory in heaven.

114. Can we resist the grace of God?

We can resist the grace of God, for our will is free, and God does not force us to accept His grace.

If you keep the brake on in the car, it is hard to push it out of the mud. God could force us, but He will not.

115. Why is sanctifying grace necessary for salvation?

Sanctifying grace is necessary for salvation because it is the supernatural life, which alone enables us to attain the supernatural happiness of heaven.

116. Is actual grace necessary for all who have attained the use of reason?

Actual grace is necessary for all who have attained the use of reason, because without it we cannot long resist the power of temptation or perform other actions which merit a reward in heaven.

C. SOURCES OF GRACE

117. What are the principal ways of obtaining grace?

The principal ways of obtaining grace are prayer and the sacraments, especially the Holy Eucharist.

118. How can we make our most ordinary actions merit a heavenly reward?

We can make our most ordinary actions merit a heavenly reward by doing them for the love of God and by keeping ourselves in the state of grace.

DISCUSSION QUESTIONS:

1. Is the Holy Ghost a dove?
2. Did the Father create the Holy Ghost?
3. Why does the Holy Ghost dwell in every soul with grace?
4. What does the Holy Ghost do for the Church?
5. Do you think we have more opportunities to grow in grace than Adam and Eve did before they sinned?
6. When we are in the state of grace, who lives in us?
7. Can we drive Him out? How?
8. What does grace do for our bodies?
9. Can we get to heaven without grace? Why not?
10. Can we see or feel grace? Why not?

TRUE OR FALSE: *(Also change each false statement to a true one.)*

1. Since Christ is in heaven He cannot live in our souls, too.
2. Actual grace lasts forever.
3. The life of sanctifying grace ends when we die.
4. It is more important to develop the life of grace in us than to develop our human life.
5. Actions with no love for God in them do not make grace grow.

FILL IN THE BLANKS:

1. The third Person of the Blessed Trinity is . . . .
2. The Holy Spirit gives to the Church the life of . . . .
3. Any gift of God can be called a . . . .
4. The two chief kinds of grace are . . . . and . . . .
5. Grace is the life of . . . . in us.
6. If we do not commit mortal sin, sanctifying grace will last

. . . .
7. Actual grace helps us to . . . . and to . . . .
8. Without grace we cannot get to . . . .
9. The principal ways of obtaining grace are . . . .

. . . .
10. The most important of these is . . . .

READ FROM THE BIBLE:

The Holy Ghost — John 14, 15-31; 16, 5-15; Romans 8.
Sanctifying Grace — John 10, 10; Eph. 1, 3-14; 2, 4-9; 1 John 3, 1-3.
Actual Grace — 2 Cor. 12, 7-10; Heb. 4, 14-16.

CLASS PROJECT:

Since grace is the life of Christ in the soul, we must imitate Christ in order to lead this life. Let each boy and girl make a poster, diagram, cartoon, or write a description of a practical way in which a modern boy or girl can imitate a particular action or virtue in the life of Christ.

PRAYER: Say the prayer "Come, Holy Spirit," on inside front cover.

LESSON 10 — The Virtues and Gifts of the Holy Ghost

VIRTUES

GIFTS OF THE HOLY GHOST

119. What are the chief supernatural powers that are bestowed on our souls with sanctifying grace?

The chief supernatural powers that are bestowed on our souls with sanctifying grace are the three theological virtues and the seven gifts of the Holy Ghost.

Supernatural means "above the natural." Something is supernatural when it is above our natural power to acquire or deserve. No matter what we might do ourselves, we could never obtain or deserve grace unless God gave it to us.

A supernatural virtue is one which is beyond the natural powers of any creature. With our natural powers we can eat, we can talk, we can run. But we cannot love our enemies, for example, with our own natural powers. God has to give us a power above the natural, that is, the virtue of charity, to enable us to do this.

A. VIRTUES

120. Why are these virtues called theological virtues?

These virtues are called theological virtues because they have God for their proper object.

Theological means "pertaining to God." Theology is the study of God.

121. What are the three theological virtues?

The three theological virtues are faith, hope, and charity.

122. What is faith?

Faith is the virtue by which we firmly believe all the truths God has revealed, on the word of God revealing them, who can neither deceive nor be deceived.

FAITH IS *BELIEF* IN GOD — Faith says, "I believe everything God has said simply because He has said it, no matter how impossible it seems; for example, the Eucharist is really Christ's Body and Blood."

123. What is hope?

Hope is the virtue by which we firmly trust that God, who is all-powerful and faithful to His promises, will in His mercy give us eternal happiness and the means to obtain it.

HOPE IS *TRUST* IN GOD — Hope says, "I trust that God will help me to get to heaven because He is able and has promised to do so, no matter how impossible it seems because of my own weakness."

124. What is charity?

Charity is the virtue by which we love God above all things for His own sake, and our neighbor as ourselves for the love of God.

CHARITY IS *LOVE* OF GOD — Charity says, " I love God above all things simply because He is good and deserves to be loved. I will try to please Him in everything by always seeking to know and do His will. I will love everyone else for His sake."

B. GIFTS OF THE HOLY SPIRIT

125. Which are the seven gifts of the Holy Spirit?

The seven gifts of the Holy Spirit are: wisdom, understanding, counsel, fortitude, knowledge, piety, and fear of the Lord.

Each gift is explained in the Dictionary and Index, page 244.

126. How do the gifts of the Holy Spirit help us?

The gifts of the Holy Spirit help us by making us more alert to discern and more ready to do the will of God.

The gifts of the Holy Spirit enable us to catch the breath of the Holy Spirit, moving the ship of our soul much faster and farther than we could ever sail it by using the virtues ourselves.

For example, we can use the virtue of faith by making an act of faith. But to use this virtue constantly, being aware of God's presence in us and about us at all times, is more than we can do ourselves unless the Holy Spirit does it in us.

Likewise, we can make an act of love. But to love our enemies for God's sake and to be willing even to die for them, we need the help of the Holy Spirit.

The power of the Holy Spirit, which our ship catches by unfolding the sails of the gifts, enables us to do even things that are humanly impossible. It is the gifts of the Holy Spirit in the souls of the saints that explain the seemingly impossible things in their lives.

127. Which are some of the effects in us of the gifts of the Holy Spirit?

Some of the effects in us of the gifts of the Holy Spirit are the fruits of the Holy Spirit and the beatitudes.

128. Which are the twelve fruits of the Holy Spirit?

The twelve fruits of the Holy Spirit are: charity joy, peace, patience, benignity, goodness, long-suffering, mildness, faith, modesty, continency, and chastity.

129. Which are the eight beatitudes?

The eight beatitudes are:

1. Blessed are the poor in spirit, for theirs is the kingdom of heaven.
2. Blessed are the meek, for they shall possess the earth.
3. Blessed are they who mourn, for they shall be comforted.
4. Blessed are they who hunger and thirst for justice, for they shall be satisfied.
5. Blessed are the merciful, for they shall obtain mercy.
6. Blessed are the clean of heart, for they shall see God.
7. Blessed are the peacemakers, for they shall be called children of God.
8. Blessed are they who suffer persecution for justice' sake, for theirs is the kingdom of heaven.

The beatitudes are eight roads to perfect happiness. They are the standards or rules Christ sets up for His followers. They are just the opposite of the standards of this world.

Those who live by the standards of this world are really living pagan lives, even though they may be Catholics in name. Only those who try to live their lives according to the beatitudes are really Catholics in practice.

STANDARDS OF CHRIST	STANDARDS OF THIS WORLD
1. Blessed are the poor in spirit, that is, those who love the humble condition of the poor.	1. Be a successful man, that is, one who makes a lot of money.
2. Blessed are the meek.	2. Get things your own way.
3. Blessed are they who mourn.	3. We have a right to enjoy life.
4. Blessed are they who hunger and thirst after justice, that is, not after the things of this world, but the grace of God and all that goes with it.	4. Love the things of this world.
5. Blessed are the merciful.	5. Get even with those who hurt you.
6. Blessed are the clean of heart, that is, those whose hearts are clean of desire for pleasure and desire only God.	6. Seek pleasure of all kinds.
7. Blessed are the peacemakers.	7. Am I my brother's keeper?
8. Blessed are they who suffer persecution.	8. Avoid all suffering, and if it comes, complain about it.
These cause a certain amount of suffering, but they lead to great happiness even here on earth, and to heaven afterwards.	These may give a certain amount of pleasure, but they lead to unhappiness even here on earth, and to hell in the next life.

130. Are there any other virtues besides the theological virtues of faith, hope, and charity?

Besides the theological virtues of faith, hope and charity there are other virtues, called moral virtues.

131. Why are these virtues called moral virtues?

These virtues are called moral virtues because they dispose us to lead moral, or good, lives by aiding us to treat persons and things in the right way, that is, according to the will of God.

132. Which are the chief moral virtues?

The chief moral virtues are prudence, justice, fortitude, and temperance; these are called cardinal virtues.

133. Why are these virtues called cardinal virtues?

These virtues are called cardinal virtues because they are like hinges on which hang all the other moral virtues and our whole moral life. The word "cardinal" is derived from the Latin word "cardo" meaning hinge.

134. How do prudence, justice, fortitude, and temperance dispose us to lead good lives?

Prudence disposes us in all circumstances to form right judgments about what we must do or not do.

Justice disposes us to give everyone what belongs to him.

Fortitude disposes us to do what is good in spite of any difficulty.

Temperance disposes us to control our desires and to use rightly the things which please our senses.

135. Which are some of the other moral virtues?

Some of the other moral virtues are:

Filial piety and patriotism, which dispose us to honor, love, and respect our parents and our country.

Obedience, which disposes us to do the will of our superiors.

Veracity, which disposes us to tell the truth.

Liberality, which disposes us rightly to use worldly goods.

Patience, which disposes us to bear up under trials and difficulties.

Humility, which disposes us to acknowledge our limitations.

Chastity, or purity, which disposes us to be pure in soul and body.

Besides these, there are many other moral virtues.

DISCUSSION QUESTIONS:

1. If a man believes only some of the truths that God has revealed, does he have the virtue of faith? Why not?

2. If someone says to you, "I can't become a saint; it is too hard," what virtue is he lacking?

3. Is charity the same as giving to the poor?

4. Is it charity to love everyone on earth except one person?

5. Does God command us to do impossible things, that is, impossible to our own unaided human powers? What, for example?

6. If Tom prays for the boy who stole his bicycle, what beatitude or beatitudes is he following?

7. If Eddie says, "Let me pitch or I will take my ball home and end the game," what standard of the world is he following?

8. Does pleasure bring happiness? Why not?

9. If Ruth, who lives next to the church, does not go to Communion on weekdays because she is afraid the other girls will tease her about being a saint, in what virtue is she weak?

10. What virtue leads us to seek advice in important matters?

TRUE OR FALSE: *(Also change each false statement to a true one.)*

1. Faith, hope and charity are the only supernatural powers that come to our soul with grace.

2. Faith means that everyone has a right to believe what he wishes.

3. If a man gives to the poor to get an income tax reduction, he is practicing the virtue of charity.

4. Charity helps us to love people we do not like.

5. We will be happy if we can get things our own way.

6. It is a greater grace if God enables a person to bear suffering than if He takes it away.

7. If a girl spends more time looking in store windows at things she would like to have than she does in praying, it shows that she is not living up to the fourth beatitude.

8. To live up to the beatitudes at all times we need the special help of the Holy Spirit.

9. If a boy keeps on playing ball when his mother calls him to go to the store, he needs more of the virtue of temperance.

10. If we try hard enough we can think of God every minute of the day even without the special help of the Holy Spirit.

FILL IN THE BLANKS:

1. The three theological virtues are ....
...................., and ....

2. The most important of these is ....

3. The seven gifts of the Holy Spirit are ....,
..................., ..., ...,
..................., ...

4. The four cardinal virtues are: . . . . , ... ,
. . . . , ...

5. If a boy could go to Communion every day without too much difficulty but just does not care to do so, it shows he is not living according to the beatitude which says . . . .
. . . .

6. Anyone who holds a grudge against someone else is not living according to the beatitude which says . . . .
. . . .

7. Listening to our conscience at all times is an act of the virtue of . . . .

8. A soldier who fights for his country is practicing the virtue of
. . . .

9. Anyone who brags about himself shows that he is weak in the virtue of . . . .

10. Looking at immodest pictures is a danger to the virtue of
. . . .

READ FROM THE BIBLE:

Virtues in general — Rom. 5, 1-5; Eph. 2, 10; 2 Pet. 1, 3-11.
Faith — Matt. 14, 22-33; John 6, 43-70; 20, 24-31; Heb. 11.
Hope — Ps. 30; 41; 42; 129; Matt. 6, 25-34; Rom. 4, 18—5, 11; Heb. 4, 14-16.
Charity — Luke 6, 27-38; John 13; 1 Cor. 13; 1 John 3, 16-18; 4, 7-16.
Humility — Matt. 11, 20-30; Luke 14, 7-11; Phil. 2, 1-11.
Gifts of the Holy Ghost — Is. 11, 1-3; 1 Cor. 2, 6-16.
Fruits of the Holy Ghost — Gal. 5, 16-25.

CLASS PROJECT:

This afternoon or tonight watch a TV program or listen to a radio program. Prepare a report for tomorrow on the following points:

1. List any of the beatitudes practiced by any of the characters on the program. List any virtues which they practiced.

2. List any of the beatitudes violated by any of the characters. List any of the standards of the world which they were following. Pay attention especially to the standards of the hero or the heroine. Would you say that they were living according to the standards of Christ?

Perhaps you might make a similar report the next day or as many days as the teacher thinks best.

PRAYER:

Acts of Faith, Hope and Love, as on pages 5 and 6.

"I believe in . . . the Holy Catholic Church . . ."

PENTECOST — the day the Church began its work. Read Acts, Chapter 2.

"You are now no longer strangers and foreigners, but you are citizens with the saints and members of God's household: you are built upon the foundation of the Apostles and prophets with Christ Jesus Himself as the chief cornerstone. In Him the whole structure is closely fitted together and grows into a temple holy in the Lord; in Him you too are being built together into a dwelling place for God in the Spirit" (Ephesians 2, 19-22).

The Church — God's building.

136. What is the Church?

The Church is the congregation of all baptized persons united in the same true faith, the same sacrifice, and the same sacraments, under the authority of the Sovereign Pontiff and the bishops in communion with him.

THE CHURCH IS THE MYSTICAL BODY OF CHRIST

ITS HEAD — Christ	ITS SOUL — The Holy Spirit
ITS MEMBERS — The faithful	ITS LIFE — Grace

Just as a human body has one head, so does the Church have one Head who is Christ. The Pope is His Vicar, or representative, on earth, the visible head of the Church.

Just as our human body is made up of many members, such as hands, feet, eyes, lungs, heart, etc., so is the Mystical Body of Christ composed of many members. The members of the Church are those who are baptized, profess the true faith, and have not left or been expelled (excommunicated) from the Church. (See Q. 169F.)

The Church is the fullness of Christ — Head and members, the whole Christ. In the Church we are all one in Christ. In a mysterious, yet true sense, the Church IS Christ.

Some symbols and comparisons the Bible uses for the Church militant on earth and triumphant in heaven are: the vine, the sheepfold, the ark of Noe, the new Jerusalem, the bride of Christ.

137. Who founded the Church?

Jesus Christ founded the Church.

138. Why did Jesus Christ found the Church?

Jesus Christ founded the Church to bring all men to eternal salvation.

139. How is the Church enabled to lead men to salvation?

The Church is enabled to lead men to salvation by the indwelling of the Holy Ghost, who gives it life.

140. When was the dwelling of the Holy Spirit in the Church first visible manifested?

The dwelling of the Holy Spirit in the Church was first visibly manifested on Pentecost Sunday, when He came down upon the apostles in the form of tongues of fire.

141. How long will the Holy Spirit dwell in the Church?

The Holy Spirit will dwell in the Church until the end of time.

142. Who sent the Holy Spirit to dwell in the Church?

God the Father and God the Son sent the Holy Spirit to dwell in the Church.

143. What does the indwelling of the Holy Spirit enable the Church to do?

The indwelling of the Holy Spirit enables the Church to teach, to sanctify, and to rule the faithful in the name of Christ.

Just as a human body has one soul to give it life, so the Mystical Body of Christ has one soul, the Holy Spirit. He dwells in the body as a whole and in each living member, filling it with divine life.

Just as a human body has a human life, so does the Mystical Body of Christ have a divine life, which we call sanctifying grace.

144. What is meant by teaching, sanctifying, and ruling in the name of Christ?

By teaching, sanctifying, and ruling in the name of Christ is meant that the Church always does the will of its Divine Founder, who remains forever its invisible Head.

THE CHURCH TEACHING	THE CHURCH SANCTIFYING	THE CHURCH RULING

Christ stands behind the preaching of the Church.	It is He who is the invisible Minister of every sacrament.	It is He who guides the Church in making its laws.

145. To whom did Christ give the power to teach, to sanctify, and to rule the members of His Church?

Christ gave the power to teach, to sanctify, and to rule the members of His Church to the apostles, the first bishops of the Church.

146. Did Christ intend that this power should be exercised by the apostles alone?

No, Christ intended that this power should be exercised also by their successors, the bishops of the Church.

147. Did Christ give special power in His Church to any one of the apostles?

Christ gave special power in His Church to Saint Peter by making him the head of the apostles and the chief teacher and ruler of the entire Church.

148. Did Christ intend that the special power of chief teacher and ruler of the entire Church should be exercised by Saint Peter alone?

Christ did not intend that the special power of chief teacher and ruler of the entire Church should be exercised by Saint Peter alone, but intended that this power should be passed down to his successor, the Pope, the Bishop of Rome, who is the Vicar of Christ on earth and the visible head of the Church.

149. Who assist the bishops in the care of souls?

The priests, especially parish priests, assist the bishops in the care of souls.

150. Who are the laity of the Church?

The laity of the Church are all its members who do not belong to the clerical or to the religious state.

151. How can the laity help the Church in her care of souls?

The laity can help the Church in her care of souls by leading lives that will reflect credit on the Church, and by co-operating with their bishops and priests, especially through Catholic Action.

CATHOLIC ACTION

| Teaching Summer School | The Legion of Mary | Volunteer work in hospitals and orphanages | Distributing Catholic literature |

151 A. What is Catholic Action?

Catholic Action is the active participation of the laity in the apostolate of the Church under the guidance of the hierarchy.

GIVE GOOD EXAMPLE AND ENCOURAGEMENT

Every Catholic is obliged to help the Church to spread. Non-Catholics are most often brought into the Church by the good example of Catholics and kept away by bad example. Be interested in non-Catholics, don't argue, but answer their sincere questions. Encourage them and, if possible, don't just *tell them,* but *take* them to see a priest.

151 B. In what ways can the laity participate actively in the apostolate of the Church?

The laity can participate actively in the apostolate of the Church when they arouse the interest of non-Catholics in the Catholic faith; promote high standards in the press, motion pictures, radio and television; participate in the work of the Confraternity of Christian Doctrine; take part in the activities of Catholic societies and organizations; represent, under proper direction, the Church's position in speaking and writing; and go as lay missionaries to foreign lands.

DISCUSSION QUESTIONS:

1. Who are the members of the Church?
2. Can you see the Mystical Body of Christ?
3. What kind of life does the Church have and what is it called?
4. How are you united with other members of the Church?
5. Can you love Christ and hate some member of His Body?
6. What three things does Christ do for us through His Church?
7. Are we obedient to Christ if we disobey the Church? Why not?
8. Who was the first Pope? Who made him Pope?

9. What does Catholic Action mean?

10. Why is it important to give good example to non-Catholics?

TRUE OR FALSE: *(Also change each false statement to a true one.)*

1. The Holy Spirit dwells in each member of the Church.

2. An excommunicated person is no longer a member of the Mystical Body of Christ.

3. If we hurt a member of the Church, we hurt Christ.

4. Some of the laws of the Church are foolish.

5. Lay people have nothing to do with the work of the Church.

FILL IN THE BLANKS:

1. The Head of the Mystical Body is ....

2. His representative on earth is ....

3. The soul of the Church is ....

4. The life of the Church is ....

5. The members of the Church are ....

6. The three powers of the Church are to ...., to ...., and to .... the faithful.

7. Christ exercises these powers chiefly through the ....

8. The ones who assist the bishops in exercising these three powers are ....

9. Lay people can assist the priests in their work, especially through ....

10. Two ways to help non-Catholics to find the true Church of Christ are .... and ....

READ FROM THE BIBLE:

The Mystical Body — Acts 9, 4-5; Rom. 12, 4-5; 1 Cor. 12, 12-27; Col. 1, 18. 24.

The Vine — Ps. 79; 127; Osee 14; John 15, 1-17.

The Sheepfold — Ps. 22; Is. 40; Ez. 34; John 10, 1-18.

The Ark of Noe — Gen. 6-9; 1 Pet. 3, 18-22.

The New Jerusalem — Ps. 121; 136; 147; Is. 60; 62; Jer. 33; Zach. 14; Gal. 4, 26; Apoc. 21.

The Bride — Ps. 44; Cant. 2; Is. 49, 14-18; Mark 2, 19-20; John 3, 29; Eph. 5, 25-27.

Spreading the Church by good example — 1 Pet. 2, 11-12; 4, 1-11.

CLASS PROJECT:

Try starting a project to assist the missions by collecting magazines, or stamps, or by writing to missionaries. Help spread the faith at home by spreading Catholic literature in your local barber shops, railroad and bus stations, etc.

PRAYER:

Graciously hear the prayers of Your Church, we beseech You, O Lord, that all adversity and error may be destroyed and she may serve You in perfect security and freedom. Through Christ Our Lord. Amen.   *(From the Roman Missal)*

THE CHURCH

MARKS

ONE
HOLY
CATHOLIC
APOSTOLIC

ATTRIBUTES

AUTHORITY
INFALLIBILITY
INDEFECTIBILITY

152. Which is the one true Church established by Christ?

The one true Church established by Christ is the Catholic Church.

A. MARKS of the Church

153. How do we know that the Catholic Church is the one true Church established by Christ?

We know that the Catholic Church is the one true Church established by Christ because it alone has the marks of the true Church.

154. What do we mean by the marks of the Church?

By the marks of the Church we mean certain clear signs by which all men can recognize it as the true Church founded by Jesus Christ.

For example, if you want me to find your house, you might tell me it is a yellow brick house on Main Avenue, between Third and Fourth Streets.

There may be many houses on Main Avenue, even many brick houses, but only one yellow brick house between Third and Fourth Streets. These signs enable me tell your house.

So do the four marks of the Church enable us to tell it as the Church of Jesus Christ.

155. What are the chief marks of the Church?

The chief marks of the Church are four: It is one, holy, catholic or universal, and apostolic.

156. Why is the Catholic Church one?

The Catholic Church is one because all its members, according to the will of Christ, profess the same faith, have the same sacrifice and sacraments, and are united under one and the same visible head, the Pope.

157. Why is the Catholic Church holy?

The Catholic Church is holy because it was founded by Jesus Christ, who is all-holy, and because it teaches, according to the will of Christ, holy doctrines, and provides the means of leading a holy life, thereby giving holy members to every age.

158. Why is the Catholic Church catholic or universal?

The Catholic Church is catholic or universal because, destined to last for all time, it never fails to fulfill the divine commandment to teach all nations all the truths revealed by God.

159. Why is the Catholic Church apostolic?

The Catholic Church is apostolic because it was founded by Christ on the apostles and, according to His divine will, has always been governed by their lawful successors.

160. How do we know that no other church but the Catholic Church is the true Church of Christ?

We know that no other church but the Catholic Church is the true Church of Christ because no other church has these four marks.

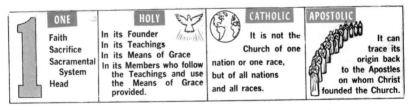

ONE	HOLY	CATHOLIC	APOSTOLIC
Faith Sacrifice Sacramental System Head	In its Founder In its Teachings In its Means of Grace In its Members who follow the Teachings and use the Means of Grace provided.	It is not the Church of one nation or one race, but of all nations and all races.	It can trace its origin back to the Apostles on whom Christ founded the Church.

Only the Catholic Church has all four of these marks. It alone is the Church Christ founded. But we must convince men of this by love. "By this will all men know that you are my disciples, if you have love for one another" (John 13, 35).

B. ATTRIBUTES (or Qualities) of the Church

161. What are the chief attributes of the Catholic Church?

The chief attributes of the Catholic Church are authority, infallibility, and indefectibility. They are called attributes because they are qualities perfecting 'the nature of the Church.

162. What is meant by the authority of the Catholic Church?

By the authority of the Catholic Church is meant that the Pope and the bishops, as the lawful successors of the apostles, have power from Christ Himself to teach, to sanctify, and to govern the faithful in spiritual matters.

Authority is the power to command others. All authority is from God, and He gives it to the Church in spiritual matters. To refuse to obey the authority of the Church is to refuse to obey Christ. He Himself said to His disciples, "He who hears you, hears Me; and he who rejects you, rejects Me" (Luke 10, 16).

163. What is meant by the infallibility of the Catholic Church?

By the infallibility of the Catholic Church is meant that the Church, by the special assistance of the Holy Ghost, cannot err when it teaches or believes a doctrine of faith or morals.

Infallibility does not mean that the Pope cannot commit a sin, but that in teaching a doctrine of faith or morals, he is prevented by the Holy Ghost from making a mistake. The Church teaches only truth.

164. When does the Church teach infallibly?

The Church teaches infallibly when it defines, through the Pope alone, as the teacher of all Christians, or through the Pope and the bishops, a doctrine of faith or morals to be held by all the faithful.

165. What is meant by the indefectibility of the Catholic Church?

By the indefectibility of the Catholic Church is meant that the Church, as Christ founded it, will last until the end of time.

Nations will rise and fall. False religions will come and go. But the Church will last forever.

166. Are all obliged to belong to the Catholic Church in order to be saved?

All are obliged to belong to the Catholic Church in order to be saved.

167. What do we mean when we say, "Outside the Church there is no salvation?

When we say, "Outside the Church there is no salvation," we mean that Christ made the Catholic Church a necessary means of salvation and commanded all to enter it, so that a person must be connected with the Church in some way to be saved.

No one can be saved except by being united to the Catholic Church. It is like Noe's Ark which saved men from the flood. Only through Christ and His Mystical Body can men be saved. They must be either in the Ark of the Church or at least hanging onto the ropes which trail from its sides. (See Question 321.)

Read Genesis 6—8; 1 Peter 3, 18-22.

Christ Himself said, "He who believes and is baptized shall be saved, but he who does not believe shall be condemned" (Mark 16, 16).

168. How can persons who are not members of the Catholic Church be saved?

Persons who are not members of the Catholic Church can be saved if, through no fault of their own they do not know that the Catholic Church is the true Church, but they love God and try to do His will, for in this way they are connected with the Church by desire.

These are really members of the Church in desire and receive grace through the Church. But we should pray that they actually enter the Church where there are more helps to be saved.

169. Why is the Catholic Church called the Mystical Body of Christ?

The Catholic Church is called the Mystical Body of Christ because its members are united by supernatural bonds with one another and with Christ, their Head, thus resembling the members and head of the living human body.

When the Father looks down from heaven at the Church, He sees Christ. THE CHURCH IS CHRIST. It is His body of which He is the Head and we are the members. (See p. 72.)

When Christ, our Head, looks down from the Cross at the Church, He sees Mary. THE CHURCH IS MARY. She is Holy Mother Church, containing, as it were, all the members of the Church in herself to unite them to Christ, our Head.

Mary is the Mother of Christ in the flesh, but in the life of grace, she is His bride. Her divine life came from His, not His from hers. (See p. 37.) What Pope Pius XII says of the Church is true of her, "As a second Eve she came forth from the side of the new Adam in His sleep on the Cross." She is the new Eve leading all her children to the Cross, the tree of life, to drink from Christ's open side the living waters of the Holy Spirit, the new wine of holy love.

MARY, MOTHER OF THE CHURCH

Our Lord showed St. John the meaning of what had happened on Mt. Calvary, using Jerusalem as a symbol for Mary, Mother of the Church.

" 'Come, I will show thee the bride, the spouse of the Lamb.' And he took me up in spirit to a mountain great and high and showed me the holy city Jerusalem, coming down out of heaven from God, having the glory of God . . . In the midst of the city street, on both sides of the river, was the tree of life " (Apoc. 21,9-11;22,2).

"Behold thy mother" (John 19, 27).

169. What conditions are necessary in order that a person be a member of the Mystical Body in the full sense?

In order that a person be a member of the Mystical Body in the full sense, it is necessary that he be baptized, that he profess the Catholic faith, and that he neither separate himself from the Mystical Body nor be excluded by lawful authority.

169 B. How does a baptized person separate himself from full incorporation in the Mystical Body?

A baptized person separates himself from full incorporation in the Mystical Body by open and deliberate heresy, apostasy or schism.

169 C. How does a baptized person separate himself from full incorporation in the Mystical Body by heresy?

A baptized person separates himself from full incorporation in the Mystical Body by heresy when he openly rejects or doubts some doctrine proposed by the Catholic Church as a truth of divine-Catholic faith, though still professing himself a Christian.

169 D. When does a baptized person separate himself from full incorporation in the Mystical Body by apostasy?

A baptized person separates himself from full incorporation in the Mystical Body by apostasy when he openly rejects the entire Christian faith.

169 E. When does a baptized person separate himself from full incorporation in the Mystical Body by schism?

A baptized person separates himself from full incorporation in the Mystical Body by schism when he openly refuses obedience to the lawful authorities of the Church, particularly to the Pope.

169 F. When is a baptized person separated from full incorporation in the Mystical Body by lawful authority?

A baptized person is separated from full incorporation in the Mystical Body by lawful authority when he incurs one of the more severe forms of excommunication.

DISCUSSION QUESTIONS:

1. How do we tell which is the true Church?
2. How can the Church be holy if there are many sinners in it?
3. Is one religion as good as another? Why not?
4. Are all non-Catholics going to hell? Why not?
5. How is Mary really our Mother when she lived so long ago?

TRUE OR FALSE: *(Also change each false statement to a true one.)*

1. The Church does not matter as long as you lead a good life.
2. Catholics have all the means they need to be holy.

3. Catholics are slaves to the Pope and the bishops.

4. Catholics are forbidden to think for themselves.

5. The Pope cannot commit a sin.

6. It is much harder for non-Catholics, even those in good faith, to be saved than it is for Catholics.

7. No one can be saved except through the Church.

8. Christ does not care whether we are Catholics or not.

9. The Church is a visible organization.

10. Mary loves us more than anyone else except God Himself.

FILL IN THE BLANKS:

1. The marks of the Church are .... which point it out as the Church of Christ.

2. The fact that the Church has the same faith, sacrifice, sacramental system, and head shows that the Church is ....

3. Members of the Church who lead good lives help to show that the Church is ....

4. The fact that the Church is governed by successors of the Apostles shows that it is ....

5. The Church is for all nations because it is ....

6. The only church which has all four marks is ....

7. The Pope cannot make a mistake in teaching a doctrine of faith or morals because of ....

8. The Church will last till the end of time because of its ....

9. The Church has power to compel our obedience because of its ....

10. Non-Catholics in good faith are members of the Church in ....

READ FROM THE BIBLE:

Attributes — Matt. 16, 13-20; 28, 16-20; John 21, 15-17.

Marks — Matt. 9, 35 — 10, 39; John 17; Eph. 4, 16.

CLASS PROJECT:

Let everyone make a poster using drawings or symbols to show Mary as Mother of the Mystical Body.

PRAYER:

Almighty and everlasting God, whose will it is that all men should be saved and that none should perish: look upon the souls deceived by the guile of Satan, so that the hearts of those who have gone astray may put aside the perverseness of heresy, and, being truly repentant, may return to Your unity. Through Christ our Lord. (*Missal*)

*"I believe in . . . the communion of saints,
the forgiveness of sins . . ."*

170. What is meant by "the communion of saints" in the Apostles' Creed?

By "the communion of saints" is meant the union of the faithful on earth, the blessed in heaven, and the souls in purgatory, with Christ as their Head.

It is an active union — a sharing of spiritual goods among the members of the Mystical Body.

It is something like the circulation of blood in the body or the circulation of steam in the heating system of a house. Grace and the virtues belong to each one of us personally, just as the steam belongs to each individual radiator. But, in a certain manner, we can share them with others and influence others by them without losing them ourselves. The heat of each radiator helps all the other radiators.

COMMUNION OF SAINTS
Circulation of Grace

MEMBERS

CHRIST

In the communion of saints each one of us either helps or hinders the circulation of spiritual life among the members of the Mystical Body by the strength or weakness of our love of God.

The word "saints" in the expression "communion of saints" means "holy ones." We are all made holy by our baptism, although only the saints in heaven have reached perfect holiness.

171. Through the communion of saints, what can the blessed in heaven do for the souls in purgatory and the faithful on earth?

Through the communion of saints, the blessed in heaven can help the souls in purgatory and the faithful on earth by praying for them.

172. Should the faithful on earth, through the communion of saints, honor the blessed in heaven and pray to them?

The faithful on earth, through the communion of saints, should honor the blessed in heaven and pray to them, because they are worthy of honor and as friends of God will help the faithful on earth.

173. Can the faithful on earth, through the communion of saints, relieve the sufferings of the souls in purgatory?

The faithful on earth, through the communion of saints, can relieve the sufferings of the souls in purgatory by prayer, fasting, and other good works, by indulgences, and by having Masses offered for them.

Indulgences will be explained in Lesson 33.

174. Can the faithful on earth help one another?

The faithful on earth, as members of the Mystical Body of Christ, can help one another by practicing supernatural charity and, especially, by performing the spiritual and corporal works of mercy.

Supernatural charity means, in the first place, LOVING GOD. The more our hearts are on fire with God's love, the more easily we can kindle that same fire in the hearts of others, even those we may never see. (See first picture on next page.) A beautiful symbol of this in the liturgy is the lighting of one another's candles in the Easter Vigil Service. The most important way we can help others is by CHARITY which means LOVING GOD OURSELVES.

Love of God moves us to show love to others by the spiritual and corporal works of mercy, chief of which is to pray for others. But to our prayers should be added something else, namely, suffering for others. The Blessed Virgin Mary at Fatima asked the children to pray and make sacrifices for sinners. The salvation of many souls depends on the prayers and penances of the members of the Mystical Body.

Briefly, the three chief ways by which we can help others are CHARITY, or love of God, PRAYER, AND PENANCE.

175. What is meant in the Apostles' Creed by "the forgiveness of sins"?

By "the forgiveness of sins" in the Apostles' Creed is meant that God has given to the Church, through Jesus Christ, the power to forgive sins, no matter how great or how many they are, if sinners truly repent.

We shall consider the forgiveness of sins more in detail when we come to the Sacrament of Penance, page 184.

DISCUSSION QUESTIONS:

1. Who are the "saints" in the communion of saints?
2. If grace and the virtues are in our own soul, how can we share them with others?
3. How can we be hindrances to the communion of saints?
4. Can we pray for the saints in heaven? Why not?
5. If a baptized baby dies, should the mother pray for the baby or the baby for the mother? Why?
6. Can the souls in purgatory help one another?
7. John says his father practices charity by giving to the poor so he will get an income tax deduction. Is that charity? Why not?
8. Can we love God if we do not love our neighbor?
9. Why are our sufferings so valuable?
10. What are the chief ways in which we can help others on earth in the communion of saints?

TRUE OR FALSE: *(Also change each false statement to a true one.)*

1. Whether we are good or bad does not matter to others.
2. Only those in heaven share in the communion of saints.
3. Everything we do, whether good or bad, influences others.
4. We in turn are influenced in a good or bad way by others.
5. The souls in purgatory want our prayers and sacrifices.
6. God does not care whether or not we honor the saints.
7. The best way to help others is to pray for them.

8. The biggest favor we can do for others is to love God more.

9. The chief work of mercy is to pray for others.

10. Penances that we perform help us, but not others.

FILL IN THE BLANKS:

1. The communion of saints is a circulation of ....
among the members of the Mystical Body.

2. The source of the spiritual life which flows through the members of the Mystical Body is ....

3. The saints in heaven help us by ....

4. The saints in heaven and those on earth can help ....
....

5. The members of the Mystical Body who do not need help of any kind are ....

6. Supernatural charity means ....

7. Charity moves us to express love to .... also.

8. Our Lady of Fatima asked the three children to ....
and .... for sinners.

9. The salvation of many souls depends on our ....
and ....

10. To be effective, prayer must always be joined to ....
....

READ FROM THE BIBLE:

The Communion of Saints — Acts 4, 32-37; 1 Cor. 12, 12-27; Col. 1; 1 John 3, 16-18.

The Forgiveness of Sins — Is. 55; John 20, 19-23.

CLASS PROJECT:

Bring in a list of the sacrifices and acts of kindness that boys and girls can do to help others and the souls in purgatory. For example, how many things can you think of to do to make life easier for your mother?

PRAYER:

To ask the intercession of the saints —

May Holy Mary and all the saints intercede for us with the Lord, that we may deserve to be helped and saved by Him who lives and reigns forever and ever. Amen.   (*Roman Breviary: Office of Prime*)

For the souls in purgatory —

Eternal rest grant unto them, O Lord, and let perpetual light shine upon them. May they rest in peace. Amen.

For others on earth —

O Jesus, through the Immaculate Heart of Mary, I offer Thee all my prayers, works, and sufferings of this day, in union with the Holy Sacrifice of the Mass throughout the world, for the wants of Holy Church, and for the conversion of sinners.

LESSON 14 — The Resurrection and Life Everlasting

*"I believe in . . . the resurrection of the body,
and life everlasting."*

THE SECOND COMING OF CHRIST

Christ has told us that He is coming again at the end of the world.
He will come sitting on the clouds of heaven and His angels with Him.
The bodies of all those who have died will rise and go to meet Him.
It is then that He will judge the living and the dead.

176. What is meant by "the resurrection of the body"?

By "the resurrection of the body" is meant that at
the end of the world the bodies of all men will rise
from the earth and be united again to their souls,
nevermore to be separated.

177. Why will the bodies of the just rise?

The bodies of the just will rise to share forever in
the glory of their souls.

**178. Has the body of any human person ever been raised from
the dead and taken into heaven?**

By the special privilege of her Assumption, the body
of the Blessed Virgin Mary, united to her immaculate
soul, was glorified and taken into heaven.

179. Why will the bodies of the damned also rise?

The bodies of the damned will also rise to share in
the eternal punishment of their souls.

180. **What is the judgment called which will be passed on all men immediately after the general resurrection?**

The judgment which will be passed on all men immediately after the general resurrection is called the general judgment.

HEAVEN   HELL

THE GENERAL JUDGMENT

"But when the Son of Man shall come in His majesty, and all the angels with Him, then He will sit on the throne of His glory; and before Him will be gathered all the nations, and He will separate them one from another, as the shepherd separates the sheep from the goats; and He will set the sheep on His right hand, but the goats on the left.

"Then the King will say to those on His right hand, 'Come, blessed of My Father, take possession of the kingdom prepared for you from the foundation of the world.' . . .

"Then He will say to those on His left hand, 'Depart from Me, accursed ones, into the everlasting fire which was prepared for the devil and his angels' " (Matthew 25, 31-34, 41).

181. **What is the judgment called which will be passed on each one of us immediately after death?**

The judgment which will be passed on each one of us immediately after death is called the particular judgment.

182. **If everyone is judged immediately after death, why will there be a general judgment?**

Although everyone is judged immediately after death, it is fitting that there be a general judgment in order that the justice, wisdom, and mercy of God may be glorified in the presence of all.

The general judgment is not really a new trial, but a judgment, that is, a public declaration and manifestation of the sentences or rewards already given or made in the particular judgment.

183. What are the rewards or punishments appointed for men after the particular judgment?

The rewards or punishments appointed for men after the particular judgment are heaven, purgatory, or hell.

184. Who are punished in purgatory?

Those are punished for a time in purgatory who die in the state of grace but are guilty of venial sin, or have not fully satisfied for the temporal punishment due to their sins.

PURGATORY IS GOD'S HOSPITAL

Purgatory is God's hospital for souls, where those who do not love God enough to enter heaven are cured by fire.

Only those who love God perfectly can enter heaven. But even many good people die with only a weak love of God. They had more interest in the people and the things of this earth than they did

PURGATORY

in God. They did not love Him with their whole heart and soul. They wasted many opportunities to please Him.

Love is purified, increased and perfected by suffering. This means not only bodily pain, but crosses of all kinds. (See Q. 425.) God sends everyone all the sufferings they need on earth to cleanse, strengthen, and perfect their love. But most people waste their sufferings. They do not want them, complain about them, and try to escape them in every manner possible, even by committing sin. Because of this attitude, the fires of their sufferings are unable to burn away the selfishness from their love, so that it will be perfect.

Then they must go to purgatory where they will have to suffer much more intensely than they would have if they had accepted the sufferings of earth. Their love is purified in purgatory, but it does not grow, whereas the sufferings of earth which we accept from God not only purify our love, but make it grow.

In purgatory, God's cleansing fires burn away the soul's selfishness till its love becomes perfect and it is ready to fly to heaven. Its sufferings only purify love, they don't increase it.

Note: The meaning of the expression "temporal punishment" is explained in Lesson 31.

185. Who are punished in hell?

Those are punished in hell who die in mortal sin; they are deprived of the vision of God and suffer dreadful torments, especially that of fire, for all eternity.

HELL IS THE LOSS OF GOD

In committing mortal sin, sinners turn their wills away from God to love themselves more than Him. After death they cannot change their wills. In hell they see their hatred of God that sin had put into their souls.

There is no love in hell and those there hate and torment one another. The fire imprisons them and prevents them from

Lazarus with Abraham, and the rich man in hell. (See Luke 16, 19-31.)

ever satisfying any of their torturing desires, while they know that those in heaven have every desire satisfied. After the final resurrection, their bodies will also be tormented.

186. Who are rewarded in heaven?

Those are rewarded in heaven who have died in the state of grace and have been purified in purgatory, if necessary, from all venial sin and all debt of temporal punishment; they see God face to face and share forever in His glory and happiness.

HEAVEN IS GOD'S HOME

Heaven is the place, or state, of perfect happiness. Happiness comes from complete union with the one we love. In heaven the saints share fully in God's life and love. They are perfectly united with Him and can never lose Him. Now at last they are perfectly free to love Him as they have desired. All their desires are satisfied, since these desires are all for the things of God.

They have the companionship with Christ as man, with our Blessed Mother and all the angels and saints. Everyone loves one another perfectly and all are completely and everlastingly happy in God.

187. What is meant by the word "Amen," with which we end the Apostles' Creed?

By the word "Amen," with which we end the Apostles' Creed, is meant "So it is," or "So be it"; the word expresses our firm belief in all the doctrines that the Creed contains.

DISCUSSION QUESTIONS:

1. When will the resurrection of the body take place?
2. Why did God take Mary's body straight to heaven?
3. Why do not souls in hell desire the resurrection?
4. What will Christ say to the good at the general judgment?
5. Why does the thought of purgatory help us to accept trials now?
6. If a boy or girl omits many easy opportunities to go to Communion, is he or she ready to go straight to heaven after death?
7. Is someone who does not study in school because he does not feel like it preparing himself for heaven or purgatory?
8. How does hell torture souls before the resurrection?
9. If God gave you a choice of going straight to heaven now, or remaining on earth many years more and dying with no greater love of Him than you have now, which would be better to take?
10. What makes heaven so different from this earth?

TRUE OR FALSE:

1. God wants us all to go to purgatory.
2. It is possible for the souls in purgatory to go to hell.
3. A good death is something to look forward to with joy.
4. Being obedient is one way to lessen the need for purgatory.
5. The fires of purgatory make our love grow.

FILL IN THE BLANKS:

1. The .... of the body will take place when Christ comes again.

2. Immediately after the resurrection of the bodies of the good and the bad, there will take place the ....

3. At the general judgment the ...., ... and .... of God will be glorified before all.

4. Immediately afer death there takes place the ....

5. After the soul has been judged by God, it may be sent to one of three places ...., ... or ....

6. Only those who love God .... when they die are ready to enter heaven immediately.

7. Others must go to .... until their love is purified.

8. Those who die in mortal sin go to ....

9. There is no love in hell because those there ..... one another.

10. Heaven is a place of perfect .... where the saints share in God's .... and ....

READ FROM THE BIBLE:

The Resurrection — Matt. 22, 23-33; 1 Cor. 15; 1 Thess. 4, 13—5, 11.

The Judgment — Matt. 25; Luke 12, 16-21; 2 Cor. 5, 1-10; 2 Pet. 3, 1-13; 1 John 4, 17-21.

Purgatory — 1 Cor. 3, 10-15.

Hell — Luke 16; Apoc 19; 20.

Heaven — John 14, 1-4; Apoc. 21, 22.

The Cloud a symbol of God's presence, power and glory — Ex. 13, 21; 14, 19-24; 24, 15-18; 40, 32-36; 3 Kings 8, 10-12; 2 Par. 5, 13-14; Ez. 10, 3-5; Matt. 17, 5; 24, 30; Luke 1, 35 (the word overshadow implying the cloud); 9, 34-35; Acts 1, 9; 1 Thess. 4, 16; Apoc. 11, 12.

CLASS PROJECT:

In our project after Lesson 13 we were looking for penances and sacrifices we could do ourselves. But in this lesson we learned how valuable are the sufferings God sends to purify our love and make it grow. Of course, we have to accept those sufferings by being willing to endure them and not needlessly complain about them. Remember no matter who else may be the instrument of our trouble, all things are under God's control. It is always He who sends the cross.

For tomorrow, then, let us see who can think of the largest number of sufferings, trials, disappointments, temptations, difficulties, annoyances, inconveniences and other crosses we can accept from God in everyday life to show Him we love Him.

PRAYER:

O my Jesus, forgive us our sins, save us from the fire of hell, and lead all souls to heaven, especially those who have most need of Your mercy.

(Prayer that Our Lady taught the children of Fatima)

PART 2. THE COMMANDMENTS

THE COMMANDMENTS OF GOD

THE LAW WAS GIVEN THROUGH MOSES

(ST. JOHN 1:17)

THE COMMANDMENTS OF THE CHURCH

Christ Sending Forth His Apostles

I HAVE NOT COME TO DESTROY THE LAW BUT TO FULFILL   (ST. MATT. 5:17)

MAKE DISCIPLES OF ALL NATIONS TEACHING THEM TO OBSERVE ALL THAT I HAVE COMMANDED YOU.
(ST. MATT. 28:19-20)

THE COMMANDMENTS SHOW HOW WE MUST LIVE. The Ten Commandments were given by God to Moses. Our Lord handed on these commandments to His Church and gave it power to make new laws as time went on.

94

LESSON 15 — The Two Great Commandments

HEAVEN

THOU SHALT

THOU SHALT NOT

EACH COMMANDMENT ORDERS US TO TAKE THE RIGHT ROAD AND FORBIDS US TO TAKE THE WRONG ROAD.

CHRISTIANITY IS A
WAY OF LIFE

THE COMMANDMENTS GUIDE US ON THE WAY.

HELL

LIFE IN CHRIST

The religion of Christ is not just a body of truths to be believed as we believe the truths in a geography book. It is above all a WAY OF LIFE. It means that we become one with Christ, living His life, imitating His actions, and following the directions of His laws.

188. Besides believing what God has revealed, what else must we do to be saved?

Besides believing what God has revealed, we must keep His law.

189. Which are the two great commandments that contain the whole law of God?

The two great commandments that contain the whole law of God are:

first, Thou shalt love the Lord thy God with thy whole heart, and with thy whole soul, and with thy whole mind, and with thy whole strength;

second, Thou shalt love thy neighbor as thyself.

LOVE is the most important of the commandments. Our love must go first to God and then to all God's children, our brothers and sisters in Christ.

All the other commandments simply show us in detail how we are to love God and our neighbor. "If you love Me, keep My commandments" (John 14, 15).

The Holy Spirit helps us to love others.

190. What must we do to love God, our neighbor, and ourselves?

To love God, our neighbor, and ourselves we must keep the commandments of God and of the Church, and perform the spiritual and corporal works of mercy.

The spiritual and corporal works of mercy are acts of love which we show to Christ in the members of His Mystical Body. Whatever we do for a member of the Body of Christ, we do for Christ. And we can help non-Catholics to become members of Christ's Body by the love we show toward them.

As Our Lord Himself says, "As long as you did it for one of these, the least of My brethren, you did it for Me" (Matt. 25, 40).

191. Which are the chief corporal works of mercy?

The chief corporal works of mercy are seven:
1. To feed the hungry.
2. To give drink to the thirsty.
3. To clothe the naked.
4. To visit the imprisoned.
5. To shelter the homeless.
6. To visit the sick.
7. To bury the dead.

CORPORAL WORKS OF MERCY — Acts of love which come from the HEART to help our neighbor in his bodily needs.

1. **To feed the hungry.** Everyone needs bodily food. It is an act of love to help others to obtain their bodily nourishment, especially those in greatest need.

Examples — Bringing food to a needy family. Sharing your candy. Going to the grocery store for your mother. Helping with the cooking. Doing the dishes. Waiting on company.

1.

HAVE SOME.

2.

2. **To give drink to the thirsty.** What was said of food applies also to the need everyone has for drink.

Examples — Giving your friends a drink on a hot day. Giving the baby its bottle. Pouring the tea at the table. Lifting up a little boy to get a drink at a fountain.

3. To clothe the naked. Everyone needs clothing. It is an act of love to help others with clothing, especially those who need help.

Examples — Bringing clothes to a needy family, or to a clothing drive for Europe or Asia. Helping your little brother dress himself. Helping your mother with the wash. Shining shoes or ironing clothes.

4. To visit the imprisoned. Besides those in prison, many others suffer hindrances or dangers to freedom. Helping them or protecting them is an act of love.

Examples — Protecting a little boy from a bigger one. Minding the baby. Fighting tor one's country. Doing patrol duty at corners.

5. To shelter the homeless. Everyone needs shelter. To help others obtain shelter or to preserve it is an act of love.

Examples — Bringing others to your home in time of fire, floods, or other disasters. Helping to take care of the furnace. Dusting the furniture. Making the beds. Cleaning the floor.

6. To visit the sick. Helping sick people in any way is an act of love.

Examples — Running an errand for an elderly lady. Reading to a sick person.

7. To bury the dead. It is an act of love to show respect for the bodies of the dead.

Examples — Going to funerals. Treating cemeteries with respect. Cutting the grass on a grave. Putting flowers on it.

192. Which are the chief spiritual works of mercy?

The chief spiritual works of mercy are seven:

1. To admonish the sinner.
2. To instruct the ignorant.
3. To counsel the doubtful.
4. To comfort the sorrowful.
5. To bear wrongs patiently.
6. To forgive all injuries.
7. To pray for the living and the dead.

SPIRITUAL WORKS OF MERCY — Acts of love toward our neighbor to help him in the needs of his soul. And since the soul is far more important than the body, the spiritual works of mercy are far more important than the corporal works of mercy.

1. **To admonish the sinner.** It is an act of love to try to make another realize how bad sin is. This might be done by trying to keep him out of sin or an occasion of sin, or by trying to get him to confession afterwards. In cases where we think it might make him worse, we do not correct him directly. We can let him know indirectly, though, especially by our example, that we do not approve of his actions.

2. **To instruct the ignorant.** It is an act of love to help others in one way or another to learn the truths they need to know to save their souls.

3. **To counsel the doubtful.** It is an act of love to help others to be certain about what they should do to love and serve God. For example, answering questions about eating meat for lunch on Ember days.

4. To comfort the sorrowful. It is an act of love to help another person in any kind of sorrow, and to refrain from doing anything that would unnecessarily cause another person more sorrow.

5. To bear wrongs patiently. It is an act of love to accept the consequences of another's thoughtlessness or carelessness, and to suffer inconveniences which another should bear.

6. To forgive all injuries. It is an act of deep love to forgive all those who have injured us in any way, even deliberately. Christ demands that His followers have great love and forgiveness for one another in imitation of His own forgiveness of His enemies as He hung on the Cross.

7. To pray for the living and the dead. We have already seen how our sharing in the communion of saints demands that we pray for everyone. This is a great means of spreading the fires of love to others, whether in this world or in purgatory.

193. Is everyone obliged to perform the works of mercy?

Everyone is obliged to perform the works of mercy, according to his own ability and the need of his neighbor.

We must remember, too, that our neighbor is everyone, even our enemies, which means those we do not like.

194. Are all the ordinary deeds done every day to relieve the corporal or spiritual needs of others true works of mercy?

All the ordinary deeds done every day to relieve the corporal or spiritual needs of others are true works of mercy, if done in the name of Christ.

Doing them in the name of Christ means doing them for the love of Christ. It is really loving Him in the members of His Mystical Body. He Himself has said of all these actions done to help others, "As long as you did it for one of these, the least of My brethren, you did it for Me" (Matt. 25, 40).

195. Which are the commandments of God?

The commandments of God are these ten:

1. I am the Lord thy God; thou shalt not have strange gods before Me.
2. Thou shalt not take the name of the Lord thy God in vain.
3. Remember thou keep holy the Lord's day.
4. Honor thy father and thy mother.
5. Thou shalt not kill.
6. Thou shalt not commit adultery.
7. Thou shalt not steal.
8. Thou shalt not bear false witness against thy neighbor.
9. Thou shalt not covet thy neighbor's wife.
10. Thou shalt not covet thy neighbor's goods.

196. Should we be satisfied merely to keep the commandments of God?

We should not be satisfied merely to keep the commandments of God, but should always be ready to do good deeds, even when they are not commanded.

Real love never says "enough." It always tries to do all it can for the one it loves, not just so much and no more.

Loving God perfectly means doing everything, every day in the way He prefers us to do it because we want to please Him.

197. What does Our Savior especially recommend that is not strictly commanded by the law of God?

Our Savior especially recommends the observance of the Evangelical Counsels — voluntary poverty, perpetual chastity, and perfect obedience.

VOCATIONS — To the Religious Life

COME, FOLLOW ME

When we say "Evangelical Counsels," we mean following the recommendations for perfect love of God found in the Gospel of Christ. Those who follow these counsels take vows to keep each one. They are called religious. Their vows consecrate them to Our Blessed Lord and give them the best possible helps to reach perfect love of Him.

Taking the vows of the religious life is the best way to walk in the footsteps of Christ and Mary.

There are three kinds of religious: PRIESTS, BROTHERS and SISTERS.

PRIESTS in religious institutes take vows and also receive Holy Orders. (See pages 211-214.) They may engage in all the works of the priesthood, but usually do missionary work of some kind.

BROTHERS take vows (but do not receive Holy Orders) and do a man's work for Christ, like St. Joseph, such as teaching young men, acting as medical aides, doing mechanical work, carpentry, etc.

SISTERS take vows and do a woman's work for Christ, teaching children and young women, nursing, social work, etc.

The life of those who take vows is called THE RELIGIOUS LIFE. The life of those who do not is called secular life. The comparison between the religious life and secular life is not a comparison between good and evil, but between good and better.

THIS IS GOOD   **THIS IS BETTER**

"I want an air rifle. I want a car. I want jewels. I want pretty clothes."

St. Francis: "You can have all that. I want Christ." (See Matthew 19, 16-22)

Our Lord's words: "If thou wilt be perfect, go, sell what thou hast, and give to the poor, and thou shalt have treasure in heaven; and come, follow Me" (Matthew 19, 21).

THIS IS GOOD

"I want to marry the person of my choice."

THIS IS BETTER

"I choose Christ as my spouse."
(See 1 Corinthians 7, 32-34).

Words of the Church: "The doctrine of the excellence of virginity and of celibacy, and of their superiority over the married state, was . . . revealed by our Divine Redeemer . . . ; so too, it was solemnly defined as a dogma of divine faith by the holy Council of Trent" (Pope Pius XII, *Encyclical on Sacred Virginity*).

THIS IS GOOD

"I want to spend the day the way I think best."

THIS IS BETTER

"I want to spend the day the way God prefers." (See Philippians 2, 5-8)

Words of Christ to all those who exercise authority in His name: "He who hears you, hears Me" (Luke 10, 16). By obedience, a religious hears the voice of Christ speaking through the superior. He wants to please God perfectly in every detail of the day's activities, and obedience always shows him how. Those not under obedience serve God in their own way, but cannot always be sure that what they are doing is what is *most* pleasing to Him.

SIGNS OF GOD'S CALL

1. Suitability (physical, mental, and moral)
2. Right intention (desire to please God)
3. Freedom from impediments (such as sick parents needing support)

Since most do not have all these signs and the majority do not have religious vocations, see page 220 for signs of vocations to the single and married states.

A vocation is God's call: "What would God prefer me to be?" — not "What would *I* prefer to be?" The big obstacle is selfishness, lack of generosity with God in little things: frequent Communion, daily Rosary, obedience, kindness to others we don't like, etc. Selfishness in little things results in selfishness concerning one's vocation. "Many are called, but few are chosen" (Matthew 22, 14). Pray daily and seek the advice of a priest to know your vocation.

DISCUSSION QUESTIONS:

1. What is the chief difference between learning the Ten Commandments and learning the multiplication table?
2. Suppose someone said to you, "God gives us laws because He wants to keep us from having any fun." What would you answer?
3. If we hate even one person on purpose, do we really love God?
4. What virtue are we especially practicing when we perform the spiritual and corporal works of mercy?
5. Why are the spiritual works of mercy more important than the corporal works of mercy?
6. Suppose you do the dishes with many complaints because your mother makes you. Why isn't that a corporal work of mercy?
7. If a boy could go to Communion on weekdays if he wanted to, but does not do it because he just does not feel like it, is he keeping the first of the two great commandments?
8. Why do religious give up money?
9. Why do not priests and Sisters get married?
10. Why do religious take a vow to obey their superiors?

TRUE OR FALSE: *(Also change each false statement to a true one.)*

1. The Ten Commandments destroy our freedom.
2. We must love God more than our parents.
3. If we deliberately let opportunities slip by to love God, we are not fulfilling perfectly the first great commandment.
4. Doing the dishes has nothing to do with love of God.
5. If someone does something to us, we ought to get even.
6. God expects us to be kind to people we don't like.
7. Selling drinks to make money is a corporal work of mercy.
8. We should think as much of the needs of others as of our own.
9. If we do what we have to and even a little more than we have to, that means we love God perfectly.

10. If a man is poor because he is unemployed, chaste because he keeps the sixth commandment, and obedient to the laws of God, he is keeping the Evangelical Counsels.

FILL IN THE BLANKS:

1. The religion of Christ is a .... of life.

2. If we disregard the commandments of God while we are on earth, we shall end up in ....

3. Our love must go first to .... and then to ....

4. If we love someone else more than God, we are not keeping the .... great commandment.

5. The acts of love we perform to help others in their bodily needs are called ....

6. Hurting others without necessity is hurting ....

7. In order for our actions in helping others to be true works of mercy, they must be done in ... .

8. The Ten Commandments show us in detail how we are to .... God and our neighbor.

9. The three recommendations Christ has given us as the best means to show perfect love for Him are ...., ..., and ....

10. Following the three counsels is the perfect way of imitating ....

READ FROM THE BIBLE:

The Ten Commandments — Ex. 20; Ps. 18; 118.
Works of mercy (love) — Luke 10:25-37; Matt. 7, 13-23; 25, 34-40.
The Counsels — Matt. 19; Mark 10; 1 Cor. 7; 1 John 2, 12-17.

CLASS PROJECTS:

I. Bring in a list with as many examples as you can think of for each corporal and spiritual work of mercy.

II. (Vocational project) Under Sister's direction, write to a religious order requesting vocational information for the class. Then be prepared to give a three-minute report on the order to which you have written, answering the following questions:

    Who founded the order? When? Where?
    What is its particular purpose and spirit?
    In what external work or works does the order engage?
    How large is it and where are its houses located (in general)?
    What does the habit look like?

PRAYER:

Deign to direct and sanctify, to rule and govern this day, O Lord God, our hearts and our bodies, our senses and our actions, according to Your law and the works of Your commandments, that here and in eternity we may be safe and free, with Your help, O Savior of the world, who live and reign forever and ever. Amen.

(Roman Breviary: Office of Prime)

LESSON 16 — The First Commandment of God

COMMANDS

FORBIDS

Worship of God

False Worship

198. What is the first commandment of God?

The first commandment of God is: I am the Lord thy God; thou shalt not have strange gods before Me.

199. What are we commanded by the first commandment?

By the first commandment we are commanded to offer to God alone the supreme worship that is due Him.

Each of the ten commandments shows us how to love God and our neighbor. The first commandment tells us to give God the reverence and adoration He deserves as the Supreme Being. It is sinful to set up some creature as (A) the chief object of our worship, or (B) the chief source of our happiness, or (C) the chief teacher of truth, or (D) the chief moral guide. These make a god out of something created.

200. How do we worship God?

We worship God by acts of faith, hope, and charity, and by adoring Him and praying to Him.

201. What does faith oblige us to do?

Faith obliges us:

first, to make efforts to find out what God has revealed;

second, to believe firmly what God has revealed;

third, to profess our faith openly whenever necessary.

LOVE OF GOD will make us want to find out what God has told us about Himself. It will make us want to be with Him in heaven and to know more and more about the way which leads there. Since we are on the way to God during all of our time on earth, love will make us always study how we can advance more surely and rapidly toward Him. We begin this study in school but we must continue it all our lives by reading and learning about God and the things of God.

LOVE OF GOD will make it easier to believe firmly what God has revealed. Love is the living of what we believe. Living our faith gives us an unshakeable conviction that it is true.

LOVE OF GOD will give us the desire and the courage to profess our faith openly whenever there is need, and even to die for it if the occasion arises.

202. What does hope oblige us to do?

Hope obliges us to trust firmly that God will give us eternal life and the means to obtain it.

LOVE OF GOD will give us the confidence we need in God's faithfulness to His promises. He has promised us heaven and all the helps for body and soul that we need to get there. For our soul we need: sanctifying and actual graces, the virtues, the gifts of the Holy Spirit, the sacraments, etc. For our body we need: food, clothing, shelter, medical care, etc. If we love God, we shall understand His loving care of us and we shall trust firmly that His love will never leave us without the things we need to serve Him.

203. What does charity oblige us to do?

Charity obliges us to love God above all things because He is infinitely good, and to love our neighbor as ourselves for the love of God.

Charity is LOVE OF GOD and this is the great commandment.

204. How can a Catholic best safeguard his faith?

A Catholic can best safeguard his faith by making frequent acts of faith, by praying for a strong faith, by studying his religion very earnestly, by living a good life, by good reading, by refusing to associate with the enemies of the Church, and by not reading books and papers opposed to the Church and her teaching.

A CATHOLIC FAMILY STUDYING RELIGION

205. How does a Catholic sin against faith?

A Catholic sins against faith by apostasy, heresy, indifferentism, and by taking part in non-Catholic worship.

Apostasy means completely leaving the faith of Christ to profess a non-Christian religion or none at all.

Heresy is a deliberate denial of one or more of the truths of faith by one who professes to be a Christian.

Indifferentism is the belief that one religion is as good as another.

These sins hurt God deeply. Apostasy and heresy show a refusal to believe what He has told us. Indifferentism would put the Mystical Body of Christ on the same footing as false religious systems.

206. Why does a Catholic sin against faith by taking part in non-Catholic worship?

A Catholic sins against faith by taking part in non-Catholic worship when he intends to identify himself with a religion he knows is defective.

207. What are the sins against hope?

The sins against hope are presumption and despair.

208. When does a person sin by presumption?

A person sins by presumption when he trusts that he can be saved by his own efforts without God's help, or by God's help without his own efforts.

An example of the first type would be a man who prays very little because he does not see the need of asking God for help.

An example of the second type would be a man who would commit a mortal sin, presuming that God would give him the grace to go to confession. God might not.

209. When does a person sin by despair?

A person sins by despair when he deliberately refuses to trust that God will give him the necessary help to save his soul.

An example would be a man who commits sins in business to make more money, because he refuses to trust that God will help him to provide for his family. God is offended when we refuse to trust in His love and care for us.

210. What are the chief sins against charity?

The chief sins against charity are hatred of God and of our neighbor, envy, sloth, and scandal.

Envy means resenting another's success because we are not as successful ourselves.

Sloth means laziness, especially in doing good to others.

Scandal is bad example which could lead another into sin.

It is easy to see how these sins are opposed to the love we should have for others as the children of God.

Are we envious when someone else takes first prize?

211. Besides the sins against faith, hope, and charity, what other sins does the first commandment forbid?

Besides the sins against faith, hope, and charity, the first commandment forbids also superstition and sacrilege.

212. When does a person sin by superstition?

A person sins by superstition when he attributes to a creature a power that belongs to God alone, as when he makes use of charms or spells, believes in dreams or fortune-telling, or goes to spiritists.

Even party games, such as reading palms, tea leaves, the ouija board, etc., are dangerous and at times even sinful.

213. When does a person sin by sacrilege?

A person sins by sacrilege when he mistreats sacred persons, places, or things.

DISCUSSION QUESTIONS:

1. How does the first commandment show us to love God?
2. Name the ways in which we worship God.
3. Why do we have to try to find out what God has revealed?
4. Why must we study our religion even after we leave school?
5. How did the martyrs show their faith?
6. Why can't we say one religion is as good as another?
7. How does the virtue of hope help us in time of temptation?
8. Can we love God if we do not love all His children?
9. Why is it a sin to go to fortune tellers?
10. How does disrespect in church break the first commandment?

TRUE OR FALSE: *(Also change each false statement to a true one.)*

1. If we graduate from a Catholic high school, we know all that we need to know about our religion.
2. If a man's family needs his support, it is all right for him to commit sins to see that they get it.
3. God is offended if we do not love Him enough to study our catechism well.
4. It is all right to go to non-Catholic churches for services.
5. Living a good life helps our faith.
6. To be pleasing to God, our worship must be an act of love.
7. God has given us freedom to believe what we want to believe.

8. Everyone should worship God the way he **feels** he should.

9. It is good luck to use horseshoes, rabbits' feet, and charms.

10. Bad example not only hurts others, but is against the love we owe to God.

FILL IN THE BLANKS:

1. To be ashamed to take part in a Holy Name parade is a sin against . . . .

2. Being angry with a girl in the class because she is popular is a sin of . . . .

3. Asking God to help us pass our examinations even though we refuse to study is a sin of . . . .

4. To deny that Christ is present in the Blessed Sacrament is a sin of . . . .

5. It breaks the first commandment to set up as the chief object of our worship some . . . .

6. The first commandment shows us one of the things we are to do to keep the great commandment of . . . .

7. By the virtue of hope we are obliged to trust that God will give us . . . . and . . . .

8. To love God above all things and our neighbor for His sake is an obligation of the virtue of . . . .

9. The belief that it does not matter what religion you practice is called . . . .

10. Giving up hope that we will ever get to heaven is called . . . .

READ FROM THE BIBLE:

Worshiping God alone — Dan. 3; 6; Matt. 4, 1-11.

Faith, Hope and Charity — See passages cited for Lesson 10.

CLASS PROJECT:

Look through the books in your home and bring to school some that you think would be helpful for you to read to increase your knowledge of your faith either now or when you get a little older. Sister can probably offer some helpful comments on the books brought in.

PRAYER:

Almighty and everlasting God, give us an increase of faith, hope and charity: and that we may deserve to attain to what You promise, make us love what You command. Through Christ Our Lord. Amen.

(Missal: Collect for Thirteenth Sunday after Pentecost)

The Saints Are God's Friends.

214. Does the first commandment forbid us to honor the saints in heaven?

The first commandment does not forbid us to honor the saints in heaven, provided we do not give them the honor that belongs to God alone.

A. WHY?

215. Why do we honor the saints in heaven?

We honor the saints in heaven because they practiced great virtue when they were on earth, and because in honoring those who are the chosen friends of God we honor God Himself.

The saints are not statues in the church. These merely represent the saints, who were real people like ourselves, whose souls are now in heaven. They loved God very much while they were on earth, so now they are His special friends. In honoring them, we really honor God, since it was by His action on their souls that they became saints.

When we read the lives of the saints, we should remember that we are reading about real people whose souls are still alive in heaven and who want to help us.

B. HOW?

216. How can we honor the saints?

We can honor the saints:

first, by imitating their holy lives;

second, by praying to them;

third, by showing respect to their relics and images.

IMITATION   PRAYING TO THEM   RESPECTING RELICS AND IMAGES

IMITATING THE SAINTS does not mean imitating their outward actions, but imitating their virtues. If you imitate a saint who slept on bare boards with no blanket, you might catch pneumonia. Imitate instead his love for penance and do what penance you can.

PRAYING TO THE SAINTS means talking with them. God lets them know what we ask them, and they are willing and able to help us. He grants our requests through their prayers to show us how much He loves them.

RESPECTING THEIR RELICS AND IMAGES means not merely showing respect to stone and wood and paper, but to the persons these things represent. Relics and images remind us of the saints whom we would otherwise tend to forget.

217. When we pray to the saints what do we ask them to do?

When we pray to the saints we ask them to offer their prayers to God for us.

218. How do we know that the saints will pray for us?

We know that the saints will pray for us because they are with God and have great love for us.

219. Why do we honor relics?

We honor relics because they are the bodies of the saints or objects connected with the saints or with Our Lord.

220. When does the first commandment forbid the making or the use of statues and pictures?

The first commandment forbids the making or the use of statues and pictures only when they promote false worship.

An example of this would be using a medal, not to remind us of a saint, but simply as a good luck charm.

221. Is it right to show respect to the statues and pictures of Christ and of the saints?

It is right to show respect to the statues and pictures of Christ and of the saints, just as it is right to show respect to the images of those whom we honor or love on earth.

222. Do we honor Christ and the saints when we pray before the crucifix, relics, and sacred images?

We honor Christ and the saints when we pray before the crucifix, relics, and sacred images because we honor the persons they represent; we adore Christ and venerate the saints.

223. Do we pray to the crucifix or to the images and relics of the saints?

We do not pray to the crucifix or to the images and relics of the saints, but to the persons they represent.

DISCUSSION QUESTIONS:

1. What is the difference between the pagan worship of idols and the veneration we pay to the statues of the saints?

2. How is it that we honor God in honoring the saints?

3. How could you imitate St. Peter the Apostle?

4. Answer this objection made by non-Catholics: "It is a waste of time to pray to the saints. It is much better to pray to God directly."

5. What is wrong with the devotion of Mrs. McAsker who prays to the saints only when she needs something?

6. Why do you have pictures or statues of saints in your home?

7. What is wrong with letting a statue in your home get all dirty?

8. Which is deserving of more respect: a golden statue of St. Martha or a plaster statue of the Sacred Heart? Why?

9. Why don't we imitate everything the saints did?

10. Why would you say that a home without crucifixes, holy pictures, or statues is not truly a good Catholic home?

TRUE OR FALSE: *(Also change each false statement to a true one.)*

1. It is foolish to kiss a holy card, since it is only paper.
2. We should pray to the saints only when we want something.
3. When we go to church, we should pay our respects to the Blessed Sacrament before we pray before the statue of a saint.
4. We should imitate everything the saints have done.
5. It is all right to throw old crucifixes in a trash barrel.
6. The more we honor the saints, the less we honor God.
7. The saints are interested in us.
8. A boy or girl who acts as if comic book characters were more real than the saints is getting things backwards.
9. To read the lives of saints helps us to imitate them.
10. To honor those who are friends of God is to honor God Himself.

FILL IN THE BLANKS:

1. Statues on earth remind us of the saints who are in ....
2. God gives us things through the prayers of the saints to show us .... He loves them.
3. Imitating the saints means chiefly imitating their ....
4. God listens to the saints because they are His ....
5. Respect paid to a holy picture is respect paid to the .... represented by the picture.
6. We may not use pictures or statues to promote false ....
7. A medal should not be used as a ....
8. When we use a crucifix, we do not pray to it, but to ....
9. The saints help us because they .... for us.
10. A piece of the body of a saint is called a ....

READ FROM THE BIBLE:

Honoring the Saints — Matt. 17, 1-8; Luke 9, 28-36. In the Transfiguration we have an example of respect for two saints of the Old Testament and conversation with them by Christ and His Apostles.

Imitation of Saints — 1 Cor. 4, 16; Phil. 3, 17.

CLASS PROJECT:

Try making a class shrine. Perhaps, too, each one might set up a shrine in his own home, then take a picture of it and bring it to class.

Another project might be to enroll in the Miraculous Medal or the Brown Scapular any in the class not yet enrolled. Those who are enrolled might explain what they are doing to live up to their enrollment.

PRAYER:

Grant to Your faithful people, we beseech You, O Lord, to rejoice always in the veneration of all the saints, and to be protected by their constant prayers. Through Christ Our Lord. Amen.

(Missal: Postcommunion for Mass of All Saints)

THE SECOND COMMANDMENT

COMMANDS

FORBIDS

Reverence for God in Word

Irreverence for God in Word

224. What is the second commandment of God?

The second commandment of God is: Thou shalt not take the name of the Lord thy God in vain.

225. What are we commanded by the second commandment?

By the second commandment we are commanded always to speak with reverence of God, of the saints, and of holy things, and to be truthful in taking oaths and faithful to them and to our vows.

226. What is an oath?

An oath is the calling on God to witness the truth of what we say.

Examples of oaths: "So help me God." "Honest to God." "By God." Many do not mean these as oaths, but that is what they are.

227. What things are necessary to make an oath lawful?

To make an oath lawful, three things are necessary:

first, we must have a good reason for taking an oath;

second, we must be convinced that what we say under oath is true;

third, we must not swear, that is, take an oath, to do what is wrong.

228. What great sin does a person commit who deliberately calls on God to bear witness to a lie?

A person who deliberately calls on God to bear witness to a lie commits the very grievous sin of perjury.

229. What is a vow?

A vow is a deliberate promise made to God by which a person binds himself under pain of sin to do something that is especially pleasing to God.

230. What is meant by taking God's name in vain?

By taking God's name in vain is meant that the name of God or the holy name of Jesus Christ is used without reverence; for example, to express surprise or anger.

A name is a word-picture of a person. Saying God's name is like using a picture of God. We should use it often, but always with reverence and love. To use a name without the proper reverence is to offend the person whose name we are using.

231. Is it a sin to take God's name in vain?

It is a sin to take God's name in vain; ordinarily, it is a venial sin.

232. What is cursing?

Cursing is the calling down of some evil on a person, place, or thing.

To wish that someone would lose his soul or would suffer some bodily harm is against the love we owe our neighbor.

233. What is blasphemy?

Blasphemy is insulting language which expresses contempt for God, either directly or through His saints and holy things.

One businessman said he would give a framed picture of the Second Beatitude to the first meek man who ever made good. This is blasphemy. (See Q. 129.)

THE THIRD COMMANDMENT
COMMANDS   FORBIDS

Keep the Lord's Day Holy.   Making the Lord's Day Profane.

234. What is the third commandment of God?

The third commandment of God is: Remember thou keep holy the Lord's day.

235. Why does the Church command us to keep Sunday as the Lord's day?

The Church commands us to keep Sunday as the Lord's day because on Sunday Christ rose from the dead, and on Sunday the Holy Spirit **descended upon the apostles.**

For these reasons the Church changed the Lord's day from Saturday to Sunday.

236. What are we commanded by the third commandment?

By the third commandment we are commanded to worship God in a special manner on Sunday, the Lord's day.

237. How does the Church command us to worship God on Sunday?

The Church commands us to worship God on Sunday by assisting at the Holy Sacrifice of the Mass.

Assisting at Mass is the first obligation of a Catholic on Sunday. However, a good Catholic should try to attend other services in his church, if they are held, and to spend more time in prayer and spiritual reading than on a weekday.

There is also more time for rest and recreation, though this should not hold the place of first importance.

238. What is forbidden by the third commandment of God?

By the third commandment of God all unnecessary servile work on Sunday is forbidden.

This type of work is forbidden, to give us more time for the things of God.

239. What is servile work?

Servile work is that which requires labor of body rather than of mind.

240. When is servile work allowed on Sunday?

Servile work is allowed on Sunday when the honor of God, our own need, or that of our neighbor requires it.

FOR EXAMPLE: Policemen, nurses, bus drivers, etc. may work on Sundays. Necessary work at home: cooking, dishes, etc., is all right.

Examples of work that should not be done on Sunday without necessity are: scrubbing floors, painting the house, keeping stores, factory work, etc. Those who co-operate in such work are also guilty of sin, such as Sunday shoppers, employers making men work on Sundays without necessity, etc.

DISCUSSION QUESTIONS:

1. What attitude does the second commandment oblige us to have toward the name of God?

2. Why does it command the same attitude toward the saints?

3. What would be a good reason for taking an oath?

4. Suppose a girl tells a lie and then says, "Honest to God, that is true." What kind of sin does she commit?

5. Why should we be careful about how we use the name of God?

6. Why is it a sin to wish evil on one who is mean to us?

7. Why don't we keep Saturday as the Lord's Day?

8. Does Sunday Mass alone fulfill perfectly the third commandment?

9. Why is servile work forbidden on Sunday?

10. Why is it a sin to shop on Sunday?

TRUE OR FALSE: *(Also change each false statement to a true one.)*

1. The second commandment forbids us to use the name of God in vain.

2. If you want others to believe you, you can take an oath.

3. There are times when it is necessary to swear.

4. If a person takes an oath to commit a sin, for example, to get revenge on someone ("By God, I'll get even with you"), he is obliged to keep it.

5. If a Catholic goes to Mass on Sunday, he can forget all about God the rest of the day.

6. It is a sin to go to the movies on Sunday.

7. Cooking on Sunday is servile work.

8. Not all servile works are forbidden on Sunday.

9. If you have plenty of time to wash the car on Saturday, you should not do it on Sunday.

10. It is all right for drugstores to be open on Sunday.

FILL IN THE BLANKS:

1. To swear means to take ....

2. To tell a lie after taking an oath is a sin of ....

3. To wish someone would break his leg is a sin of ....

4. To insult God is a sin of ....

5. Servile work is allowed on Sunday if it is ....

6. A name represents a ....

7. A sacred promise to lead a life consecrated to God is a ....

8. Recreation on Sunday should not hold the place of .... importance.

9. We are commanded to keep Sunday holy by ....

10. It is a sin to .... in unnecessary servile work of others on Sunday.

READ FROM THE BIBLE:

God's Name — Deut. 5, 11; Ps. 112; Acts 3; 4, 8-12; Col. 3, 17.
Oaths — Matt. 5, 33-37.
The Sabbath — Ex. 16, 23-30; 31, 12-17; Matt. 12, 8.

CLASS PROJECT:

BOYS: Make posters illustrating each of the Divine Praises.

GIRLS: Make posters suggesting different things that can be done to make Sunday the Lord's Day.

PRAYER:

Grant us, O Lord, to have a perpetual fear and love for Your holy name, for You never forsake in Your guidance those whom You establish in the strength of Your love.

(Missal: Collect for Second Sunday after Pentecost)

THE FOURTH COMMANDMENT

COMMANDS	FORBIDS

Obedience to Authority	Disrespect for Authority

241. What is the fourth commandment of God?

The fourth commandment of God is: Honor thy father and thy mother.

242. What are we commanded by the fourth commandment?

By the fourth commandment we are commanded to respect and love our parents, to obey them in all that is not sinful, and to help them when they are in need.

243. Does the fourth commandment oblige us to respect and to obey others besides our parents?

Besides our parents, the fourth commandment obliges us to respect and obey all our lawful superiors.

All authority comes from God. When God gives authority to people, He uses those people as signposts to show us what pleases Him in a particular case. To refuse to obey anyone with true authority, as parents, teachers, etc., is to refuse to obey God and to reject His will.

What makes obedience the hardest, though, is not the person we must obey, but our own likes and dislikes, our own love for ourself.

When we obey quickly in something we like, this is really loving ourselves. When we obey quickly in what we do not like, this is true love of God.

However, authority has its limits. If someone in authority goes outside those limits, then in that case, he no longer represents God and is not a signpost of His will. An example would be a parent commanding a child to do something sinful or forbidding that child to follow a religious vocation.

Father: "No daughter of mine will ever enter a convent."

Daughter: "Then I will have to wait until I am old enough and go anyway, since our parish priest and the Sisters tell me I have a religious vocation."

244. What duty have parents toward their children and superiors toward those under their care?

Parents must provide for the spiritual and bodily welfare of their children; superiors, according to their varying degrees of responsibility, must care for those entrusted to them.

Parents must care especially for the spiritual needs of their children, since these are the most important: teaching them to pray, developing their virtues, such as obedience, truthfulness, unselfishness, etc. They must see to it that they receive a thorough Catholic education, not merely a few instructions before First Communion and Confirmation.

245. What are the duties of a citizen toward his country?

A citizen must love his country, be sincerely interested in its welfare, and respect and obey its lawful authority.

246. How does a citizen show a sincere interest in his country's welfare?

A citizen shows a sincere interest in his country's welfare by voting honestly and without selfish motives, by paying just taxes, and by defending his country's rights when necessary.

247. Why must we respect and obey the lawful authority of our country?

We must respect and obey the lawful authority of our country because it comes from God, the Source of all authority.

248. Why are we obliged to take an active part in works of good citizenship?

We are obliged to take an active part in works of good citizenship because right reason requires citizens to work together for the public welfare of the country.

249. What are the chief duties of those who hold public office?

The chief duties of those who hold public office are to be just to all in exercising their authority and to promote the general welfare.

250. What does the fourth commandment forbid?

The fourth commandment forbids disrespect, unkindness, and disobedience to our parents and lawful superiors.

THE FIFTH COMMANDMENT

COMMANDS   FORBIDS

Respect for Life and Health   Injuring Life or Health

251. What is the fifth commandment of God?

The fifth commandment of God is: Thou shalt not kill.

252. What are we commanded by the fifth commandment?

By the fifth commandment we are commanded to take proper care of our own spiritual and bodily well-being and that of our neighbor.

The fifth commandment obliges us to show love for our neighbor by respecting his person and not injuring him in any way.

Some things this commandment obliges us to do are easy, such as eating and drinking; others are hard, such as taking medicine when necessary. If we love God we do all the things He commands, hard or easy, simply because it pleases Him.

253. What does the fifth commandment forbid?

The fifth commandment forbids murder and suicide, and also fighting, anger, hatred, revenge, drunkenness, reckless driving, and bad example.

We are forbidden to kill or to injure our neighbor's body by murder, fighting, etc., or our own by suicide or neglect of health. We are also forbidden to injure anyone's soul by bad example.

THE SIXTH COMMANDMENT

COMMANDS	FORBIDS

Chastity in Word, Action and Dress   Impurity and Immodesty

254. What is the sixth commandment of God?

The sixth commandment of God is: Thou shalt not commit adultery.

255. What are we commanded by the sixth commandment?

By the sixth commandment we are commanded to be pure and modest in our behavior.

Our bodies are temples of the Holy Spirit and we should therefore respect them and cover them modestly. We must also respect those of the opposite sex.

256. What does the sixth commandment forbid?

The sixth commándment forbids all impurity and immodesty in words, looks, and actions, whether alone or with others.

Examples of this would be: touching one's own body or that of another without necessity simply to satisfy sinful curiosity, impure conversations, dirty jokes, looking at bad pictures, undue familiarity with the opposite sex.

257. What are the chief dangers to the virtue of chastity?

The chief dangers to the virtue of chastity are: idleness, sinful curiosity, bad companions, drinking, immodest dress, and indecent books, plays, and motion pictures.

258. What are the chief means of preserving the virtue of chastity?

The chief means of preserving the virtue of chastity are to avoid carefully all unnecessary dangers, to seek God's help through prayer, frequent confession, Holy Communion, and assistance at Holy Mass, and to have a special devotion to the Blessed Virgin.

Many fall because they do not avoid dangers. They go to movies which are objectionable, or which only adults should see. They read dangerous magazines, or newspapers. They associate too much with the opposite sex and try to excuse themselves by saying that they have no bad intentions. Good intentions alone are not sufficient. Human nature is very weak where purity is concerned, and we must keep far from all dangers, or sooner or later we shall fall.

DISCUSSION QUESTIONS:

1. What has the fourth commandment to do with love of God?
2. Why should we always obey our parents?
3. Why do parents who fail to give their children a Catholic education violate the fourth commandment?
4. Why is it that parents who allow their children to be disobedient are committing a sin?
5. Why is drunkenness against the fifth commandment?
6. How does bad example injure others?
7. Name some easy things commanded by the fifth commandment.
8. Why should we show respect to the human body?
9. Is it all right for a girl to wear a dress that does not cover her very well simply because other girls wear the same kind?
10. Why must we always be on our guard against dangers to purity?

TRUE OR FALSE: *(Also change each false statement to a true one.)*

1. It is sufficient for parents to provide a Catholic grammar school education for their children.

2. Citizens in a democracy have an obligation to try to find out which candidate for office is best qualified and to vote for him regardless of his party or personal friendship.

3. We can break the fifth commandment in regard to recreation by playing too little and also by playing too much.

4. It is all right to go to the movies without checking the Legion of Decency list first.

5. Any girl who always "hangs out" with boys, or any boy who always "hangs out" with girls, is in danger of some day committing sin.

FILL IN THE BLANKS:

1. The fourth commandment obliges us to obey our . . . . and . . . .

2. What makes obedience easy is . . . . of God.

3. What makes obedience hard is our own love for . . . .

4. Parents who never correct their children's faults are violating the . . . . commandment.

5. Paying taxes is a duty of a citizen to his . . . .

6. Bad example is an injury to the . . . . of our neighbor.

7. "Getting even" is a sin against the . . . . commandment.

8. We must treat our bodies with reverence because they are temples of . . . .

9. Indecent books, magazines, and movies are dangers to the virtue of . . . .

10. One way to preserve purity is a special devotion to . . . .

READ FROM THE BIBLE:

Fourth Commandment — Gen. 22 (Obedience of Abraham); Eph. 6, 1-4; Col. 3, 18-21; 1 Pet. 2, 13-17.

Fifth Commandment — Matt. 5, 21-24; 18, 5-7; 1 Cor. 13, 1-3; 1 John 2, 9-11.

Sixth Commandment — Dan. 13; 1 Cor. 3, 16-17; Gal. 5, 16-26; 1 Thess. 4, 1-8; Heb. 13; 2 Pet. 2.

CLASS PROJECT:

In the comic section of tonight's paper look for every violation you can find of the fourth, fifth or sixth commandments. Tell whether it is actually presented as a sin or as being all right. In each case tell how the commandment should have been kept instead of violated.

PRAYER:

Holy St. Joseph, father and protector of virgins, to whose faithful keeping Christ Jesus and Mary, the Virgin of Virgins, were committed, by these dearest pledges, Jesus and Mary, I beseech and conjure You that I may always serve Jesus and Mary in perfect chastity with a spotless mind, a clean heart, and a chaste body. *(From The Raccolta)*

THE SEVENTH COMMANDMENT

COMMANDS FORBIDS

Respect for the Property of Others   Stealing

259. What is the seventh commandment of God?

The seventh commandment of God is: Thou shalt not steal.

260. What are we commanded by the seventh commandment?

By the seventh commandment we are commanded to respect what belongs to others, to live up to our business agreements, and to pay our just debts.

The seventh commandment applies the great commandments of love of God and neighbor by telling us to respect the property of our neighbor.

The seventh and the tenth commandments go together. The tenth makes it easy to keep the seventh by telling us not even to desire the property of our neighbor.

Remember Christ's warning on the danger of riches. Anyone who desires to be rich, that is, to have more material possessions than he needs will find it hard to respect the property of others and to let it alone. And the more we love the things of this earth, the harder we shall find it to love God.

We need a certain amount of material things, such as food, clothing, shelter, etc. But God has promised to see to it by His Providence that we always have enough of these things to enable us to get to heaven, if we ask Him, work hard, and trust Him for them. To possess more than we need is dangerous for our soul.

261. What does the seventh commandment forbid?

Besides stealing, the seventh commandment forbids cheating, unjust keeping of what belongs to others, unjust damage to the property of others, and the accepting of bribes by public officials.

262. Are we obliged to restore to the owner stolen goods, or their value?

We are obliged to restore to the owner stolen goods, or their value, whenever we are able.

Not only is it forbidden to steal, but even to buy a stolen article, or to accept it as a gift. If we have a stolen article in our possession, we must give it back to the owner. However, if we bought it, we have a right to the money back from the one who sold it to us.

263. Are we obliged to repair damage unjustly done to the property of others?

We are obliged to repair damage unjustly done to the property of others, or to pay the amount of the damage, as far as we are able.

THE EIGHTH COMMANDMENT

COMMANDS — Truth

FORBIDS — Lying

264. What is the eighth commandment of God?

The eighth commandment of God is: Thou shalt not bear false witness against thy neighbor.

Christ said, "I am . . . the truth." He died on the Cross for the truth. The eighth commandment tells us to love truth and to show love for others by respecting their reputation.

265. What are we commanded by the eighth commandment?

By the eighth commandment we are commanded to speak the truth in all things, but especially in what concerns the good name and honor of others.

266. What does the eighth commandment forbid?

The eighth commandment forbids lies, rash judgment, detraction, calumny, and the telling of secrets we are bound to keep.

We may never tell a lie. When people have a right to know the truth, we must tell them the truth, even though we have to suffer for it. When they have no right to know the truth, or when we have to keep a secret, we may answer evasively, or throw them off the track, but we may never directly make a false statement.

267. When does a person commit the sin of rash judgment.

A person commits the sin of rash judgment when, without sufficient reason, he believes something harmful to another's character.

268. When does a person commit the sin of detraction.

A person commits the sin of detraction when, without a good reason, he makes known the hidden faults of another.

269. When does a person commit the sin of calumny or slander?

A person commits the sin of calumny or slander when by lying he injures the good name of another.

270. When are we obliged to keep a secret?

We are obliged to keep a secret when we have promised to do so, when our office requires it, or when the good of another demands it.

271. What must a person do who has sinned by detraction or calumny, or has told a secret he is bound to keep?

A person who has sinned by detraction or calumny, or who has told a secret he is bound to keep, must repair the harm he has done to his neighbor, as far as he is able.

NINTH and TENTH COMMANDMENTS

COMMAND US TO GUARD OUR THOUGHTS	FORBID SINS OF THOUGHT

The ninth commandment forbids in desire what the sixth forbids in action. The tenth commandment forbids in desire what the seventh forbids in action.

272. What is the ninth commandment of God?

The ninth commandment of God is: Thou shalt not covet thy neighbor's wife.

273. What are we commanded by the ninth commandment?

By the ninth commandment we are commanded to be pure in thought and desire.

274. Are mere thoughts about impure things always sinful in themselves?

Mere thoughts about impure things are not always sinful in themselves, but such thoughts are dangerous.

275. When do thoughts about impure things become sinful?

Thoughts about impure things become sinful when a person thinks of an unchaste act and deliberately takes pleasure in so thinking, or when unchaste desire or passion is aroused and consent is given to it.

276. What is forbidden by the ninth commandment?

The ninth commandment forbids all thoughts and desires contrary to chastity.

That is to say, it forbids all willful thoughts. We know from Question 64 that no thought can be a sin unless it is willful. A willful thought is one we want, one we take deliberate pleasure in and do not try to put out of our minds.

An unchaste thought that we do not want and try to get rid of is not a sin but a temptation. It is not possible to avoid all temptations. When the devil wants to put an unchaste thought in our minds, he is usually able to do so. But this is nothing to worry about and will never be a sin as long as we do not want the thought and do our best to put it out by a little prayer and by keeping busy. The best remedy against this type of temptation is prayer and flight. Run away from it by thinking about something else as much as you can. Above all, avoid idleness, as the devil has trouble tempting busy people.

277. What is the tenth commandment of God?

The tenth commandment of God is: Thou shalt not covet thy neighbor's goods.

278. What does the tenth commandment forbid?

The tenth commandment forbids all desire to take or to keep unjustly what belongs to others, and also forbids envy at their success.

DISCUSSION QUESTIONS:

1. Why do we have to respect the property of others?
2. Why are riches dangerous to the soul?
3. Why is it a sin to keep a borrowed article a long time when we can presume the owner would prefer to have it back?
4. Why do we have to return things that we find?
5. What kind of a sin is committed when someone hurts another's good name by telling what is not true?
6. What kind of sin is committed when one tells without necessity some fault of another?
7. How can we break the eighth commandment by telling the truth?
8. Is every impure thought that comes to your mind a sin?
9. What is the best remedy against temptations concerning purity?
10. Why is envy a sin?

TRUE OR FALSE: *(Also change each false statement to a true one.)*

1. It is all right to tell a white lie to keep peace in the family.
2. To want more material things than we need to get to heaven is harmful to the soul.
3. All bad thoughts are sins.
4. If we break the tenth commandment, we shall find it hard to keep the seventh, too.
5. Idleness makes it easy for the devil to tempt us.

FILL IN THE BLANKS:

1. Copying from another during an examination breaks the
. . . . commandment.

2. A bad thought which we do not want is a . . . .

3. To make known another's sins without necessity is the sin of
. . . .

4. If we have a stolen article in our possession we have to return
it to . . . .

5. To believe something evil of another on a slight suspicion is
a sin of . . . .

6. Envy is forbidden by the . . . . commandment.

7. Possession of too many things for the body is harmful to the
. . . .

8. The seventh commandment obliges us to respect the . . . .
of others.

9. Making known a secret is a sin against the . . . .
commandment.

10. Keeping something we find without trying to discover the owner
is against the . . . . commandment.

READ FROM THE BIBLE:

Seventh and Tenth Commandments — Mark 10, 23-27; Luke 12, 13-21; Eph. 4, 28; 1 Tim. 6, 7-10; James 5, 1-6.

Eighth Commandment — Sirach (Ecclus.) 4, 25-28; Eph. 4, 25; James 3 1-14.

Ninth Commandment — Matt. 5, 27-42; Mark 7, 14-23; 1 Cor. 6, 18-20.

CLASS PROJECT:

Read in the Bible and explain how Our Lord suffered in His Passion from those who broke the commandments explained in this lesson: the seventh (the soldiers — see John 19, 23-24), the Eighth (the witnesses — see Mark 14, 55-65), the Ninth (Luke 23, 8-11 — see Mark 6, 14-29), the Tenth (Judas — see Mark 14, 10-11). Discuss in class how to make reparation to Our Lord for these sins.

PRAYER:

O God, to whom every heart is open and every desire is known, and to whom no secret is hid, cleanse the thoughts of our hearts by pouring into them Your Holy Spirit, so that we may be worthy to love You perfectly and to praise You worthily.

(Roman Breviary: Prayers before ·Mass)

LESSON 21 — The Commandments of the Church; The First and Second Commandments

"And I will give thee the keys of the kingdom of heaven; and whatever thou thou shalt bind on earth shall be bound in heaven, and whatever thou shalt loose on earth shall be loosed in heaven." (Matt. 16, 19).

Keys are a symbol of authority since the rulers of fortified cities in ancient times used to keep the keys to the gates.

279. Whence has the Catholic Church the right to make laws?

The Catholic Church has the right to make laws from Jesus Christ, who said to the apostles, the first bishops of His Church: "Whatever you bind on earth shall be bound also in heaven."

We have seen that the purpose of laws is to guide us to God. Christ sent His Church into the world as a living guide to point out new dangers that would arise in the course of time, and to apply the laws of God to new times and circumstances.

The Church has power from God to make laws and to change the laws that it makes. It has no power, however, over the laws of God themselves. The Church can never change them to make it all right, for example, to steal, or to lie.

280. By whom is this right to make laws exercised?

This right to make laws is exercised by the bishops, the successors of the apostles, and especially by the Pope, who as the successor of the chief of the apostles, Saint Peter, has the right to make laws for the Universal Church.

281. Which are the chief commandments, or laws, of the Church?

The chief commandments, or laws, of the Church are these six:

1. To assist at Mass on all Sundays and holydays of obligation.
2. To fast and to abstain on the days appointed.
3. To confess our sins at least once a year.
4. To receive Holy Communion during the Easter time.
5. To contribute to the support of the Church.
6. To observe the laws of the Church concerning marriage.

These are the chief laws of the Church, but there are many others. Besides the general laws of the Church, each diocese has particular laws for those who live in that diocese.

282. What sin does a Catholic commit who through his own fault misses Mass on a Sunday or holyday of obligation?

A Catholic who through his own fault misses Mass on a Sunday or holyday of obligation commits a mortal sin.

1st COMMANDMENT

It hurts Christ tremendously if we do not love Him enough even to assist at Mass on Sunday after all He suffered to give us the Mass.

283. Which are the holydays of obligation in the United States?

The holydays of obligation in the United States are these six:

Christmas Day (December 25)
The Octave of the Nativity (January 1)
Ascension Thursday (40 days after Easter)
The Assumption (August 15)
All Saints' Day (November 1)
The Immaculate Conception (December 8)

284. What else does the Church oblige us to do on holydays of obligation?

The Church obliges us to abstain from servile work on holydays of obligation, just as on Sundays, as far as we are able.

285. Why were holydays instituted by the Church?

Holydays were instituted by the Church to remind us of the mysteries of our religion and of the important events in the lives of Christ and of His Blessed Mother, and to recall to us the virtues and the rewards of the saints.

286. What is a fast day?

A fast day is a day on which only one full meal is allowed, but in the morning and evening some food may be taken, the quantity and quality of which are determined by approved local custom.

2nd COMMANDMENT

Today in this country a fast day means:

1. One full meal, with meat if desired.

2. Two other meals without meat, sufficient to maintain one's strength; the quantity, when added up, should be less than a full meal.

3. No eating between meals.

The penance of this usually comes from not being able to eat between meals or at night before going to bed, and from not being able to take bacon at breakfast, or meat sandwiches, etc. at lunch.

287. Who are obliged to observe the fast days of the Church?

All baptized persons between the ages of twenty-one and fifty-nine are obliged to observe the fast days of the Church, unless they are excused or dispensed.

288. What is a day of abstinence?

A day of abstinence is a day on which we are not allowed the use of meat.

On a day of partial abstinence we may eat meat only once.

289. Who are obliged to observe the abstinence days of the Church?

All Catholics who have passed their fourteenth birthday and have attained the use of reason are obliged to observe the abstinence days of the Church, unless excused or dispensed.

290. Why does the Church command us to fast and to abstain?

The Church commands us to fast and to abstain in order that we may control the desires of the flesh, raise our minds more freely to God, and make satisfaction for sin.

Our Lord tells us we need penance. This means making ourselves do things we don't feel like doing to control our feelings (the desires of the flesh). For example, study when you don't feel like it, etc.

291. Why does the Church make Fridays of Lent days of abstinence?

The Church makes Fridays of Lent days of abstinence in order that we may do penance for our sins, and also in order that we may prepare ourselves more worthily for God Friday, when we commemorate the death of Jesus Christ.

292. How can we know the days appointed for fast or abstinence?

We can know the days appointed for fast or abstinence from the instructions of our bishops and priests.

DISCUSSION QUESTIONS:

1. If God gives us laws, why does the Church give us more laws?
2. What laws has the Church the power to change?
3. Can you think why it is that no civil government has a right to interfere with the laws of the Church?
4. Why is it a mortal sin to miss Mass on Sunday?
5. Why do we abstain from servile work on Sunday?
6. If a boy goes to Mass on Sunday, but does nothing else of a religious nature during the day, has he fully made it the Lord's Day?
7. What are the rules of fasting in this country today?
8. What advantages are there in fasting?

9. Can the Church change the laws of fasting? Why?
10. Why do Catholics abstain from meat on Friday?

TRUE OR FALSE: *(Also change each false statement to a true one.)*

1. Only God can make laws.
2. The Pope can change the laws of God.
3. There are only six commandments of the Church.
4. A bishop has the right to make laws for his diocese.
5. If you miss Mass on Sunday because you are sick, you have to tell it in confession.
6. Adults as well as children must assist at Mass every Sunday.
7. The chief reason why we do not work on Sunday is to give us more time for recreation. *(See Questions 237 and 238.)*
8. Besides assisting at Mass on Sunday we should try to spend more time on the things of God.
9. Catholics must eat fish on Friday.
10. The Church's laws of fast and abstinence give us one way of keeping Christ's general command to do penance.

FILL IN THE BLANKS:

1. No civil government has the right to interfere with the Church laws, since the Church's power to make laws comes from . . . .
2. The right to make laws belongs to the . . . . . . and the . . . . . .
3. Missing Mass deliberately on Sunday is a . . . . sin.
4. Besides Sundays, we must also assist at Mass on the . . . .
5. We must refrain from all unnecessary servile work on holydays of obligation just as we would on . . . .
6. A day on which we cannot eat meat is called a . . . .
7. Catholics between the ages of . . . . . and . . . . . must fast.
8. Those obliged to fast cannot eat between meals on a . . . .
9. The purpose of fasting is to enable us to do . . . .
10. Catholics abstain from meat on Friday in memory of . . . .

READ FROM THE BIBLE:

First Commandment — Acts 2, 42.
Second Commandment — Matt. 6, 16-18; 9, 14-15.

CLASS PROJECT:

Christ commands us all to do penance, especially during Lent. See how many practical penances you can think up that would be possible for boys and girls to do during Lent.

PRAYER:

In Your kindness, O Lord, pour forth, we beseech You, Your grace into our hearts, that, repressing our sins by voluntary chastisement, we may suffer in time rather than be sentenced to eternal punishment.   *(Missal: Collect for Friday after Passion Sunday)*

LESSON 22 — The Third, Fourth, Fifth and Sixth Commandments of the Church

3rd COMMANDMENT

To confess our sins at least once a year.

4th COMMANDMENT

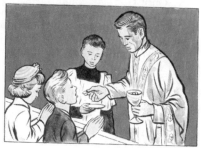

To receive Holy Communion during the Easter time.

293. What is meant by the commandment to confess our sins at least once a year?

By the commandment to confess our sins at least once a year is meant that we are strictly obliged to make a good confession within the year, if we have a mortal sin to confess.

However, anyone who lets confession go for a whole year is in danger of falling into mortal sin. We need the help of frequent confession to keep out of sin.

294. Why should we go to confession frequently?

We should go to confession frequently because frequent confession greatly helps us to overcome temptation, to keep in the state of grace, and to grow in virtue.

295. What sin does a Catholic commit who neglects to receive Holy Communion worthily during the Easter time?

A Catholic who neglects to receive Holy Communion worthily during the Easter time commits a mortal sin.

Anyone who receives Communion only once a year is also in danger of falling into mortal sin. Communion is food for the soul. Eating only once a year is certainly starvation. Even once a month is not often, and the result frequently is that the soul starves to death, death being mortal sin.

296. What is the Easter time in the United States?

The Easter time in the United States begins on the first Sunday of Lent and ends on Trinity Sunday.

5th COMMANDMENT

6th COMMANDMENT

To contribute to the support of the Church.

To observe the marriage laws of the Church.

297. What is meant by the commandment to contribute to the support of the Church?

By the commandment to contribute to the support of the Church is meant that each of us is obliged to bear his fair share of the financial burden of the Holy See, of the diocese, and of the parish.

298. What is the ordinary law of the Church to be observed at the wedding of a Catholic?

The ordinary law of the Church to be observed at the wedding of a Catholic is this: A Catholic can contract a true marriage only in the presence of an authorized priest and two witnesses.

A Catholic who is married by a justice of the peace or a Protestant minister is really not married at all, but simply living in sin. (See Question 465.) If a Catholic is "married" in this way it is hypocrisy and a mockery of God. God puts no bond of marriage around such a couple, as He does around couples who are married by a priest.

When a Catholic is "married" at a civil or non-Catholic ceremony, other Catholics are not allowed to be present, or even to send gifts or show any approval, since this is not a real marriage, but simply a terrible agreement to live together in sin. If the "marriage" takes place at a religious ceremony, the Catholic party is excommunicated. To have this sin forgiven, the couple must be married by a priest, or separate from each other.

299. Does the Church forbid Catholics to contract marriage with certain persons?

The Church does forbid Catholics to contract marriage with certain persons, and the following are examples:

first, a marriage with a non-Catholic; this is a mixed marriage;

second, a marriage with a second cousin, or any relative closer than a second cousin.

300. Why does the Church forbid Catholics to marry non-Catholics?

The Church forbids Catholics to marry non-Catholics because mixed marriages often bring about family discord, loss of faith on the part of the Catholic, and neglect of the religious training of the children.

301. Does the Church ever permit mixed marriages or marriages between close relatives?

For grave reasons the Church sometimes permits mixed marriages or marriages between close relatives; such a permission is called a dispensation.

There must always be a serious reason to ask for a dispensation. The reason given most often is that the Catholic party is so weak in the faith that he (or she) would leave the Church if the dispensation were not granted. So-called "love" is not a good reason.

302. Does the Church allow Catholics to marry during Lent and Advent?

The Church allows Catholics to marry during Lent and Advent, though they should do so without much festivity. A Nuptial Mass is now allowed during these seasons.

303. What is a Nuptial Mass?

A Nuptial Mass is a Mass which has special prayers to beg God's blessing on the married couple.

DISCUSSION QUESTIONS:

1. If a Catholic has no mortal sins on his soul, how often is he strictly obliged to go to confession?
2. Why is it hard to keep from sin with only one confession a year?
3. Name three advantages of going to confession often.
4. Why is it bad for the soul to go to Communion only once a year?
5. Can you give at least one reason why we should go to Communion frequently?
6. Is everyone in a parish obliged to contribute exactly the same to the support of the parish?
7. How must a Catholic be married?
8. If a Catholic man is married by a justice of the peace, what must he do to have his sin forgiven?
9. Why does the Church forbid mixed marriages?
10. If a Catholic girl wants to marry a non-Catholic man simply because she falls in love with him, will the Church allow her to do so?

TRUE OR FALSE: *(Also change each false statement to a true one.)*

1. Catholics should go to confession only once a year.
2. Confession not only forgives past sins, but helps us to stay out of sin in the future.
3. Only very holy people should go to Communion frequently.
4. We need Communion to help us to keep out of sin.
5. God does not put a marriage bond on a Catholic who attempts marriage outside the Church.
6. Catholics who marry outside the Church can never be forgiven.
7. It is all right to send a wedding present to a Catholic who is going to be "married" by a justice of the peace.
8. Mixed marriages are forbidden by the Church.
9. For a Catholic to get a dispensation to marry a non-Catholic a very serious reason is necessary, much more than what is called "falling in love."
10. To have God's blessing on their married life, Catholics should be married at a Nuptial Mass.

FILL IN THE BLANKS:

1. It is hard to grow in virtue without going to confession . . . .
2. All Catholics must receive Communion during the . . . .
3. Infrequent Communion does to the soul what . . . . does to the body.
4. Contributing in the collection basket on Sunday is fulfilling the . . . . commandment of the Church.
5. A Catholic can be married only in the presence of . . . . and . . . .

6. A Catholic who tries to get married in any other way is really not married at all and commits a.................

7. If Catholics who are living together as husband and wife have never been married by a priest, then in order to get their sin forgiven they must either .... or ....

8. No Catholic man and woman have the right to live together as husband and wife, even if they have children, until they have been married by a ....

9. If two Catholics are only civilly "married" and cannot get really married because one of them is divorced, then in order to have their sin forgiven they must ....

10. To protect Catholics from great dangers to their souls, the Church .... mixed marriages.

READ FROM THE BIBLE:

Third Commandment — Matt. 9, 1-8.
Fourth Commandment — 1 Cor. 11, 17-34.
Fifth Commandment — Luke 21, 1-4; 1 Cor. 16, 1-4.
Sixth Commandment — 2 Cor. 6, 14-18.

CLASS PROJECT:

Give a report on one issue of your diocesan Catholic paper:
What pages carry news items of national interest?
What pages carry news items of local interest?
List the features of the paper (editorials, question box, marriage column, etc.) What is the purpose of each?
What sections or features apply the laws of God and the Church to modern conditions? (For example, the movie guide)
How does reading his Catholic paper each week help a Catholic to keep the laws of God and the Church better?
For what other reason should a Catholic read his diocesan paper each week?
List five Catholic magazines that help Catholics to lead a better life. How does each do this?

PRAYER:

Jesus, Mary and Joseph, bless us and grant us the grace of conforming our lives fully, as we are bound to do, to the commandments of God's law and that of His Holy Church, so as to live always in that charity which they set forth.

(From The Raccolta)

PART 3. THE SACRAMENTS AND PRAYER

THE SACRAMENTS GIVE POWER TO LIVE. They are actions of Christ on our souls. They are channels or streams flowing from the open side of Christ through Mary's hands to us.

LESSON 23 — The Sacraments

A sign represents something other than itself.

Smoke is a sign of fire.
A red light is a sign of danger.
Dark clouds are a sign of rain.
A siren is a sign of some emergency, fire, accident, etc.
A flag is a sign of one's country.

A sign is something we can see or hear which tells us of something else which we cannot see or hear at the moment.

A SACRAMENT IS A SIGN OF CHRIST

It indicates that Christ is in action, working in our souls to produce grace.

Note: The Greek letters XP mean in English CHR. It is an abbreviation of the name of Christ. (*See Lesson 7.*)

304. What is a sacrament?

A sacrament is an outward sign instituted by Christ to give grace.

A light switch is a sign of three things:

1. A Dynamo is the Source of Electricity

2. Electricity Itself

3. Light is the Result of Electricity

A sacrament is a sign of grace and a sign of Christ in three ways:

PAST	PRESENT	FUTURE

The Passion of Christ— the source of grace

Grace itself—the life of Christ in us (See Q. 111)

The result of grace— our share in the glory of the risen Christ.

305. How many sacraments are there?

There are seven sacraments: Baptism, Confirmation, Holy Eucharist, Penance, Anointing of the Sick, Holy Orders, and Matrimony.

306. From whom do the sacraments receive their power to give grace?

The sacraments receive their power to give grace from God, through the merits of Jesus Christ.

Merit is a right to a reward. The reward to which Christ had a right as a result of His Passion and Death was that we should receive grace. He won it for us.

307. Do the sacraments give sanctifying grace?

The sacraments do give sanctifying grace.

A SACRAMENT IS A CHANNEL OF GRACE

Since grace is divine life in our souls, we can better understand the sacraments by comparing them with the functions of human life.

I. INDIVIDUAL LIFE

	Begins with **BIRTH**	BAPTISM is birth in the life of grace.
	Grows to strong **ADULTHOOD**	CONFIRMATION gives us power to become adults in the life of grace.
	Needs the nourishment of **FOOD**	HOLY EUCHARIST is the Flesh and Blood of Christ as the food and drink of our soul.
	When sick or wounded is healed by **MEDICINE**	The sacrament of PENANCE is the medicine of the soul to heal sins.
	Is restored to full health by **CONVALESCENCE**	If the body is dying, EXTREME UNCTION gives the power for the full restoration of the health of the soul, lost by sin.

II. LIFE OF THE CHURCH

HOLY ORDERS provides new priests to teach, rule, and sanctify the Mystical Body.

MATRIMONY provides new members for the Mystical Body.

308. Does each of the sacraments also give a special grace?

Each of the sacraments also gives a special grace, called sacramental grace, which helps one to carry out the particular purpose of that sacrament.

The sacramental grace of BAPTISM helps us to live as children of God, makes it easier for us to believe in God and to act accordingly, and lessens our inclinations to evil.

The sacramental grace of CONFIRMATION gives us strength to profess our faith even under difficulties and persecutions and to give good example to others.

The sacramental grace of the HOLY EUCHARIST nourishes our love of God and one another and helps to overcome our natural self-love, or selfishness.

The sacramental grace of PENANCE helps to cure the deeper inclinations to evil that actual sins have put in our soul and makes it easier for us to keep out of sin in the future.

The sacramental grace of ANOINTING OF THE SICK helps us to accept sickness as a purifying cross sent by God and even to accept death willingly from His hands whenever He chooses to send it.

The sacramental grace of HOLY ORDERS helps a priest to fulfill his sacred duties and to be a good priest.

The sacramental grace of MATRIMONY helps married people to bear with each other's defects and to fulfill the duties of their state, chiefly bringing children into the world and rearing them for God.

309. Do the sacraments always give grace?

The sacraments always give grace if we receive them with the right dispositions.

For example, the necessary dispositions to receive the Sacrament of Penance are sorrow for sin and a firm purpose of amendment. If someone were to go to confession without being sorry, he would not have the proper dispositions. God would pour out the living waters of grace through the sacrament, but the lack of sorrow in the heart would block the pipelines, so that no grace would actually enter the soul.

310. Why are Baptism and Penance called sacraments of the dead?

Baptism and Penance are called sacraments of the dead because their chief purpose is to give the supernatural life of sanctifying grace to souls spiritually dead through sin.

311. Why are Confirmation, Holy Eucharist, Anointing of the Sick, Holy Orders, and Matrimony called sacraments of the living?

Confirmation, Holy Eucharist, Anointing of the Sick, Holy Orders, and Matrimony are called sacraments of the living because their chief purpose is to give more grace to souls already spiritually alive through sanctifying grace.

312. What sin does one commit who knowingly receives a sacrament of the living in mortal sin?

He who knowingly receives a sacrament of the living in mortal sin commits a mortal sin of sacrilege, because he treats a sacred thing with grave irreverence.

313. Which are the sacraments that can be received only once?

The sacraments that can be received only once are Baptism, Confirmation, and Holy Orders.

314. Why can Baptism, Confirmation, and Holy Orders be received only once?

Baptism, Confirmation, and Holy Orders can be received only once because they imprint on the soul a spiritual mark, called a character, which lasts forever.

A character is a mark on the soul like a seal on soft wax. It stamps the image of Christ on the soul and gives the soul a share in the priestly powers of Christ.

The character of Baptism gives the power to share in the Mass and to receive the other Sacraments.

The character of Confirmation gives power to fight spiritually with Christ and for Christ against the enemies of the Faith.

The character of Holy Orders gives a full share in the priesthood of Christ, power to offer Mass, to forgive sins, etc.

DISCUSSION QUESTIONS:

1. Of whom is a sacrament a sign?

2. Of what actions of Christ is a sacrament a sign?

3. What is the connection between grace and the Passion of Christ?

4. What is the connection between grace and our resurrection with Christ?

5. What is sacramental grace?

6. What does the sacramental grace of Holy Orders do for the one who receives it?

7. Why does the grace God ꞌgives through the sacraments sometimes fail to reach a person's soul?

8. What is meant by the merits of Christ?

9. Why is it a sacrilege to receive Communion in mortal sin?

10. What is a sacramental character?

CHOOSE THE BEST ANSWER:

1. The sacraments always have the power to give: (a) forgiveness (b) grace (c) a character (d) faith. ☐

2. One of the sacraments of the dead is: (a) Confirmation (b) Baptism (c) Extreme Unction (d) Matrimony. ☐

3. A character on the soul remains: (a) till the use of reason (b) till a sin is committed (c) till death (d) forever. ☐

4. A sacrament is a sign of all these except one: (a) grace (b) sin (c) the Passion (d) the Resurrection. ☐

5. The sacrament of: (a) Penance (b) Extreme Unction (c) Matrimony (d) Holy Orders can be received only once. ☐

FILL IN THE BLANKS:

1. Baptism symbolizes death and ....

2. The seven sacraments are: ....
....
....

3. The sacrament which begins the life of grace in our soul is
....

4. The sacrament which helps us to fight and even to die for Christ is ....

5. The sacrament which cures sickness in the life of grace is
....

6. The sacrament which has the power to restore full spiritual health is ....

7. The special help each sacrament gives to fulfill the purpose of that sacrament is called ....

8. In order to receive grace through the sacraments we must have the ....

9. Sacraments are channels of ....

10. The sacraments which imprint a character on the soul are
.............., ..., and ....

READ FROM THE BIBLE:

The sacraments as channels of the living waters of grace — Is. 12; 49, 8-10; John 4, 14; 7, 37-39; 10, 10; 1 John 5, 8; Apoc. 22, 1-2.

CLASS PROJECT:

An interesting project in connection with the sacraments is to have a class poster contest to see who can make the best poster explaining each of the seven sacraments. Symbols or drawings may be used.

PRAYER:

Those whom You strengthen with Your sacraments, O Lord, lift up in Your goodness by Your constant helps; that we may obtain the effect of Your redemption both by these mysteries and by our manner of living.

(Missal: Postcommunion of the Mass for the Ordination of a Priest)

LESSON 24 — Baptism

BAPTISM IS BIRTH IN THE LIFE OF GRACE

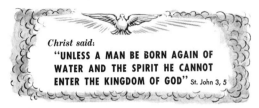

Christ said:
"UNLESS A MAN BE BORN AGAIN OF WATER AND THE SPIRIT HE CANNOT ENTER THE KINGDOM OF GOD" St. John 3, 5

HOW BEING BORN AGAIN TOOK PLACE IN THE LIFE OF CHRIST:

Christ's FIRST BIRTH was in the flesh.

He died for our sins and was buried.

His SECOND BIRTH was from the tomb.

HOW THIS IS SYMBOLIZED IN BAPTISM BY IMMERSION:

At its FIRST BIRTH a child has sin on its soul.

Going under the water in Baptism, the child dies to sin and is buried with Christ.

Coming up out of the water (SECOND BIRTH) symbolizes rising with Christ to the new life of grace.

St. Paul says, "Do you not know that all we who have been baptized into Christ Jesus have been baptized into His death? For we were buried with Him by means of Baptism into death, in order that, just as Christ has arisen from the dead through the glory of the Father, so we also may walk in newness of life" (Rom. 6, 3-4).

(This is also symbolized, though not so expressly, when the water is only poured on the person being baptized.)

"Make disciples of all nations, baptizing them in the name of the Father, and of the Son, and of the Holy Spirit, teaching them to observe all that I have commanded you" (Matt. 28, 19-20).

315. What is Baptism?

Baptism is the sacrament that gives our souls the new life of sanctifying grace by which we become children of God and heirs of heaven.

Since it is God who gives us birth in this new life, we become His children. St. Paul says: "If we are sons (of God), we are heirs also: heirs indeed of God and joint heirs with Christ, provided, however, we suffer with Him that we may also be glorified with Him" (Rom. 8, 17).

316. What sins does Baptism take away?

Baptism takes away original sin; and also actual sin and all the punishment due to them, if the person baptized be guilty of any actual sins and truly sorry for them.

317. What are the effects of the character imprinted on the soul by Baptism?

The effects of the character imprinted on the soul by Baptism are that we become members of the Church, subject to its laws, and capable of receiving other sacraments.

St. Paul says we are baptized "into Christ," that is, we become members of His Mystical Body, we are branches grafted onto the vine which is Christ. Baptism is called the "gateway of the sacraments," because unless we pass through this gateway, it is impossible to receive any of the other sacraments.

318. Who can administer Baptism?

The priest is the usual minister of Baptism, but if there is danger that someone will die without Baptism, anyone else may and should baptize.

319. How would you give Baptism?

I would give Baptism by pouring ordinary water on the forehead of the person to be baptized, saying while pouring it: "I baptize thee in the name of the Father, and of the Son, and of the Holy Spirit."

320. Why is Baptism necessary for the salvation of all men?

Baptism is necessary for the salvation of all men because Christ has said: "Unless a man be born again of water and the spirit, he cannot enter into the kingdom of God."

321. How can those be saved who through no fault of their own have not received the sacrament of Baptism?

Those who through no fault of their own have not received the sacrament of Baptism can be saved through what is called baptism of blood or baptism of desire.

However, only Baptism of water actually makes a person a member of the Church. It might be compared to a ladder up which one climbs into the Bark of Peter, as the Church is often called.

Baptism of blood or desire makes a person a member of the Church in desire. These are the two lifelines trailing from the sides of the Church to save those who are outside the Church through no fault of their own. (See Questions 166-168.)

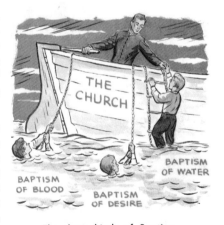

The three kinds of Baptism

322. How does an unbaptized person receive the baptism of blood?

An unbaptized person receives the baptism of blood when he suffers martyrdom for the faith of Christ.

323. How does an unbaptized person receive the baptism of desire?

An unbaptized person receives the baptism of desire when he loves God above all things and desires to do all that is necessary for his salvation.

324. When should children be baptized?

Children should be baptized as soon as possible after birth.

325. What sin do Catholic parents commit who put off for a long time, or entirely neglect, the Baptism of their children?

Catholic parents who put off for a long time, or entirely neglect, the Baptism of their children, commit a mortal sin.

326. What do we promise through our godparents in Baptism?

We promise through our godparents in Baptism to renounce the devil and to live according to the teachings of Christ and of His Church.

We renounce the devil and his work—sin. Even though Baptism cleanses us from sin, the devil will tempt us to fall back into it. We promise through our godparents not to fall back into it, but to hate sin and to live for God. St. Paul says, "Thus do you consider yourselves also as dead to sin, but alive to God in Christ Jesus" (Rom. 6,11).

327. Why is the name of a saint given in Baptism?

The name of a saint is given in Baptism in order that the person baptized may imitate his virtues and have him for a protector.

328. What is the duty of a godparent after Baptism?

The duty of a godparent after Baptism is to see that the child is brought up a good Catholic, if this is not done by the parents.

329. Who should be chosen as godparents for Baptism?

Only Catholics who know their faith and live up to the duties of their religion should be chosen as godparents for Baptism.

DISCUSSION QUESTIONS:

1. What happens to original sin at Baptism?
2. How are we born again in Baptism?
3. Why do we have to suffer as children of God?
4. What is the inheritance of the children of God?
5. How does Baptism make us members of the Church?
6. If an unbaptized man goes to confession, can he receive absolution? Why not?
7. How do we know it is necessary to be baptized in order to get to heaven?
8. Why is it a mortal sin to delay Baptism?
9. At Baptism what attitude toward sin did we, through our godparents, promise we would have?
10. Why should only good Catholics be chosen as godparents?

CHOOSE THE BEST ANSWER:

1. Baptism is a second: (a) grace (b) death (c) birth (d) love. ☐
2. In case of necessity Baptism may be given: (a) by anyone (b) only by a priest (c) only by a bishop (d) only by a Catholic. ☐
3. The water needed for such a Baptism is: (a) holy water (b) Easter water (c) baptismal water (d) ordinary water. ☐
4. To be an actual member of the Church we must receive: (a) Baptism of water (b) Baptism of blood (c) Baptism of desire (d) all the sacraments. ☐
5. Baptism removes from the soul: (a) every sin (b) only original sin (c) only mortal sin (d) only venial sin. ☐

FILL IN THE BLANKS:

1. Baptism is the birth of . . . . in our souls.
2. In Baptism we are born again of . . . . and the

. . . .

3. The one who ordinarily administers Baptism is . . . .
4. The way to give Baptism in case of necessity is to . . . .
. . . . and to say at the same time . . . .
. . . .
. . . .

5. Those outside the Church can be saved through Baptism of
. . . . or of . . . .

6. The only ones who can be saved through these types of Baptism are those who are outside the Church through no . . . . of their own.

7. In Baptism we renounce . . . . and promise to follow
. . . .

8 The way of the devil is the way of . . . ., the way of Christ is the way of . . . .

9. It is harder to follow the way of . . . .

10. After Baptism we must be dead to . . . . . . but alive to . . . .

READ FROM THE BIBLE:

Ez. 36, 22-38; John 3; Rom. 6; 1 Cor. 12, 13; Eph. 4, 1-5. — See also passages on Noe's ark given after Lesson 8.

CLASS PROJECT:

I. Perhaps the class could be split into small groups and get permission for each group to witness a Baptism at the parish church, or demonstrate a Baptism in class. It would be well to follow the rite of Baptism, which is contained in pamphlet form. A report could then be made by the different groups on the following points: **a.** Prayers which emphasize the driving out and renouncing of Satan. **b.** Prayers which emphasize the renouncing of sin. **c.** Prayers which emphasize the new birth. **d.** Prayers which concern the work of the Holy Spirit. **e.** Prayers which emphasize the power of the Cross of Christ. **f.** Prayers which bring out the Christlike life the one baptized must lead.

II. Read in your Missal the Renewal of Baptismal Promises at the Easter Vigil service and explain why you think these Promises are renewed each year.

PRAYER:

May almighty God, the Father of Our Lord Jesus Christ, who caused us to be born anew by water and the Holy Spirit, and who granted us remission of sins, keep us by His grace unto everlasting life in the same Jesus Christ Our Lord. Amen.
(Missal: Prayer after renewal of baptismal promises in the new Easter Vigil)

The Manner in Which a Lay Person Is to Baptize in Case of Necessity

Pour ordinary water on the forehead of the person to be baptized, and say while pouring: "I baptize thee in the name of the Father, and of the Son, and of the Holy Ghost."

N.B. Any person of either sex who has reached the use of reason can baptize in case of necessity, but the same person must say the words while pouring the water.

LESSON 25 — Confirmation

Peter and John Confirming the Samaritans (Acts 8, 14-17).

330. What is Confirmation?

Confirmation is the sacrament through which the Holy Spirit comes to us in a special way and enables us to profess our faith as strong and perfect Christians and soldiers of Jesus Christ.

In Baptism we are born again of water and the Holy Spirit. In Confirmation the Holy Spirit gives us power to grow from infancy to adulthood in the life of grace, with the strength of a soldier to fight for Christ.

Power is given, as it was to the Apostles on Pentecost, to love God as a soldier loves his country and to spread our Faith.

331. Who is the usual minister of Confirmation?

The bishop is the usual minister of Confirmation.

332. What does the bishop do when he gives Confirmation?

The bishop extends his hands over those who are to be confirmed, prays that they may receive the Holy Ghost, and, while laying his hand on the head of each person, anoints the forehead with holy chrism in the form of a cross.

333. What does the bishop say in anointing the person he confirms?

In anointing the person he confirms, the bishop says: "I sign you with the sign of the cross and I confirm you with the chrism of salvation, in the name of the Father, and of the Son, and of the Holy Spirit."

334. What is holy chrism?

Holy chrism is a mixture of olive oil and balm, blessed by the bishop on Holy Thursday.

In ancient times athletes used to a-noint their bodies with oil to limber up their muscles. The oil used in the sacraments symbolizes strength of soul.

335. What does the anointing of the forehead with chrism in the form of a cross signify?

The anointing of the forehead with chrism in the form of a cross signifies that the Catholic who is confirmed must always be ready to profess his faith openly and to practice it fearlessly.

The anointing is in the form of a cross because the strength given is strength to bear crosses for the love of God. We ALL have to take up our cross after Christ and even die for Him if we are given that privilege.

336. Why does the bishop give the person he confirms a slight blow on the cheek?

The bishop gives the person he confirms a slight blow on the cheek to remind him that he must be ready to suffer everything, even death, for the sake of Christ.

337. What are the effects of Confirmation?

Confirmation increases sanctifying grace, gives its special sacramental grace, and imprints a lasting character on the soul.

See Questions 308 and 314.

338. What does the sacramental grace of Confirmation help us to do?

The sacramental grace of Confirmation helps us to live our faith loyally and to profess it courageously.

339. What is the character of Confirmation?

The character of Confirmation is a spiritual and indelible sign which marks the Christian as a soldier 'in the army of Christ.

The character of Confirmation gives us the power to be soldiers in Christ's army, fighting with Him against the enemies of the Faith. We do not fight against *persons,* but for them as an army of liberation to free them from the enemies of their soul.

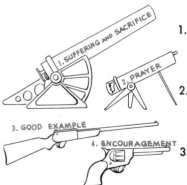

The amount of good we can do is shown by the *power* of different kinds of weapons.

OUR WEAPONS ARE:

1. *Sufferings and sacrifices* not only help to cure our own soul of the inclination to do wrong, but also help to save the souls of others.

2. Our Lady told the children at Fatima, "Many souls go to hell because they have no one to *pray* and make sacrifices for them."

3. Many non-Catholics are encouraged to inquire into the Catholic Faith by the good *example* of Catholics.

4. Encourage those who are interested. If you can, TAKE them to see a priest.

A Catholic who never tries to work for the conversion of non-Catholics or to bring bad Catholics back to the sacraments is a soldier who lets the enemy win without putting up a fight.

340. What is necessary to receive Confirmation properly?

To receive Confirmation properly it is necessary to be in the state of grace, and to know well the chief truths and duties of our religion.

341. After we have been confirmed, why should we continue to study our religion even more earnestly than before?

After we have been confirmed, we should continue to study our religion even more earnestly than before, so that we may be able to explain and defend our faith, and thus co-operate with the grace of Confirmation.

We cannot possibly explain the Faith to intelligent non-Catholics unless we know it well, nor can we live it ourselves as adults, unless our knowledge of our Faith grows as our bodies and minds grow. The knowledge acquired in school is a good foundation to build on, but all our lives we must continue to read and deepen our knowledge of the mysteries of our Faith. (See Question 204.)

342. Why should all Catholics be confirmed?

All Catholics should be confirmed in order to be strengthened against the dangers to salvation and to be prepared better to defend their Catholic faith.

Confirmation is not necessary to salvation, but tremendously helpful. To neglect it deliberately would be a sin.

DISCUSSION QUESTIONS:

1. What does the Holy Spirit do in our soul in Confirmation?
2. How does this differ from what He does in Baptism?
3. What does holy chrism symbolize?
4. What two ceremonies of Confirmation remind us that we have to bear crosses?
5. What does "bearing the cross" mean?
6. What does the character of Confirmation do for the soul?
7. How do we fight in the army of Christ?
8. Should we argue with non-Catholics about the faith?
9. Why should we read more about our faith after we leave school?
10. Can we get to heaven without Confirmation?

CHOOSE THE BEST ANSWER:

1. Confirmation is usually given by: (a) the Pope (b) a bishop (c) a Sister (d) anyone over twelve. ☐

2. The oil in Confirmation symbolizes: (a) joy (b) peace (c) strength (d) purity. ☐

3. Confirmation helps us to: (a) make a good confession (b) keep out of sin (c) spread our Faith (d) go straight to heaven. ☐

4. The bishop gives a blow on the cheek to remind us that: (a) all men must die (b) life will always be hard (c) we must be willing to suffer for Christ (d) everyone must go to purgatory. ☐

5. We should study our religion until: (a) the end of grammar school (b) the end of high school (c) we grow up (d) we die. ☐

FILL IN THE BLANKS:

1. The weapons of a soldier of Christ are: ....
................., ..., and ....

2. Confirmation is administered by ....

3. Confirmation gives us strength to grow to ....
in Christ.

4. To symbolize the strength given by the sacrament of Confirmation to bear crosses, the bishop anoints the forehead in the form of a ....

5. Catholics should be confirmed in order to be strengthened against dangers to .... and be prepared better to .... their Catholic faith.

6. The character of Confirmation makes the Christian a .... of Christ.

7. The bishop anoints those being confirmed with ....

8. In this sacrament the .... comes to strengthen the soul so that we can become a soldier of Christ.

9. Confirmation gives us the strength to bear ....

10. Confirmed Catholics must always study their ....

READ FROM THE BIBLE:

Luke 10, 1-20; Acts 2; 1 Pet. 4.

CLASS PROJECT:

List the Catholic radio and TV programs in your area. Describe each program. Write a letter to thank your local station for carrying the program. (Most Catholic programs depend on such letters to keep them on the air, as the stations give the time free.) Try to interest a non-Catholic in listening to a Catholic program.

PRAYER:

Almighty and eternal God, Who in Your kindness have given to me, Your servant, a new birth through water and the Holy Spirit, and granted to me the remission of all my sins, send forth from heaven upon me Your sevenfold Spirit, the Holy Paraclete. Amen.

(Adapted from the Roman Ritual)

LESSON 26 — The Holy Eucharist

THE HOLY EUCHARIST AS A SACRAMENT

"The bread that I will give is My flesh for the life of the world" (John 6, 52).

"Because the bread is one, we, though many, are one body, all of us who partake of the one bread" (1 Cor. 10, 17).

343. What is the Holy Eucharist?

The Holy Eucharist is a sacrament and a sacrifice. In the Holy Eucharist, under the appearances of bread and wine, the Lord Christ is contained, offered, and received.

The Eucharist is a SACRAMENT. Like all sacraments it is a SIGN OF CHRIST. But unlike the other sacraments, the Eucharist is not only an ACTION OF CHRIST, but also really CONTAINS CHRIST PERSONALLY.

In this lesson we consider the way in which Christ is contained in this sacrament; in the next lesson we consider this sacrament as the sign of Christ's sacrifice, and in the lesson after that we consider this sacrament as the food of our soul.

344. When did Christ institute the Holy Eucharist?

Christ instituted the Holy Eucharist at the Last Supper, the night before He died.

The Last Supper was a banquet, a ceremonial meal called the Passover or Paschal Supper. It was eaten each year in commemoration of the freeing of the Jews from slavery in Egypt.

At this meal, the Jews ate the Paschal Lamb which had been sacrificed by a priest. This was the principal sacrifice of the Jews and was a symbol of the future sacrifice of Christ.

At the Last Supper, Christ instituted the Eucharist as the ceremony under which His sacrifice of the next day on Calvary was to be continued through the centuries. Our Mass is the continuation of this ceremony (with prayers added by the Church), but it is a SACRAMENT, not merely an empty ceremony; it really contains what the ceremony signifies — the sacrifice of Christ.

345. Who were present when Our Lord instituted the Holy Eucharist?

When Our Lord instituted the Holy Eucharist the apostles were present.

346. How did Christ institute the Holy Eucharist?

Christ instituted the Holy Eucharist in this way: He took bread, blessed and broke it, and giving it to His apostles, said: "Take and eat; this is My body"; then He took a cup of wine, blessed it, and giving it to them, said: "All of you drink of this; for this is My blood of the new covenant which is being shed for many unto the forgiveness of sins"; finally, He gave His apostles the commission: "Do this in remembrance of Me."

This same ceremony is the basic ceremony of our Mass today.

347. What happened when Our Lord said: "This is My body . . . this is My blood"?

When Our Lord said, "This is My body," the entire substance of the bread was changed into His body; and when He said, "This is My blood," the entire substance of the wine was changed into His blood.

348. Did anything of the bread and wine remain after their substance had been changed into Our Lord's body and blood?

After the substance of the bread and wine had been changed into Our Lord's body and blood, there remained only the appearances of bread and wine.

349. What do we mean by the appearances of bread and wine?

By the appearances of bread and wine we mean their color, taste, weight, shape, and whatever else appears to the senses.

The *substance* of anything is what it is. The *appearances* are what it looks like, or feels like, or tastes like. For *example,* an apple is a substance. It looks red and round. It feels smooth. It tastes sweet. Redness, roundness, smoothness, and juiciness are appearances.

350. What is the change of the entire substance of the bread and wine into the body and blood of Christ called?

The change of the entire substance of the bread and wine into the body and blood of Christ is called Transubstantiation.

There are different kinds of changes which may take place in things.

A. A change of appearances. For example, a green apple grows to be a full, ripe, red apple.

B. A partial change of substance. For example, oil burns and changes into smoke. The appearances change also.

C. A complete change of substance. This is transubstantiation.

The only example of this kind of change is found in the Consecration of the Mass. The appearances of bread would also change into those of Christ if God did not prevent this by a miracle.

When the priest says, "This is My body," at Mass, you would immediately see Christ, and not the appearances of bread, if God did not prevent it by a miracle. He keeps the appearances of bread in existence to enable us to eat the flesh of Christ without difficulty.

351. Is Jesus Christ whole and entire both under the appearances of bread and under the appearances of wine?

Jesus Christ is whole and entire both under the appearances of bread and under the appearances of wine.

Christ is present whole and entire even under a tiny particle of the Host. Now that He has risen from the dead He can die no more, nor can He be divided.

352. How was Our Lord able to change bread and wine into His body and blood?

Our Lord was able to change bread and wine into His body and blood by His almighty power.

353. Does this change of bread and wine into the body and blood of Christ continue to be made in the Church?

The change of bread and wine into the body and blood of Christ continues to be made in the Church by Jesus Christ, through the ministry of His priests.

354. When did Christ give His priests the power to change bread and wine into His body and blood?

Christ gave His priests the power to change bread and wine into His body and blood when He made the apostles priests at the Last Supper by saying to them: "Do this in remembrance of Me."

355. How do priests exercise their power to change bread and wine into the body and blood of Christ?

Priests exercise their power to change bread and wine into the body and blood of Christ by repeating at the Consecration of the Mass the words of Christ: "This is My Body . . . this is My blood."

356. Why does Christ give us His own body and blood in the Holy Eucharist?

Christ gives us His own body and blood in the Holy Eucharist:

> *first,* to be offered as a sacrifice commemorating and renewing for all time the sacrifice of the cross;
>
> *second,* to be received by the faithful in Holy Communion;
>
> *third,* to remain ever on our altars as the proof of His love for us, and to be worshiped by us.

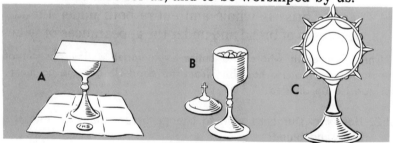

A. The Mass is a sacrament.   B. The Host received in Communion is a sacrament.   C. The Host in the monstrance at Benediction is a sacrament.

And still the Eucharist is only ONE sacrament in which we offer, receive, and adore Christ really present.

DISCUSSION QUESTIONS:

1. In what manner is Jesus Christ contained in the Eucharist?
2. What is the big difference between the Eucharist and the other sacraments?
3. What was the Last Supper?

4. What was the greatest thing that happened at the Last Supper?
5. What words did Our Lord use in instituting the Eucharist?
6. What is the difference between a substance and its appearances?
7. Why does Our Lord remain in the tabernacle?
8. What event did the Jewish Paschal Supper commemorate?
9. With what words were the Apostles given power to say Mass?
10. For what three reasons was the Eucharist instituted?

CHOOSE THE BEST ANSWER:

1. The Mass is the continuation of the: (a) Sermon on the Mount (b) Last Supper (c) wedding feast at Cana (d) Incarnation. ☐
2. A broken host contains: (a) all of Christ (b) part of Christ (c) none of Christ (d) Christ in pain. ☐
3. If you put a host under a microscope you would see: (a) the body of Christ (b) the face of Christ (c) the wounds of Christ (d) only bread. ☐
4. At Mass the bread and wine change in: (a) appearance (b) substance (c) condition (d) size. ☐
5. All who receive the Eucharist are one body in Christ because the bread is: (a) holy (b) good (c) one (d) universal. ☐

FILL IN THE BLANKS:

1. We call what something is, its ....
2. We call what it looks like, its ....
3. The chief sacrifice of the Jews before Christ was the ....
4. A complete change of substance is called ....
5. The Mass is the same ceremony as ....
6. Christ remains on our altars as a sign of His .... for us.
7. The bread and wine are changed into Christ's Body and Blood at the .... of the Mass.
8. God feeds us with the flesh of His Son under the appearances of bread so that we can eat it without ....
9. God hides His Son's appearances by a ....
10. The Eucharist is a sign under which Christ is ...., ... and ....

READ FROM THE BIBLE:

Matt. 26, 17-24; Mark 14, 12-26; Luke 22, 7-30; 1 Cor. 10, 16-17.

CLASS PROJECT:

Write and produce a one-act play about the Eucharist, based on St. John's Gospel, chapter 6, verses 25 to 70. It contains Christ's teaching on the nature of the Eucharist, the arguments which His words caused, the departure of many followers, and St. Peter's profession of faith.

PRAYER: O God, under a marvelous sacrament You have left us the memorial of Your Passion; grant us, we beseech You, so to venerate the sacred mysteries of Your Body and Blood, that we may ever perceive within us the fruit of Your Redemption. Who live and reign, world without end. Amen.   *(From Mass of the Blessed Sacrament)*

THE HOLY EUCHARIST AS A SACRIFICE

"Walk in love, as Christ also loved us and delivered Himself up for us an offering and a sacrifice to God" (Eph. 5, 2).

A. THE MASS — A SACRIFICE

357. What is the Mass?

The Mass is the sacrifice of the New Law in which Christ, through the ministry of the priest, offers Himself to God in an unbloody manner under the appearances of bread and wine.

The Mass is the sacrifice of Christ offered in a sacramental manner. This means that it is offered, not under its natural appearances, as it was on Calvary, but under other appearances, the appearances of the sacramental signs. The reality is the same but the appearances differ.

The Mass is the sacrament, or sign, of Christ's sacrifice. It is a sign of Christ in action, offering Himself in love to the Father as He did on the Cross. In brief, the Mass is an act of love, our share in the great act of love that Christ made on the Cross.

358. What is a sacrifice?

A sacrifice is the offering of a victim by a priest to God alone, and the destruction of it in some way to acknowledge that He is the Creator of all things.

SACRIFICE is an action in which we give a gift to God as a sign of our devotion. It shows Him we love Him.

When you give your mother a birthday present, it shows her you love her. She will gladly accept it, not only because she is pleased with the gift itself, but much more because she is pleased with your love which the gift represents.

Cain and Abel offered gifts, or sacrifices, to God. God was pleased with Abel's gift and accepted it because the gift represented the love and devotion of Abel's heart. He did not accept Cain's gift because He could see that Cain did not really love Him. The fire is a symbol of the love and devotion of the heart going up to God.

A gift offered to God in sacrifice we call a VICTIM.

One who offers sacrifice to God in the name of all the people we call a PRIEST.

B. THE CROSS — The Perfect Sacrifice

359. Who is the principal priest in every Mass?

The principal priest in every Mass is Jesus Christ, who offers to His heavenly Father, through the ministry of His ordained priest, His body and blood which were sacrified on the cross.

I. CHRIST GIVES

The perfect sacrifice was that of Christ on the Cross. The PRIEST was the Son of God made man. He was also the VICTIM, since the gift was Himself, His own human life. It cost Him every last drop of His Precious Blood. He gave it to His Father to show Him His love and devotion.

As Christ hung on the Cross, every beat of His Sacred Heart said to His Father, "Father, I love You."

II. THE FATHER ACCEPTS

The Father was most pleased. He accepted the gift His Son offered Him and showed it by raising Him from the dead on Easter and bringing Him to heaven forty days later, on Ascension Day.

THE RESURRECTION

Father's Glory
Raising Christ

These acts marked the completion of Christ's sacrifice. He is now in heaven showing His Father His five wounds as a sign of His love. He is forever an accepted VICTIM OF SACRIFICE.

THE ASCENSION

Father Welcoming
Christ into Heaven

C. THE MASS—The Perfect Sacrifice
(Continued)

The Mass continues the Sacrifice of the Cross. Each time Mass is offered, the Sacrifice of Christ is repeated. A new sacrifice is not offered, but by divine power, one and the same sacrifice is repeated. "As often as you shall eat this bread and drink the cup, you proclaim the death of the Lord, until He comes" (1 Corinthians 11, 26).

In the Mass Christ continues to offer Himself to the Father as He did on the Cross.

And in the Mass the Father continues to accept His Son's gift, just as He did in the Resurrection and Ascension.

That is why the priest says immediately after the Consecration of the Mass:

"Mindful, therefore, O Lord, not only of the blessed passion of the same Christ, Your Son, our Lord, but also of His resurrection from the dead, and finally His glorious ascension into heaven, we, Your ministers, as also Your holy people, offer to Your supreme Majesty, of the gifts bestowed upon us, the pure ✠ Victim, the holy ✠ Victim, the all-perfect ✠ Victim: the holy ✠ Bread of life eternal and the Chalice ✠ of unending salvation."

THE MASS — A Memorial of the Passion, Resurrection and Ascension of our Lord.

360. Why is the Mass the same sacrifice as the sacrifice of the cross?

The Mass is the same sacrifice as the sacrifice of the cross because in the Mass the victim is the same, and the principal priest is the same, Jesus Christ.

D. THE MASS — As a Ceremony

The Mass is a sacrifice. But it is also a ceremony. Our Blessed Lord did not want His sacrifice continued in the same bloody way in which He offered it on the Cross. That would be too hard for us. So at the Last Supper He gave us a ceremony under which we could continue His Sacrifice. The Mass is the same basic ceremony as the Last Supper, with other prayers and actions that have been added by the Church in the course of time.

But it is not an empty ceremony. It is a ceremony which is a sacrament, that is, a sign of the action of Christ, a channel of grace. It is a sign of His action on the Cross. On the Cross and in the Mass there is the same Priest, the same Gift, or Victim, and the same act of offering.

ON THE CROSS	IN THE MASS
Priest	*Priest*
Jesus Christ.	Jesus Christ, the invisible priest of every Mass. The ordained priest takes His place.
Victim (Gift)	*Victim*
Christ's Body and Blood.	Christ's Body and Blood (under the appearances of bread and wine).
Act of Offering	*Act of Offering*
The act of love of the Sacred Heart, shown by shedding all Its Precious Blood.	The same act of love of the Sacred Heart, shown by the separate consecration of bread and wine to symbolize the death of Christ on the Cross.

THE MASS IS THE SACRAMENT OF THE PASSION OF CHRIST

E. PURPOSES of the Mass

361. What are the purposes for which the Mass is offered?

The purposes for which the Mass is offered are:

first, to adore God as our Creator and Lord; *second,* to thank God for His many favors; *third,* to ask God to bestow His blessings on all men; *fourth,* to satisfy the justice of God for the sins committed against Him.

These purposes are realized in every Mass regardless of the dispositions of the priest or people. In addition, there flow from each Mass special fruits, or blessings, upon the celebrant, servers, those present, those for whom it is offered, and all mankind, especially all members of the Church and the souls in purgatory. These blessings may be increased or decreased by the good or bad disposition of each person concerned.

The Mass stipend — Sometimes people give a priest an offering to say Mass for some intention they desire, or some person, living or dead, for whom they want to pray. This offering is not buying a Mass, since the Mass is beyond price and all the money in the world would not buy one Mass. The value of the Mass is the value of the Precious Blood of Christ. But the Mass stipend is given to help support the priest who says the Mass. In former centuries people would make an offering of food, articles of clothing, firewood, etc., to the priest, but nowadays they usually find it easier simply to make a donation.

362. Is there any difference between the sacrifice of the cross and the Sacrifice of the Mass?

The manner in which the sacrifice is offered is different. On the Cross Christ physically shed His blood and was physically slain, while in the Mass there is no physical shedding of blood nor physical death, because Christ can die no more; on the cross Christ gained merit and satisfied for us, while in the Mass He applies to us the merits and satisfaction of His death on the cross.

F. The MASS—Our Sacrifice

Although the Mass is essentially the same sacrifice as that of the Cross, yet there are some differences.

ON THE CROSS	IN THE MASS
Christ really died.	Christ does not really die.
There were shouts of the crowd, darkness, an earthquake, soldiers casting lots, and so forth.	These details are not continued in the Mass.
Christ alone was the Priest and He alone was the Victim.	Christ unites all the members of His Mystical Body in His priesthood and in His victimhood.

In the Mass, the Sacred Heart does not only say to the Father, "Father, I love You," but He also says, "Father, I love You, and so do all these who are here with Me united as members of My Mystical Body."

The Mass is the sacrifice of the whole Christ, the Mystical Body united with its Head. Christ offers us up with Himself, including all our prayers, works, and sufferings of every day. He offers these together with His own as our gift to tell the Father we love him.

In the Mass the Father gives us the Flesh of His Son to eat as a sign that He is pleased and will one day raise our bodies from the dead to be with Him forever as accepted VICTIMS OF SACRIFICE.

THE MASS — OUR ACT OF LOVE

G. How to Assist at Mass

363. How should we assist at Mass?

We should assist at Mass with reverence, attention, and devotion.

364. What is the best method of assisting at Mass?

The best method of assisting at Mass is to unite with the priest in offering the Holy Sacrifice, and to receive Holy Communion.

364 A.   How can we best unite with the priest in offering the Holy Sacrifice?

We can best unite with the priest in offering the Holy Sacrifice by joining in mind and heart with Christ, the principal Priest and Victim, by following the Mass in a missal, and by reciting or chanting the responses.

The responses for the Dialogue Mass begin on page 256.

WHAT WE SEE   WHAT WE SHOULD THINK OF

365. Who said the first Mass?

Our Divine Savior said the first Mass, at the Last Supper, the night before He died.

DISCUSSION QUESTIONS:

   1. Why do we offer sacrifice to God?

   2. Why does Abel's smoke go up and Cain's go down in the picture?

   3. Name three ways of assisting at Mass.

   4. Give four reasons why Christ offers each Mass.

   5. What was the most important aspect of the sacrifice of the Cross: The Cross itself, the body of Christ hanging on it, His Precious Blood, or the love in His Sacred Heart?

   6. Why was the Father pleased with the sacrifice of the Cross?

   7. Why does Christ still keep His five wounds in heaven?

   8. Of what action of Christ is the Mass the sign?

   9 .How did Christ show His love for His Father on the Cross and how is this symbolized in the Mass?

   10. In what way does the Mass continue Christ's Passion?

CHOOSE THE BEST ANSWER:

1. The Mass and the Cross are the same in: (a) appearance (b) every detail (c) priest and victim (d) those present. ☐

2. The Mass is the same ceremony as the: (a) Cross (b) Last Supper (c) Paschal Lamb (d) Resurrection. ☐

3. The principal priest at every Mass is: (a) the Pope (b) the bishop (c) the priest who says the Mass (d) Jesus Christ. ☐

4. In every Mass Christ: (a) dies (b) suffers (c) is born (d) offers Himself in love. ☐

5. The separate consecration of bread and wine symbolizes: (a) the birth of Christ (b) the death of Christ (c) the Resurrection (d) the Ascension. ☐

FILL IN THE BLANKS:

1. The Mass is the sacrament of Christ's ....

2. The sacrifice of the Mass is offered in an .... manner.

3. Christ offers each Mass through the ministry of ....

4. A gift offered in sacrifice is called a ....

5. The Mass is the sacrifice of the Cross offered under the appearances of .... and ....

6. The Mass as a ceremony was instituted by Christ at ....
....

7. The principal priest at every Mass is ....

8. The victim at every Mass is ....

9. The Father showed His pleasure with the sacrifice of His Son by .... Him from the ....

10. On the Last Day the Father will raise our bodies and accept us as .... forever.

READ FROM THE BIBLE:

The Paschal Lamb — Ex. 12; John 1, 29; 1 Peter 1, 19; Apoc. 5.
God's acceptance of sacrifice — 3 Kings 18.
The Mass a sacrifice — 1 Cor. 11, 17-34.

CLASS PROJECT:

Many projects relating to the Mass could be undertaken, such as: a study of the vestments; the Missal (Ordinary and Proper); the making of a small model altar (with tabernacle, candlesticks, missal stand, etc.) by the boys; the dressing of dolls (in vestments of priest and servers) by the girls.

PRAYER:

Grant us, we beseech You, O Lord, worthily to frequent these mysteries, since as often as the commemoration of this victim is celebrated, the work of our redemption is performed. Through Christ Our Lord. Amen.   *(Missal: Secret for Ninth Sunday after Pentecost)*

LESSON 28 — Holy Communion

RECEIVING THE HOLY EUCHARIST

MULTIPLICATION OF LOAVES AND FISHES

NEXT DAY

CHRIST IN SYNAGOGUE AT CAPHARNAUM

"AND ALL ATE AND WERE SATISFIED" (Matthew 14, 20)

"You seek Me . . . because you have eaten of the loaves and have been filled. Do not labor for the food that perishes, but for that which endures unto life everlasting. . . . The bread that I will give is My flesh for the life of the world" (John 6, 26-27, 52).

366. What is Holy Communion?

Holy Communion is the receiving of Jesus Christ in the sacrament of the Holy Eucharist.

Communion is an action. It is the sharing to the full in the Eucharistic sacrifice, by eating the Flesh of Christ as the food of our soul.

By our sacrifice we have offered a gift to God. God is pleased and has accepted our gift. He is so pleased that He invites us to eat of the gift we have given Him. He invites us to eat as guests at His table. Communion is the action by which all of us eat together the Flesh and Blood of Christ as the food and drink of our souls.

367. What is necessary to receive Holy Communion worthily?

To receive Holy Communion worthily it is necessary to be free from mortal sin, to have a right intention, and to obey the Church's laws on the fast required before Holy Communion out of reverence for the body and blood of Our Divine Lord. However, there are some cases in which Holy Communion may be received without fasting.

368. Does he who knowingly receives Holy Communion in mortal sin receive the body and blood of Christ and His graces?

He who knowingly receives Holy Communion in mortal sin receives the body and blood of Christ; but he does not receive His graces and he commits a grave sin of sacrilege.

**Healthy People
Can Eat**

SOULS WITHOUT SIN CAN
RECEIVE COMMUNION

**Sick People Can Eat,
Though it is Harder**

SOULS WITH VENIAL SIN CAN
RECEIVE, BUT GET LESS GRACE

**Dead People
Cannot Eat**

SOULS IN MORTAL SIN
CANNOT RECEIVE

Only the living can eat bodily food. So, too, only those living the life of grace can be nourished by the food of the Eucharist. If someone in mortal sin goes to Communion, he receives no more nourishment than a dead man would if food were forced down his throat. It would even be worse, since it would be a sacrilege.

369. What should we do to receive more abundantly the graces of Holy Communion?

To receive more abundantly the graces of Holy Communion we should strive to be most fervent and to free ourselves from deliberate venial sin.

JOHN, YOUR HANDS ARE DIRTY. GO WASH THEM.

If our hands are dirty at meal time, we wash them before coming to table. So too, if our souls are soiled with venial sin before Communion, we wash them with an act of contrition. That is why we say the Confiteor at Mass.

To get our souls really clean, we should often take a good bath in the Precious Blood of Christ in the Sacrament of Penance. The more often we do this, the cleaner our souls will be to approach the table of the Eucharist. We should never stay away from Communion, though, because we have venial sins on our soul. Even though we may not be as clean as we should be, our souls need the food.

370. Does the Church now command us to fast from midnight before Holy Communion?

The Church does not now command us to fast from midnight before Holy Communion, as it did formerly. The laws enacted by Pope Pius XII now regulate this matter by the number of hours we must fast.

371. When may Holy Communion be received without fasting?

Holy Communion may be received without fasting when one is in danger of death, or when it it necessary to save the Blessed Sacrament from insult or injury.

372. What are the laws enacted by Pope Pius XII regarding the fast required before Holy Communion?

The laws enacted by Pope Pius XII regarding the fast required before Holy Communion are the following:

1. Water may be taken at any time before Holy Communion without breaking the fast.

2. Sick persons, though not confined to bed, may receive Holy Communion after taking medicine or non-alcoholic drinks. A priest's permission is not necessary.

3. All Catholics may receive Holy Communion after fasting one hour from food and drink including even alcoholic beverages in moderation. This rule applies to Holy Communion at midnight Mass as well as at Masses celebrated in the morning, afternoon or evening. A priest's permission is not needed.

4. One may not receive Holy Communion a second time on the same day, unless the danger of death arises, when he can receive the Blessed Sacrament as Viaticum. But one who has received the Holy Eucharist at the midnight Mass of Christmas or at the Mass of the Easter Vigil may receive again in the course of the day. These rules show the Church's desire that all Catholics partake of the Holy Eucharist frequently.

373. How should we prepare ourselves for Holy Communion?

We should prepare ourselves for Holy Communion by thinking of Our Divine Redeemer whom we are about to receive, and by making fervent acts of faith, hope, love, and contrition.

It is good to prepare ourselves for Communion, even before Mass begins, by thinking about what we are going to do and asking Our Lord to come to us. This is a good time to say the prayers before Communion in our prayer book or missal.

374. What should we do after Holy Communion?

After Holy Communion we should spend some time adoring Our Lord, thanking Him, renewing our promises of love and of obedience to Him, and asking Him for blessings for ourselves and others.

The fifteen or twenty minutes that Our Lord is in us bodily after Communion is the best time of the whole day for prayer.

375. What are the chief effects of a worthy Holy Communion?

The chief effects of a worthy Holy Communion are:

first, a closer union with Our Lord and a more fervent love of God and of our neighbor;

second, an increase of sanctifying grace;

third, preservation from mortal sin and the remission of venial sin;

fourth, the lessening of our inclinations to sin and the help to practice good works.

Holy Communion is eating food for the soul. Our Lord said, "He who eats Me, he also shall live because of Me" (John 6, 58). But Christ is love. This food is a flaming food, flaming with the fire of divine love. This love unites us most closely to Our Blessed Lord. It fills us with His fires of love for His Father and for all men, and makes our own fires of love strong with His.

376. When are we obliged to receive Holy Communion?

We are obliged to receive Holy Communion during Easter time each year and when in danger of death.

377. Why is it well to receive Holy Communion often, even daily?

It is well to receive Holy Communion often, even daily, because this intimate union with Jesus Christ, the Source of all holiness and the Giver of all graces, is the greatest aid to a holy life.

EVERYTHING IS READY

COME TO THE MARRIAGE FEAST

(MATT 22:4)

WEEKLY COMMUNION

If we appreciate what Communion really is, we will do our best to receive at least on Sundays. Our Lord must certainly be disappointed on Sundays when He sets out such a banquet and then sees so many people at Mass who do not come up to eat. They simply watch others eating and then go away with hungry souls.

DAILY COMMUNION

Most people could go to Communion daily if they really wanted to, though it might cost a little sacrifice. They could perhaps skip the late TV show at night, get to bed a little earlier, and be able to get up for early Mass and Communion. Daily Communion is highly recommended by the Church.

THIS - OR - THIS

10:00 PM

7:00 AM

Those who cannot go to daily Communion, but would if they could, can make a spiritual communion. This means a real desire to go to Communion when it is impossible to receive sacramentally. This desire obtains for us from Our Lord the graces of Communion in proportion to the strength of the desire.

378. How should we show our gratitude to Our Lord for remaining always on our altars in the Holy Eucharist?

We should show our gratitude to Our Lord for remaining always on our altars in the Holy Eucharist by visiting Him often, by reverence in church, by assisting every day at Mass when this is possible, by attending parish devotions, and by being present at Benediction of the Blessed Sacrament.

"Come to Me all you who labor and are burdened, and I will give you rest" (Matt. 11, 28).

Christ loves to have us visit Him in the Blessed Sacrament just as He loved to have people come to Him on earth. He loves us so much that He wants us to come with our troubles so that He can help us. And even if we do not have any special troubles, He loves to have us come just to talk to Him in our own words and spend some time with Him.

If we learn to listen to Him with our hearts, to hear anything He wants us to hear, He will teach our hearts what to do to love Him. Those who visit the Blessed Sacrament often, and really learn to be silent for some time before Christ in the tabernacle, find that their desire to be there gets stronger every day, and it becomes easier and easier to converse in love with Him.

DISCUSSION QUESTIONS:

1. Why do we eat the Flesh of Christ in Holy Communion?
2. Why is it that those in mortal sin cannot receive Communion?
3. What should we do before Communion if we have venial sins?
4. Why is the time after Communion the best time of the day?
5. How should we spend it?
6. Why does frequent confession help us to receive Communion more worthily?
7. What is a spiritual Communion?
8. What should we do before Communion?

9. How long do we have to fast before Communion?

10. Can Communion ever be received more than once a day?

CHOOSE THE BEST ANSWER:

1. To receive Communion worthily we must be free from: (a) venial sin (b) mortal sin (c) all sin (d) all imperfections. ☐

2. Before Communion we are urged to fast: (a) one hour (b) three hours (c) all day (d) from midnight. ☐

3. The Eucharistic fast is broken by: (a) water (b) food (c) medicine. ☐

4. To take medicine before Communion we must ask: (a) the bishop (b) a priest (c) a Sister (d) no one. ☐

5. To please Our Lord most it is best to go to Communion: (a) once a year (b) every month (c) every Sunday (d) daily. ☐

FILL IN THE BLANKS:

1. In Holy Communion we eat the Flesh and drink the Blood of

. . . .

2. Holy Communion is taking food and drink for our . . . .

3. We must receive Communion during . . . . and when

. . . .

4. Someone who receives Communion in mortal sin commits a

. . . .

5. To get the full grace of Communion we should try to be free from . . . .

6. If we use the privileges of Pope Pius XII, we should also do works of . . . . and . . . .

7. The Eucharistic fast from solids must be kept for . . . . hours.

8. Sick persons may go to Communion after taking . . . .

. . . .

9. We should often receive the Sacrament of Penance to get our . . . . really clean before Holy Communion.

10. We should try to spend the time after Communion in . . . .

READ FROM THE BIBLE:

Ex. 16; Ps. 22; Matt. 22; John 6.

CLASS PROJECT:

The best project is actually to receive daily Communion if possible, but without pressure on anyone. Perhaps a few volunteers each day could receive Communion as class representatives, going in rotation. Have a minute of silence morning and afternoon for a spiritual Communion in class.

PRAYER:

Having received these holy gifts, we beseech You, O Lord, that with the frequentation of this mystery, the effect of our salvation may increase. Through Christ, Our Lord, Amen.

(Missal: Postcommunion for First Sunday after Pentecost)

LESSON 29 — Penance

"Take courage, son; thy sins are forgiven thee" (Matthew 9, 2).

379. What is the sacrament of Penance?

Penance is the sacrament by which sins committed after Baptism are forgiven through the absolution of the priest.

PENANCE — The MEDICINE for our Soul

The sacrament of Penance is a SIGN.

Like every sacrament it is a sign of three things: past, present, and future.

1. It is a sign of the **Passion of Christ** and of His Precious Blood, which is the medicine He uses to heal our souls.

2. It is a sign of the **healing action of Christ** on the soul through the absolution of the priest.

3. It is a sign of the **spiritual health** which this sacrament gives.

380. Whence has the priest the power to forgive sins?

The priest has the power to forgive sins from Jesus Christ, who said to His apostles and to their successors in the priesthood: "Receive the Holy Spirit; whose sins you shall forgive, they are forgiven them; and whose sins you shall retain, they are retained."

Only God can forgive sins. But He can decide for Himself how He wants to do it. And the way He has decided upon is to use priests as His instruments.

We can truly say that Christ forgives sins, using the lips and hands of the priest, or we can say that the priest forgives sins by the power Christ gives him.

381. With what words does the priest forgive sins?

The priest forgives sins with the words: "I absolve thee from thy sins in the name of the Father, and of the Son, and of the Holy Spirit. Amen."

382. What are the effects of the sacrament of Penance, worthily received?

The effects of the sacrament of Penance, worthily received, are:

first, the restoration or increase of sanctifying grace;

second, the forgiveness of sins;

third, the remission of the eternal punishment, if necessary, and also of part, at least, of the temporal punishment, due to our sins;

fourth, the help to avoid sin in future;

fifth, the restoration of the merits of our good works if they have been lost by mortal sin.

FIVE FRUITS OF A GOOD CONFESSION

1. Those who are dead in mortal sin are raised by Christ to the life of grace. Those who are sick with venial sin have this life made healthy and strong.

2. Just as light drives out darkness, so does the life given by this sacrament drive out the darkness of sin.

3. See Questions 421-425.

4. The sacramental grace of Penance is a spring from which flow the helps we need to keep out of sin for the future.

5. It is something like a man who returns from a hospital cured and is now able to use his possessions again. (See Question 118.)

383. What else does the sacrament of Penance do for us?

The sacrament of Penance also gives us the opportunity to receive spiritual advice and instruction from our confessor.

384. What must we do to receive the sacrament of Penance worthily?

To receive the sacrament of Penance worthily, we must:

first, examine our conscience;

second, be sorry for our sins;

third, have the firm purpose of not sinning again;

fourth, confess our sins to the priest;

fifth, be willing to perform the penance the priest gives us.

STEPS TO A GOOD CONFESSION

Our share in the fruits of a good confession depends in large measure on our preparation. Here are the five steps to the reception of the sacrament of Penance. Think of these steps slowly and carefully. Don't rush. Exact words are not important, but each step must be climbed.

5 ACCEPT YOUR PENANCE	Q. 420-425
4 CONFESS YOUR SINS	Q. 408-419
3 HAVE PURPOSE OF AMENDMENT	Q. 406-407
2 BE TRULY SORRY	Q. 388-405
1 EXAMINE YOUR CONSCIENCE	Q. 385-387

385. What is an examination of conscience?

An examination of conscience is a sincere effort to call to mind all the sins we have committed since our last worthy confession.

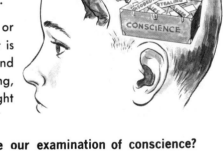

Our conscience is the judgment or decision our mind makes on what is right and wrong. It does not depend on what we *feel* is right and wrong, but on what Our Lord tells us is right and wrong.

386. What should we do before our examination of conscience?

Before our examination of conscience we should ask God's help to know our sins and to confess them with sincere sorrow.

387. How can we make a good examination of conscience.

We can make a good examination of conscience by calling to mind the commandments of God and of the Church, and the particular duties of our state of life, and by asking ourselves how we may have sinned with regard to them.

DISCUSSION QUESTIONS:

1. What are the fruits of a good confession?
2. With what words did Christ institute this sacrament?
3. Why should we pray before confession?
4. What are the steps to a good confession?
5. How is this sacrament a sign of the Passion?

CHOOSE THE BEST ANSWER:

1. The sacrament of Penance is a sign of: (a) sin   (b) sickness (c) medicine   (d) courage.   ☐
2. Our conscience is in our: (a) mind   (b) heart   (c) feelings (d) imagination.   ☐
3. The priest forgives sins in the name of: (a) the Pope   (b) the bishop   (c) the people   (d) God.   ☐
4. In giving absolution the priest: (a) prays that sins will be forgiven   (b) gives advice   (c) asks questions   (d) forgives sin.   ☐
5. Thinking over our past sins is called: (a) repentance   (b) sorrow   (c) examination of conscience   (d) temporal punishment.   ☐

FILL IN THE BLANKS:

1. In the Sacrament of Penance our sins are forgiven by . . . . who takes the place of . . . .
2. Penance is to the soul what . . . . is to the body.
3. This sacrament heals diseases of . . . .
4. The priest gets his power to forgive sins from . . . .
5. Trying to remember our sins is called . . . .

READ FROM THE BIBLE:

God's Forgiveness of Sins — Ps. 129; 142; Luke 15; John 8, 1-11; Apoc. 7, 13-17.

CLASS PROJECT:

Read the miracle of Christ healing the paralyzed man (Matt. 9, 2-8). Discuss the following points in class:

Why did Christ heal the man's sins before He cured his body?

Why did not Christ ask the man to tell Him his sins?

How did this miracle prove Christ's power to forgive sins?

Why do you think Christ worked a miracle of healing to prove His power to forgive sins, rather than another type of miracle?

Which was a greater act of Christ's power, healing the man's body or forgiving his sins? Why?

PRAYER:

May the Almighty God have mercy on me, and forgive me my sins, and bring me to everlasting life. Amen.

May the almighty and merciful Lord grant me pardon, absolution and remission of all my sins. Amen.

"And Peter went out and wept bitterly" (Luke 22, 62).

388. What is contrition?

Contrition is sincere sorrow for having offended God, and hatred for the sins we have committed, with a firm purpose of sinning no more.

This is the most necessary part of the sacrament of Penance. There are times when sins can be forgiven without confession or without satisfaction afterward, but there are never times when sins can be forgiven without sorrow in the heart.

389. Will God forgive us any sin unless we have true contrition for it?

God will not forgive us any sin, whether mortal or venial, unless we have true contrition for it.

390. When is sorrow for sin true contrition?

Sorrow for sin is true contrition when it is interior, supernatural, supreme, and universal.

The garment of contrition must have all four of these qualities or it will not please God and win for us His pardon.

Qualities of the garment of contrition

- 189 -

QUALITIES OF TRUE CONTRITION

1. Interior

391. When is our sorrow interior?

Our sorrow is interior when it comes from our heart, and not merely from our lips.

THIS

This means we must not only *say* we are sorry, but we must *mean* it. We *must want* to be sorry even though we cannot always *feel* it.

NOT THIS

2. Supernatural

392. When is our sorrow supernatural?

Our sorrow is supernatural when, with the help of God's grace, it arises from motives which spring from faith and not merely from natural motives.

THIS

I'M SORRY I STOLE THAT APPLE BE- CAUSE IT OFFENDS GOD. I'LL PUT AN EXTRA DIME IN THE POOR BOX

NOT THIS

I'M SORRY I TOOK THIS. HE MIGHT CATCH ME.

This means we must be sorry because we have offended God and may lose our soul, not just because we may have been caught or because something bad happened to us.

Supernatural means "above the natural." It is *natural* to be sorry for our actions when something unpleasant happens to us. It is *supernatural* to be sorry for sins because of what God has told us, either about the danger of hell or about how sin offends Him, even though nothing unpleasant may have happened to us yet.

3. Supreme

393. When is our sorrow supreme?

Our sorrow is supreme when we hate sin above every other evil, and are willing to endure any suffering rather than offend God in the future by sin.

THIS

"DEATH RATHER THAN SIN"

ST. DOMINIC SAVIO

NOT THIS

"I'LL TRY TO KEEP OUT OF SIN." (MEANING,- IF IT'S NOT TOO HARD)

This means that we know that sin is the greatest, the supreme, evil in the world and we would do anything to keep out of it.

4. Universal

394. When is our sorrow universal?

Our sorrow is universal when we are sorry for every mortal sin which we may have had the misfortune to commit.

THIS

WATERS OF SORROW

I'LL PUT THEM ALL IN.

MISSING MASS LYING QUARRELING

NOT THIS

WATERS OF SORROW

I'LL KEEP THIS ONE OUT.

MISSING MASS

This means we must be sorry at least for all our mortal sins, if we have any.

If we do not wash all our dirty clothes of sin, then none will be clean.

395. Should we always try to have sorrow for all our venial sins when receiving the sacrament of Penance?

We should try to have sorrow for all our venial sins when receiving the sacrament of Penance, and, when we have only venial sins to confess, we must have sorrow for at least one of them or for some sin of our past life which we confess.

396. Why should we have contrition for mortal sin?

We should have contrition for mortal sin because it is the greatest of all evils, gravely offends God, keeps us out of heaven, and condemns us forever to hell.

397. Why should we have contrition for venial sin?

We should have contrition for venial sin because it is displeasing to God, merits temporal punishment, and may lead to mortal sin.

398. How many kinds of contrition are there?

There are two kinds of contrition: perfect contrition and imperfect contrition.

399. When is our contrition perfect?

Our contrition is perfect when we are sorry for our sins because sin offends God, whom we love above all things for His own sake.

400. When is our contrition imperfect?

Our contrition is imperfect when we are sorry for our sins because they are hateful in themselves or because we fear God's punishment.

401. To receive the sacrament of Penance worthily, what kind of contrition is sufficient?

To receive the sacrament of Penance worthily, imperfect contrition is sufficient.

402. Should we always try to have perfect contrition in the sacrament of Penance?

We should always try to have perfect contrition in the sacrament of Penance because perfect contrition is more pleasing to God, and because with His help we can always have it.

403. How can a person in mortal sin regain the state of grace before receiving the sacrament of Penance?

A person in mortal sin can regain the state of grace before receiving the sacrament of Penance by making an act of perfect contrition with the sincere purpose of going to confession.

404. What should we do if we have the misfortune to commit a mortal sin?

If we have the misfortune to commit a mortal sin, we should ask God's pardon and grace at once, make an act of perfect contrition, and go to confession as soon as we can.

It is much worse to commit a mortal sin than to catch a bodily disease. If a man has a heart attack, will he wait a month to call a doctor? Anyone who has committed a mortal sin should go to confession immediately and cancel all other appointments so as to be there at the first possible opportunity. Since that might be a few days away, he should do his best to make an act of perfect contrition as explained in the preceding question.

LET'S GO TO THE MOVIES THIS AFTERNOON.

I CAN'T. I'LL BE BUSY

(TO HIMSELF) I HAVE TO GO TO CONFESSION. I HAVE A MORTAL SIN ON MY SOUL.

242-5

405. May we receive Holy Communion after committing a mortal sin if we merely make an act of perfect contrition?

We may not receive Holy Communion after committing a mortal sin if we merely make an act of perfect contrition; one who has sinned grievously must go to confession before receiving Holy Communion. The Church permits an exception in the case of one who has an urgent need to receive Holy Communion (which rarely happens) and cannot get to confession; such a person an act of perfect contrition.

406. What is the firm purpose of sinning no more?

The firm purpose of sinning no more is the sincere resolve not only to avoid sin but to avoid as far as possible the near occasions of sin.

Suppose someone says, "God, I am sorry I have offended You, but I intend to do it again." Is he really sorry? Of course not.

Suppose someone says, "I promise not to steal again, but I will not stay away from my companions who steal." Is he really sorry? Of course not. He is fooling himself if he thinks he can keep out of sin without giving up the occasions of sin.

407. What purpose of amendment must a person have if he has only venial sins to confess?

If a person has only venial sins to confess, he must have the purpose of avoiding at least one of them.

He *should* want to avoid all of them, but he *must* have the purpose of avoiding at least one of them or his confession is worthless.

DISCUSSION QUESTIONS:

1. Why do we have to be sorry for our sins?
2. Is it enough to say we are sorry for our sins?
3. State difference between saying and making an act of contrition.
4. What is the difference between natural and supernatural sorrow?
5. Why do we have to be sorry for at least all mortal sins?
6. What is the difference between perfect and imperfect contrition?
7. How can we arouse ourselves to perfect contrition for our sins?
8. How soon should we go to confession if we ever have the terrible misfortune of committing a mortal sin?
9. Since we cannot always be sure we have perfect contrition, what do we have to do if we have committed a mortal sin?
10. Why do we have to be determined to avoid occasions of sin?

CHOOSE THE BEST ANSWER:

1. Interior sorrow must come from our: (a) lips (b) mind
(c) heart (d) feelings. ☐

2. When we go to confession we must have: (a) at least natural
sorrow (b) imperfect contrition (c) perfect contrition (d) a feeling of sorrow. ☐

3. Supreme sorrow comes from knowing that sin: (a) hurts others
(b) makes us feel bad (c) is the worst evil in the world (d) cannot be forgiven. ☐

4. Universal sorrow must include: (a) some mortal sins (b) many
mortal sins (c) at least one mortal sin (d) all mortal sins if there
are any. ☐

5. Before a person in mortal sin can go to Communion he must:
(a) make an act of perfect contrition (b) go to confession (c) say
his penance (d) be supremely sorry. ☐

FILL IN THE BLANKS:

1. God will never forgive sins unless we have . . . .
for them.

2. Sorrow that is deep in our heart is called . . . .

3. Sorrow that comes from knowing that sin is the worst thing
on earth is called . . . .

4. Sorrow that comes from what God has told us about sin is
called. . . . .

5. Sorrow that includes all our sins is called . . . .

6. We have to have sorrow for our . . . . sins and
should try hard to be sorry also for our . . . . sins.

7. If someone is dying in mortal sin, he should try to make an
act of . . . .

8. To be sorry for sin because we are afraid God will do something to us is to have . . . .

9. Real sorrow means that we have a firm . . . . not to
sin again.

10. If we are truly sorry, we are determined to . . . .
near occasions of sin.

READ FROM THE BIBLE:

Ps. 6; 40; 76; Is. 1; Luke 7, 36-50; John 21, 15-17.

CLASS PROJECT:

Let each boy and girl in the class bring in a simple cartoon illustrating one of the qualities of true contrition or the difference between perfect and imperfect contrition.

PRAYER:

Act of Contrition, as on page 6.

LESSON 31 — Confession

"Peace be to you! As the Father has sent Me, I also send you . . . . Receive the Holy Spirit; whose sins you shall forgive, they are forgiven them; and whose sins you shall retain, they are retained" (John 20, 21-23).

408. What is confession?

Confession is the telling of our sins to an authorized priest for the purpose of obtaining forgiveness.

409. Why must we confess our sins?

We must confess our sins because Jesus Christ obliges us to do so in these words, spoken to the apostles and to their successors in the priesthood: "Whose sins you shall forgive, they are forgiven them; and whose sins you shall retain, they are retained."

410. How do these words of Christ oblige us to confess our sins?

These words of Christ oblige us to confess our sins because the priest cannot know whether he should forgive or retain our sins unless we tell them to him.

Christ never asked men to confess their sins to Him as He could read their hearts. He could see both their sins and their sorrow.

However, He rarely gives the power of reading hearts to priests. He wants people to tell their sins since this humbles that pride which is the root of all sin. If we were to tell our sins to God alone, pride would not be humbled and would remain strong.

411. Is it necessary to confess every sin?

It is necessary to confess every mortal sin which has not yet been confessed and forgiven; it is not necessary to confess our venial sins, but it is better to do so.

Anyone who deliberately omits a venial sin in confession does not make a bad confession but loses much of the grace of the sacrament which would help him overcome this sin. Besides, there is the danger that he might convince himself that a sin is only venial which is really mortal. In doubt, it is always safer to tell even venial sins.

412. What are the chief qualities of a good confession?

The chief qualities of a good confession are three: it must be humble, sincere, and entire.

NO EXCUSES	NO FALSEHOODS	NO OMISSIONS

HUMBLE	SINCERE	ENTIRE
It was my fault.	I am telling the truth.	I am leaving nothing out.

413. When is our confession humble?

Our confession is humble when we accuse ourselves of our sins with a conviction of guilt for having offended God.

414. When is our confession sincere?

Our confession is sincere when we tell our sins honestly and frankly.

415. When is our confession entire?

Our confession is entire when we confess at least all our mortal sins, telling their kind, the number of times we have committed each sin, and any circumstances changing their nature.

416. What are we to do if without our fault we forget to confess a mortal sin?

If without our fault we forget to confess a mortal sin, we may receive Holy Communion, because we have made a good confession and the sin is forgiven; but we must tell the sin in confession if it again comes to our mind.

417. What happens if we knowingly conceal a mortal sin in confession?

If we knowingly conceal a mortal sin in confession, the sins we confess are not forgiven; moreover, we commit a mortal sin of sacrilege.

418. What must a person do who has knowingly concealed a mortal sin in confession?

A person who has knowingly concealed a mortal sin in confession must confess that he has made a bad confession, tell the sin he has concealed, mention the sacraments he has received since that time, and confess all the mortal sins he has committed since his last good confession.

STORY OF A BAD CONFESSION

JOHN HAS FOUR MORTAL SINS — HE GOES TO CONFESSION — HE TELLS THREE, BUT IS ASHAMED OF THE OTHER — HE COMES OUT WITH **FIVE**

And no matter how often John goes to confession after this, no sin will ever be forgiven until he tells the one he deliberately left out. As often as he goes to confession without telling this sin, all his confessions will be bad. And if he goes to Communion, this will be a sacrilege, too.

419. Why should a sense of shame and fear of telling our sins to the priest never lead us to conceal a mortal sin in confession?

A sense of shame and fear of telling our sins to the priest should never lead us to conceal a mortal sin in confession because this is a grave sacrilege, and also because the priest, who represents Christ Himself, is bound by the seal of the sacrament of Penance never to reveal anything that has been confessed to him.

A priest must always keep his lips locked about what he hears in confession. One priest even died a martyr's death, because he refused to reveal what he had heard in confession. His name was St. John Nepomucene.

PRIEST'S LIPS
LOCKED

420. Why does the priest give us a penance after confession?

The priest gives us a penance after confession that we may make some atonement to God for our sins, receive help to avoid them in the future, and make some satisfaction for the temporal punishment due to them.

421. What kinds of punishment are due to sin?

Two kinds of punishment are due to sin: the eternal punishment of hell, due to unforgiven mortal sins, and temporal punishment, lasting only for a time, due to venial sins and also to mortal sins after they have been forgiven.

Eternal punishment is God's angry punishment, which balances the scales of justice, upset by sin. This punishment is reserved for those in hell, since they refused to let God correct them on earth.

Temporal punishment is God's loving, corrective punishment like medicine a mother gives a child. This punishment is given either on earth or in purgatory.

422. Does the sacrament of Penance, worthily received, always take away all punishment?

The sacrament of Penance, worthily received, always takes away all eternal punishment; but it does not always take away all temporal punishment.

423. Why does God require temporal punishment for sin?

God requires temporal punishment for sin to satisfy His justice, to teach us the great evil of sin, and to warn us not to sin again.

The wound caused by sin in the will is healed by the medicine of the sacrament of Penance.

But there are also wounds in the other powers of the soul. These are healed by the further medicine of temporal punishment. Temporal punishment repairs all the damage done to the soul by sin.

424. Where do we pay the debt of our temporal punishment?

We pay the debt of our temporal punishment either in this life or in purgatory.

425. What are the chief means of satisfying the debt of our temporal punishment, besides the penance imposed after confession?

Besides the penance imposed after confession, the chief means of satisfying the debt of our temporal punishment are: prayer, attending Mass, fasting, almsgiving, the works of mercy, the patient endurance of sufferings, and indulgences.

The secret of healing the effects of sin quickly is love of the Cross. Our Lord tells us to take up our cross daily. But what is our cross?

Our cross is everything that happens to us during the day that we do not like. When these things happen to us, it is a sign of God's love. He is sending crosses to heal the wounds of our soul. Crosses heal us quickly if we accept them and even love them the way Our Lord did. We must pray for help to recognize and love the crosses God sends us each day.

DISCUSSION QUESTIONS:

1. How do we know we have to tell our sins to get them forgiven?
2. Why isn't it enough just to tell God we are sorry?
3. Why is it a bad practice to omit venial sins in confession?
4. Why is it good to try always to tell our venial sins?
5. Why is it so bad to leave out a mortal sin on purpose?
6. What is eternal punishment?
7. Why is temporal punishment needed after sins are forgiven?
8. What are some means of avoiding purgatory?
9. How can we quickly heal the effects of sin?
10. Give one reason why God sends us crosses.

CHOOSE THE BEST ANSWER:

1. Christ wants us to admit our sins to a priest to destroy our: (a) punishment (b) humility (c) pride (d) remorse. ☐

2. It is a bad confession if we leave out: (a) one venial sin (b) all venial sins (c) one mortal sin (d) sins we forget.

3. The debt of temporal punishment is paid either in this life or in: (a) hell (b) heaven (c) purgatory (d) limbo. ☐

4. Temporal punishment is a sign of God's: (a) anger (b) power (c) love (d) hatred. ☐

5. To heal all the effects of sin, God must send us: (a) medicine (b) crosses (c) temptations (d) occasions of sin. ☐

FILL IN THE BLANKS:

1. In confession the priest represents . . . .

2. The purpose of confession it to obtain . . . .

3. When we admit we have done wrong through our own fault, our confession is . . . .

4. When we do not leave out any sins, our confession is . . . .

5. When we tell the truth about our sins, our confession is . . . .

6. Deliberately leaving out a mortal sin in confession is a sin of
. . . .

7. Two kinds of punishment are . . . . and . . . .

8. The secret of healing the effects of sin quickly is . . . .

9. If we refuse the crosses God sends us, we may escape hell, but we cannot escape. . . . .

10. The priest's obligation to keep silence about what he hears in confession we call the . . . . of the Sacrament of Penance.

READ FROM THE BIBLE:

4 Kings 5; Ps. 50; John 20, 19-23.

CLASS PROJECT:

Since our cross is everything God allows to happen each day that we do not like, or each thing He wants us to do that we do not like, let each boy and girl make a list of crosses that ordinarily come up in the life of a schoolboy or girl.

Here are some examples: being willing to have someone tease you, being willing to lose a ball game, being willing to pay attention in class when you do not feel like it, being willing to do your homework well, being willing to help with the dishes. Doing these things willingly when you do not feel like it is bearing a cross.

PRAYER:

The Confiteor, as on page 5.

PREPARE   TELL YOUR SINS   THANK GOD

426. Before entering the confessional, how should we prepare ourselves for a good confession?

Before entering the confessional, we should prepare ourselves for a good confession by taking sufficient time not only to examine our conscience but, especially, to excite in our hearts sincere sorrow for our sins and a firm purpose not to commit them again.

Never enter the confessional box without at least a few minutes of preparation. Often you will have to wait in line. But even if there is no line outside the box, spend at least five minutes to prepare yourself well.

After you have examined your conscience well, arouse in your heart real sorrow for sin. The best way to do this is to think of some detail of the Passion of Our Lord. Perhaps His crown of thorns, perhaps one nail wound, perhaps the smarting of His eyes from the blood and sweat and tears. This will make you wish you had never offended Him by sin and make you willing to do anything or give up anything to keep out of sin in the future.

427. How should we begin our confession?

We should begin our confession in this manner: Entering the confessional, we kneel, and making the sign of the cross we say to the priest: "Bless me, Father, for I have sinned"; and then we tell how long it has been since our last confession.

For example: "Bless me, Father, for I have sinned. It is two weeks since my last confession."

428. After telling the time of our last confession, what do we confess?

After telling the time of our last confession, if we have committed any mortal sins since that time we must confess them, and also any that we have forgotten in previous confessions, telling the nature and number of each; we may also confess any venial sins we wish to mention.

For example: "I missed Mass once. I was disobedient ten times. I told lies five times. I quarreled once. I was unkind eight times."

429. What should we do if we cannot remember the exact number of our mortal sins?

If we cannot remember the exact number of our mortal sins, we should tell the number as nearly as possible, or say how often we have committed the sins in a day, a week, a month, or a year.

For example: "During the summer I missed Mass twice a month."

430. What should we do when we have committed no mortal sin since our last confession?

When we have committed no mortal sin since our last confession, we should confess our venial sins or some sin told in a previous confession, for which we are again sorry, in order that the priest may give us absolution.

And this is what should ordinarily be the case, because if we really love God, we will rarely, if ever, commit a mortal sin. But it is always best to tell all our sins, even the slightest.

431. How should we end our confession?

We should end our confession by saying: "I am sorry for these and all the sins of my past life, especially for . . ."; and then it is well to tell one or several of the sins which we have previously confessed and for which we are particularly sorry.

For example: "especially for disobedience."

432. What should we do after confessing our sins?

After confessing our sins, we should answer truthfully any question the priest asks, seek advice if we feel that we need any, listen carefully to the spiritual instruction and counsel of the priest, and accept the penance he gives us.

For example: The priest might ask if you were sick when you missed Mass. You might answer, "No, Father, but my mother overslept and did not wake me up." Then listen to the priest's advice.

If you have any questions to ask about sins, you should ask the priest in confession. For example: "Father, is it a sin to see movies that are unobjectionable for adults?" Then do what he tells you. If you ever wonder whether something is right or wrong, it is much better to ask the priest before you do it than afterward.

433. What should we do when the priest is giving us absolution?

When the priest is giving us absolution, we should say from our heart the act of contrition in a tone to be heard by him.

Remember that you are telling Our Lord you are sorry you have hurt Him. Be sure to mean what you are saying.

434. What should we do after leaving the confessional?

After leaving the confessional we should return thanks to God for the sacrament we have received, beg Our Lord to supply for the imperfections of our confession, and promptly and devoutly perform our penance.

Always spend a few minutes in thanksgiving after Our Lord has healed your soul. Thank Him from the bottom of your heart for all He went through in His Passion, since His sufferings paid the price for this medicine of the Sacrament of Penance. He bought it with His blood so that He could give it to us free.

Say your penance from your heart and then think over what you can do to improve. Think over any advice the priest has given you.

Take at least five minutes for your thanksgiving. It gives the healing medicine of Christ's Precious Blood more time to sink into your soul and it will do much more good than if you said your penance quickly and ran out of church.

DISCUSSION QUESTIONS:

1. What is the best way to make ourselves sorry for our sins?

2. If you enter church to go to confession and there is no one waiting outside the box, what should you do?

3. Suppose you do not know whether or not it is a sin to throw snowballs. What should you do?

4. What should you think of when you say your Act of Contrition?

5. What should you think of after you leave the confessional box?

CHOOSE THE BEST ANSWER:

1. We begin confession by telling when our last: (a) sin (b) confession (c) communion was. ☐

2. We must tell the: (a) nature and number (b) details (c) causes of each sin. ☐

3. It is best to tell: (a) only mortal sins (b) some venial sins (c) all our sins. ☐

4. We should say our Act of Contrition: (a) aloud (b) silently (c) after leaving the confessional. ☐

5. Thanksgiving should last at least: (a) a minute (b) five minutes (c) an hour. ☐

FILL IN THE BLANKS:

1. Before entering the confessional box we should try especially to arouse in our hearts ....

2. To do this it is a big help to think about some detail of the .... of Our Lord.

3. As we start our confession we should make the ....

4. If we are doubtful whether or not something is a sin we should

....

5. After confession we should first .... God for healing our sins.

READ FROM THE BIBLE:

Ps. 31; Acts 5, 1-11; 1 John 1, 5-8.

CLASS PROJECT:

Let each boy and girl in the class bring in on paper a good practical suggestion for keeping occupied while waiting in line for confession. Then let the class vote on the five best suggestions.

PRAYER:

O God, Who are offended by our faults and appeased by our penance, look with favor on the prayers of Your people who beseech You, and turn away the scourges of Your anger which we have deserved by our sins. Through Christ Our Lord. Amen.

(Missal: Collect for Thursday after Ash Wednesday)

SPIRITUAL TREASURY OF THE CHURCH
SATISFACTION OF CHRIST, OUR LADY, AND THE SAINTS

INDULGENCES

435. What is an indulgence?

An indulgence is the remission granted by the Church of the temporal punishment due to sins already forgiven.

After sin has been healed by the medicine of the sacrament of Penance, the wounds left by sin must be healed by the further medicine of temporal punishment (See page 200.)

An indulgence remits punishment. In other words it removes the need for the bitter medicine of suffering and substitutes an easier but more effective one to assist and even complete the healing process.

As a medicine to heal the soul, indulgences are better than our own acts of self-denial and the acceptance of suffering. But as fuel to make the fires of love grow — which is much more important than mere healing — suffering is much better.

436. How many kinds of indulgences are there?

There are two kinds of indulgences, plenary and partial.

437. What is a plenary indulgence?

A plenary indulgence is the remission of all the temporal punishment due to our sins.

A plenary indulgence heals completely the damage to the soul done by sin so that there is no longer any need of temporal punishment.

438. What is a partial indulgence?

A partial indulgence is the remission of part of the temporal punishment due to our sins.

A partial indulgence hastens the healing process. A 300 days indulgence, for example, has the healing power of 300 days of great bodily penance, such as was customary in the early church.

439. How does the Church by means of indulgences remit the temporal punishment due to sin?

The Church by means of indulgences remits the temporal punishment due to sin by applying to us from her spiritual treasury part of the infinite satisfaction of Jesus Christ and of the superabundant satisfaction of the Blessed Virgin Mary and of the saints.

The satisfaction of Jesus Christ means the power of His Precious Blood to make up for our sins and to heal all the wounds left by sin. It is like a great reservoir of medicine He has left for us to draw on as we need it. This is the spiritual treasury of the Church.

440. What is the superabundant satisfaction of the Blessed Virgin Mary and of the saints?

The superabundant satisfaction of the Blessed Virgin Mary and of the saints is that which they gained during their lifetime but did not need, and which the Church applies to their fellow members of the communion of saints.

Mingled with the Precious Blood of Christ in the treasury of the Church are the sorrows of Mary and the sufferings of the saints as they bore their crosses after Christ. These were the healthy members of the Mystical Body of Christ who were able to help sinners, the sick members. We can draw on this treasury and we can also contribute to it. The sufferings we bear through love can help others.

441. What must we do to gain an indulgence for ourselves?

To gain an indulgence for ourselves we must be in the state of grace, have at least a general intention of gaining the indulgence, and perform the works required by the Church.

To gain a plenary indulgence we must be free from all sin, since an indulgence applies only to the healing of wounds left by sin, not to the healing of sin itself. We must also be free from any intention to commit sin or to stay in an occasion of sin.

442. Can we gain indulgences for others?

We cannot gain indulgences for other living persons, but we can gain them for the souls in purgatory, since the Church makes most indulgences applicable to them.

Living persons are in a position to help themselves, but the souls in purgatory are not. (See Lesson 13.)

DISCUSSION QUESTIONS:

1. What is temporal punishment?
2. What is the spiritual treasury of the Church?
3. Why must we be in the state of grace to gain an indulgence?
4. What is the satisfaction of Jesus Christ?
5. Why cannot those in venial sin gain a plenary indulgence?

CHOOSE THE BEST ANSWER:

1. Indulgences take away: (a) sins (b) penance (c) temporal punishment. ☐

2. Indulgences act on the soul like: (a) medicine (b) confession (c) penance. ☐

3. Indulgences complete the process of: (a) healing (b) suffering (c) loving. ☐

4. One in mortal sin can gain: (a) plenary (b) partial (c) no indulgences. ☐

5. We can gain indulgences for others: (a) on earth (b) in purgatory (c) in heaven.

FILL IN THE BLANKS:

1. There are two kinds of indulgences: .... and ....

2. We can gain indulgences only for ourselves and for ....

3. The satisfactions of the Blessed Virgin Mary and the other saints can be applied to our souls because of that circulation of graces through the Mystical Body of Christ which we call ....

4. When we gain an indulgence, we draw on the .... of the Church.

5 Indulgences are granted by ....

READ FROM THE BIBLE:

Heb. 12, 1-13; 1 Pet. 1, 3-7. Here suffering is shown as a purification of the effects of sin (temporal punishment).

CLASS PROJECT:

Find prayers or actions to which indulgences are attached, especially plenary indulgences.

PRAYER:

I wish to gain all the indulgences attached to the prayers I shall say and to the good works I shall perform this day. (Recommended to be said after the morning offering.)

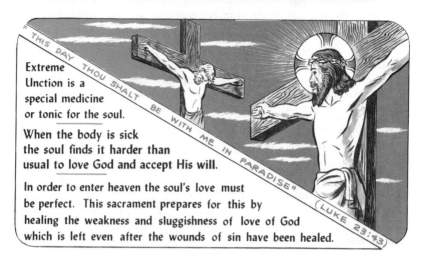

Extreme Unction is a special medicine or tonic for the soul.

When the body is sick the soul finds it harder than usual to love God and accept His will.

In order to enter heaven the soul's love must be perfect. This sacrament prepares for this by healing the weakness and sluggishness of love of God which is left even after the wounds of sin have been healed.

"THIS DAY THOU SHALT BE WITH ME IN PARADISE" (LUKE 23:43)

443. What is Extreme Unction?

Extreme Unction is the sacrament which, through the anointing with blessed oil by the priest, and through his prayer, gives health and strength to the soul and sometimes to the body when we are in danger of death from sickness, accident, or old age.

444. Who should receive Extreme Unction?

All Catholics who have reached the use of reason and are in danger of death from sickness, accident, or old age should receive Extreme Unction.

445. What are the effects of the sacrament of Extreme Unction?

The effects of the sacrament of Extreme Unction are:

first, an increase of sanctifying grace;

second, comfort in sickness and strength against temptation;

third, preparation for entrance into heaven by the remission of our venial sins and the cleansing of our souls from the remains of sin;

fourth, health of body when it is good for the soul.

1. This means an increase of divine life within us. As St. Paul puts it, "Even though our outer man is decaying, yet our inner man is being renewed" (2 Cor. 4, 16).

2. The comfort comes from a deeper realization of the purpose of suffering and the help to bear it which the sacrament gives. St. Peter says, "Rejoice, in so far as you are partakers of the sufferings of Christ, that you may also rejoice with exultation in the revelation of His glory" (1 Pet. 4, 13).

The strength is strength to resist the devil at a time when he wants to tempt us most to resist God's will.

3. It makes us desire our heavenly home. No one goes there who does not desire it ardently. It strengthens the weakness of our love so that we can have the attitude of St. Paul when he says, "Knowing that while we are in the body we are exiled from the Lord . . . we even have the courage to prefer to be exiled from the body to be at home with the Lord" (2 Cor. 5, 6, 8).

4. If a longer life would prepare the soul better for heaven, then God prolongs life through this sacrament.

446. When does Extreme Unction take away mortal sin?

Extreme Unction takes away mortal sin when the sick person is unconscious or otherwise unaware that he is not properly disposed, but has made an act of imperfect contrition.

447. How should we prepare ourselves to receive Extreme Unction worthily?

We should prepare ourselves to receive Extreme Unction worthily by a good confession, by acts of faith, hope, charity, and, especially, by resignation to the will of God.

448. Who can administer Extreme Unction?

Only a priest can administer Extreme Unction.

449. When is it advisable to call the priest to visit the sick?

It is advisable to call the priest to visit the sick in any serious illness, even though there be no apparent danger of death, as it is the duty of the priest to visit the sick and to administer to them the sacraments they need.

It is dangerous and even sinful to delay Extreme Unction because it might frighten the sick person. Extreme Unction has a calming effect and helps sick people overcome their fear. Even if a sick person might be frightened, it is better to be frightened than to die without the last sacraments.

450. In case of sudden or unexpected death, should a priest be called?

In case of sudden or unexpected death a priest should be called always, because absolution and Extreme Unction can be given conditionally for some time after apparent death.

THE PRIESTHOOD

A PRIEST is a MEDIATOR, a GO-BETWEEN, whose work is to unite God and man.

1. GOD AND MAN SEPARATED BY SIN

2. THE WORK OF CHRIST, THE PRIEST, RECONCILIATION

3. THE WORK OF THE ORDAINED PRIEST, THE MINISTRY OF RECONCILIATION

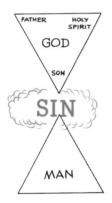

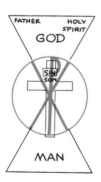

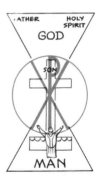

"From the offense of the one man the result was unto condemnation to all men" (Rom. 5, 18). See Question 56.

"The decree against us, which was hostile to us . . . He has taken it completely away, nailing it to the cross" (Col. 2, 14). See Question 90.

"God was truly in Christ, reconciling the world to Himself by not reckoning against men their sins and by entrusting to us the message of reconciliation" (2 Cor. 5, 19). See Question 454.

451. What is Holy Orders?

Holy Orders is the sacrament through which men receive the power and grace to perform the sacred duties of bishops, priests, and other ministers of the Church.

452. What are some of the requirements that a man may receive Holy Orders worthily?

That a man may receive Holy Orders worthily it is necessary:

first, that he be in the state of grace and be of excellent character;

second, that he have the prescribed age and learning;

third, that he have the intention of devoting his life to the sacred ministry;

fourth, that he be called to Holy Orders by his bishop.

452 A. *What is meant essentially by a vocation to the priesthood?*

By a vocation to the priesthood is meant essentially that invitation to receive Holy Orders given by the proper ecclesiastical superior to a man who, after a sufficient period of preparation and trial, gives signs that he has been called by God to the priesthood.

452 B. *What are the chief signs that a man has been called by God to the priesthood?*

The chief signs that a man has been called by God to the priesthood are: a sincere desire to become a priest, a virtuous life, and sufficient bodily health and intellectual ability to enable him to make the required studies and to perform the duties of the priestly life.

452 C. *Do religious brothers and sisters receive the sacrament of Holy Orders?*

No; religious brothers and sisters do not receive the sacrament of Holy Orders, but they have received from God a vocation to dedicate their lives to His service.

453. What are the effects of ordination to the priesthood?

The effects of ordination to the priesthood are:

first, an increase of sanctifying grace;

second, sacramental grace, through which the priest has God's constant help in his sacred ministry;

third, a character, lasting forever, which is a special sharing in the priesthood of Christ and which gives the priest special supernatural powers.

Christ is *THE ONE* priest in whom the fullness of the priesthood is found. All other priests share in the priesthood of Christ, as a mirror shares in the light of the sun. But just as a mirror really sheds light, so does the ordained priest really show forth the priesthood which he has from Christ through the priestly character.

CHRIST OUR
HIGH PRIEST
IN HEAVEN

———

"always living
to make
intercession
for us."
(Hebrews 7, 25)

THE PRIEST
ON EARTH
ANOTHER
CHRIST

———

The faithful
sharing through
the ordained
priest in the
Priesthood
of Christ

454. What are the chief supernatural powers of the priest?

The chief supernatural powers of the priest are: to change bread and wine into the body and blood of Christ in the Holy Sacrifice of the Mass, and to forgive sins in the sacrament of Penance.

The chief power of the priest is to offer the Sacrifice of the Mass. Here he exercises his office of reconciliation by applying to the people the power of the Cross of Christ to unite man to God in love.

The priest also administers the Sacrament of Penance to remove the chief obstacle to reconciliation, which is sin.

455. Why should Catholics show reverence and honor to the priest?

Catholics should show reverence and honor to the priest because he is the representative of Christ Himself and the dispenser of His mysteries.

"The priest is indeed another Christ, or in some way he is himself a continuation of Christ" (Pope Pius XI, Encyclical on the Priesthood).

456. Who is the minister of the sacrament of Holy Orders?

The bishop is the minister of the sacrament of Holy Orders.

DISCUSSION QUESTIONS:

1. How does Extreme Unction comfort us in sickness?
2. When should we receive Extreme Unction?
3. When does Extreme Unction make sick people better?
4. Why can't babies receive Extreme Unction?
5. What qualities does a boy need to enter a seminary?
6. What does the sacramental grace of Holy Orders do for a priest?
7. Why does the human race need the priesthood?
8. What is the greatest power a priest has?
9. Why is it a great privilege to be a priest?
10. Whose work does the priest continue on earth?

CHOOSE THE BEST ANSWER:

1. Extreme Unction helps us desire: (a) health (b) heaven (c) confession. □

2. Extreme Unction usually: (a) heals (b) calms (c) frightens the sick person. □

3. A candidate for Holy Orders must have the intention of devoting his life to: (a) good works (b) the priesthood (c) the religious life. □

4. A priest receives his priestly powers from: (a) the Pope (b) the Church (c) Jesus Christ. □

5. The chief work of the priest is: (a) preaching (b) hearing confessions (c) reconciling man to God. □

FILL IN THE BLANKS:

1. To receive Extreme Unction we must have reached the use of .... and be in danger of ....

2. Extreme Unction gives strength against ....

3. Extreme Unction must be given by a ....

4. Extreme Unction sometimes helps the .... if God sees it is good for the soul.

5. Extreme Unction cleanses the soul from ....

6. Our great High Priest is ....

7. A priest is a .... between .... and ....

8. A priest must be ordained by a ....

9. The greatest power of the priest is to change bread and wine into ....

10. The chief signs that God is calling a boy to the priesthood are

....

....

READ FROM THE BIBLE:

Extreme Unction — Luke 23, 39-43; James 5, 13-15.

Holy Orders — 1 Cor. 11, 23-26; 2 Cor. 5, 18—6, 10; Heb. 5, 1-10; 7, 24—10, 10.

CLASS PROJECT:

1. Set up in the class a model sick table with different ones assigned to bring in the necessary objects.

2. Let two or three of the boys be assigned to present to the class a report on "A day in the life of a priest." They could interview one of the parish priests to get the necessary information.

PRAYER:

O God, who for the glory of Your majesty and the salvation of the human race didst constitute Your Only-begotten Son as the supreme and eternal Priest, grant that those whom He has chosen as His ministers and the dispensers of His mysteries may be found faithful in the fulfillment of the ministry they have embraced. Through the same Christ Our Lord. Amen.

(Missal: Collect for the Mass of Jesus Christ, the High Priest)

LESSON 35 — Matrimony

"Husbands, love your wives, just as Christ also loved the Church and delivered Himself up for her" (Ephesians 5, 25).

MATRIMONY IS A SIGN OF CHRIST.

IT IS A SIGN OF THE PASSION OF CHRIST.

The grace of Matrimony which a husband and wife receive to love each other and their children unselfishly comes from the Passion of Christ. They receive the grace to make their love a reflection of the love of Christ for His Bride, the Church, personified in Mary. In the flesh Mary was His Mother, but in the spirit she was His bride.

Children, seeing such love in their parents, can more easily learn what love Christ had for them on the Cross.

457. What is the sacrament of Matrimony?

Matrimony is the sacrament by which a baptized man and a baptized woman bind themselves for life in a lawful marriage and receive the grace to discharge their duties.

458. What are the chief duties of husband and wife in the married state?

The chief duties of husband and wife in the married state are to be faithful to each other, and to provide in every way for the welfare of the children God may give them.

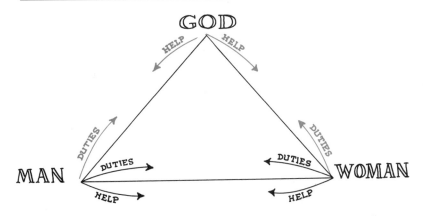

Their duties are to God, each other, and their children. Help to fulfill these duties comes first from God, then from each other, and finally from the children.

Married people must learn to love unselfishly, to forget themselves so that they can spend themselves for each other. They surrender themselves to God's plans for marriage to bring children into the world and to care for them.

459. Why does the bond of the sacrament of Matrimony last until the death of husband or wife?

The bond of the sacrament of Matrimony lasts until the death of husband or wife because Christ has said: "What therefore God has joined together, let no man put asunder."

Love should be permanent or it is not true love. It is not a feeling which comes and goes, but a power to give which should be there even when feeling dies out.

DIVORCE IS FORBIDDEN BY GOD. Furthermore, it is useless, since if a couple gets a divorce in a court, God refuses to remove the marriage bond. They might walk out of

the court and think they are no longer married and can each go to look for a new partner. But God keeps the marriage bond on them, and if either of them attempts a new marriage, it will not be a real marriage, but adultery. The first marriage lasts, even though they no longer live together.

460. What is meant by the unity of the sacrament of Matrimony?

By the unity of the sacrament of Matrimony is meant that the husband cannot during the life of his wife have another wife, nor the wife during the life of her husband have another husband.

461. Why is every true marriage between a baptized man and a baptized woman a sacrament?

Every true marriage between a baptized man and a baptized woman is a sacrament because Christ Himself raised every marriage of this kind to the dignity of a sacrament.

In order to love each other the way Christ loves us, husband and wife need special graces. A Christian marriage demands far more love and ability to make sacrifices than does a pagan marriage. That is why Christ made it a sacrament.

462. Why has the Catholic Church alone the right to make laws regulating the marriages of baptized persons?

The Catholic Church alone has the right to make laws regulating the marriages of baptized persons because the Church alone has authority over the sacraments and over sacred matters affecting baptized persons.

463. What authority has the State regarding the marriages of baptized persons?

Regarding the marriages of baptized persons, the State has the authority to make laws concerning their effects that are merely civil.

464. What is necessary to receive the sacrament of Matrimony worthily?

To receive the sacrament of Matrimony worthily it is necessary to be in the state of grace, to know the duties of married life, and to obey the marriage laws of the Church.

465. In whose presence do the laws of the Church require a Catholic to be married?

The laws of the Church require a Catholic to be married in the presence of the parish priest, or the bishop of the diocese, or a priest delegated by either of them, and before two witnesses.

THIS	**NOT THIS**

For a Catholic marriage there must be:
A PRIEST plus TWO WITNESSES.
NO PRIEST equals NO MARRIAGE.

Some Catholics attempt to get married by a justice of the peace. This is a civil marriage, but not a real marriage. It is a mortal sin.

In so-called marriages before a justice of the peace, even if only one party is a Catholic, there is no marriage. God will not forgive him unless he gives up his sin and is married by a priest. If this is impossible, then the couple ordinarily must separate, even if they have children, since they are not really married and cannot keep on living in sin. The man must support the children, but he cannot live with the woman, since she is not really his wife. (See Question 298.)

466. What are the chief effects of the sacrament of Matrimony?

The chief effects of the sacrament of Matrimony are:

first, an increase of sanctifying grace;

second, the special help of God for husband and wife to love each other faithfully, to bear with each other's faults, and to bring up their children properly.

God gives married people special helps to bear the crosses of married life. He even guarantees them all the material things they need (such as food, clothing, and shelter) provided they keep His laws in marriage, trust Him, and pray for their needs.

467. What should Catholics do to prepare for a holy and happy marriage?

To prepare for a holy and happy marriage, Catholics should:

first, pray that God may direct their choice;

second, seek the advice of their parents and confessors;

third, practice the virtues, especially chastity:

fourth, frequently receive the sacraments of Penance and Holy Eucharist.

They should first seek advice from a priest to be sure that marriage is their vocation. There are three signs of a marriage vocation:

1. Absence of a religious vocation. (If they have a religious vocation, that is a call to give to God a gift even more pleasing to Him than marriage. They should not prepare for marriage until they are sure God does not have even greater plans for them. *See page 101.*)

2. The qualities needed for marriage.

3. Meeting a suitable partner. (If a girl, for example, has no religious vocation and the only possible partners she meets are not suitable ones, such as non-Catholics or bad Catholics, then that is usually a sign of a vocation to the single state. She could marry an unsuitable partner, even though God would not prefer it, but she would find it harder to be happy and even to save her soul.)

468. How can Catholics best obtain God's blessing for their marriage?

Catholics can best obtain God's blessing for their marriage by being married at a Nuptial Mass and by receiving Holy Communion devoutly.

MARRIAGE AT MASS
(ABUNDANCE OF GRACE)

MARRIAGE WITHOUT MASS
(LESS GRACE)

DISCUSSION QUESTIONS:

1. How is the Sacrament of Matrimony a sign of the Passion?

2. What can children learn from parents who really love each other?

3. Why did Christ make marriage a sacrament?

4. Why should married people not worry about whether they will be able to support their children if God sends them a large family?

5. What did Christ have to say about divorce?

6. If civilly married Catholics are not free to be married by a priest, what must they ordinarily do to be forgiven?

7. If Catholics who have been civilly married are sorry for their sin and separate, who must support the children?

8. Why does the religious state please God more than marriage?

9. How can a vocation to the single state usually be recognized?

10. What happens if one enters a state God does not prefer for him?

CHOOSE THE BEST ANSWER:

1. In Christian marriage husbands should love their wives as Christ loves: (a) sinners (b) the souls in purgatory (c) the Church (d) His Father. ☐

2. Marriage lasts: (a) until there is a divorce (b) until the partners separate (c) until death (d) forever. ☐

3. The power to dissolve a marriage belongs to: (a) the state (b) the supreme court (c) the Pope (d) God alone. ☐

4. A civil divorce: (a) does nothing to (b) breaks (c) stretches (d) tightens the marriage bond. ☐

5. A Catholic married by a justice of the peace is: (a) illegally married (b) not married at all (c) sinfully married (d) temporarily married. ☐

FILL IN THE BLANKS:

1. The chief obligations of married people are to be . . . . to each other and to . . . . for their children.

2. Laws concerning the sacraments can be made only by . . . .

3. Married people have duties to . . . ., to . . . . and to . . . .

4. If a girl never meets a suitable partner, this is a sign she has no marriage . . . .

5. Catholics must be married in the presence of . . . . and . . . .

6. The virtue Catholics need especially in preparing for marriage is . . . .

7. Before marriage, Catholics should seek advice from . . . . and . . . .

8. Marriage was raised to the dignity of a sacrament by . . . .

9. Laws made by the State concerning the marriages of Catholics are just laws if they concern the . . . . effects of marriage only.

10. Married people need special helps to bear the . . . . of married life.

READ FROM THE BIBLE:

Matt. 19, 3-9; Mark 10, 2-12; John 4, 16-18; Eph. 5, 22-33.

CLASS PROJECT:

A happy marriage demands long preparation. Even children can develop the virtues needed in marriage and the habits that will help make marriage happy. Some of the things in marriage are easy to do and need no preparation, like kissing each other. But other things are hard and need preparation. Let each boy and girl in the class make a list, with the help of their parents, of virtues, habits and abilities they can develop now to prepare for a happy marriage, should that be their vocation.

Examples: GIRLS: patience, understanding, sympathy, learning to cook, to sew, washing dishes, making beds, taking care of children, cleaning the house, letting others have their own way, etc.

BOYS: kindness, thoughtfulness, helpfulness, learning to fix things in the house, keeping one's room clean, not throwing clothes on the floor, respect for girls, willingness to do hard work, etc.

PRAYER:

O my God, You who are the God of wisdom and good counsel, You who read in my heart a sincere desire to please You alone and to direct myself in regard to my choice of a state of life in conformity with Your holy will in all things; by the intercession of the most holy Virgin, my Mother, and of my Patron Saints, grant me the grace to know that state of life which I ought to choose, and to embrace it when known, in order that thus I may seek Your glory and increase it, work out my own salvation, and deserve the heavenly reward which You have promised to those who do Your holy will. Amen.

(From The Raccolta. Indulgence of 300 days)

"Daddy, that statue of the Sacred Heart reminds us that God is here protecting us."

Sacramentals are signs. They remind us of God, the saints and spiritual truths. They are something like sacraments, but there is this big difference: The sacraments were instituted by Christ to produce grace of themselves and are signs of His direct action on souls. The sacramentals were instituted by the Church and obtain graces for us indirectly by arousing us to those acts of virtue which draw down God's graces on us.

469. What are sacramentals?

Sacramentals are holy things or actions of which the Church makes use to obtain for us from God, through her intercession, spiritual and temporal favors.

470. How do the sacramentals obtain favors from God?

The sacramentals obtain favors from God through the prayers of the Church offered for those who make use of them, and through the devotion they inspire.

471. What are the chief benefits obtained by the use of the sacramentals?

The chief benefits obtained by the use of the sacramentals are:

first, actual graces;
second, the forgiveness of venial sins;
third, the remission of temporal punishment;
fourth, health of body and material blessings;
fifth, protection from evil spirits.

472. Which are the chief kinds of sacramentals?

The chief kinds of sacramentals are:

first, blessings given by priests and bishops;

second, exorcisms against evil spirits;

third, blessed objects of devotion.

BLESSINGS	EXORCISMS	BLESSED OBJECTS

"O water, creature of God, I exorcise you . . . so that you may put to flight all the power of the enemy . . . with his apostate angels."

FATHER, PLEASE BLESS MY ROSARY.

Always ask a priest for his blessing. He represents Christ and his blessing obtains special graces.

Exorcism means freeing persons or things from the power of the devil. He rarely possesses persons now, but uses things to tempt us. Exorcisms destroy this power.

Have articles of devotion blessed by a priest. This blessing obtains God's grace to arouse devotion.

473. Which are the blessed objects of devotion most used by Catholics?

The blessed objects of devotion most used by Catholics are: holy water, candles, ashes, palms, crucifixes, medals, rosaries, scapulars, and images of Our Lord, the Blessed Virgin, and the saints.

Examples of other sacramentals which are not in the possession of individual Catholics but are used by them together are: a church building, the ceremonies of Benediction, the Stations of the Cross.

474. How should we make use of sacramentals?

We should make use of the sacramentals with faith and devotion, and never make them objects of superstition.

Using sacramentals with faith means believing in what they represent and treating them as signs of spiritual things. We break the first commandment by superstition in using them as good luck charms.

DISCUSSION QUESTIONS:

1. What are exorcisms?
2. Why do we use sacramentals?
3. How are sacramentals like the sacraments?
4. How are they different?
5. How does one use sacramentals with faith, not superstition?

CHOOSE THE BEST ANSWER:

1. Sacramentals inspire: (a) fear (b) grace (c) devotion in us. ☐
2. They are signs of: (a) spiritual things (b) good luck (c) the Church. ☐
3. They were instituted by: (a) Christ (b) the Church (c) holy persons. ☐
4. They are: (a) exactly (b) somewhat (c) nothing like the sacraments. ☐
5. Exorcism means freeing from: (a) harm (b) sin (c) evil spirits. ☐

FILL IN THE BLANKS:

1. A sacramental is a .... of spiritual things.

2. Objects of devotion should be .... before we use them.

3. We should not make sacramentals objects of ....

4. Sacramentals can obtain for us protection from ....

5. Sacramentals obtain favors through the intercession of ....

READ FROM THE BIBLE:

Blessings — Gen. 48, 9; Exorcism — Luke 10, 17-20; Blessed Objects — Deut. 28, 3-5.

CLASS PROJECT:

The new Latin-English Ritual lists 26 blessings. Let 26 pupils in the class each give a report to the class on one of these blessings, explaining the purpose and manner of the blessing. (The Latin Ritual lists over 150 blessings.)

PRAYER:

May whatever this touches or sprinkles be rid of all uncleanness and protected from every assault of evil spirits. (This is a good prayer to say when using holy water.) *(Roman Ritual, Blessing of Water.)*

"All these (the Apostles) with one mind continued steadfastly in prayer with the women and Mary, the mother of Jesus, and with His brethren" (Acts 1, 14).

475. What is prayer?

Prayer is the lifting up of our minds and hearts to God.

Prayer is an act of love. It is sometimes called conversation with God — but conversation of love — a heart-to-heart talk with God who is Love and loves us.

476. Why do we pray?

We pray:

first, to adore God, expressing to Him our love and loyalty;

second, to thank Him for His favors;

third, to obtain from Him the pardon of our sins and the remission of their punishment;

fourth, to ask for graces and blessings for ourselves and others.

477. How should we pray?

We should pray:

first, with attention;

second, with a conviction of our own helplessness and our dependence upon God;

third, with a great desire for the graces we beg of
Him;

fourth, with loving trust in His goodness;

fifth, with perseverance.

478. For whom should we pray?

We should pray especially for ourselves, for our
parents, relatives, friends, and enemies, for sinners,
for the souls in purgatory, for the Pope, bishops, and
priests of the Church, and for the officials of our
country.

**479. How do we know that God always hears our prayers if we
pray properly?**

We know that God always hears our prayers if we
pray properly because Our Lord has promised: "If
you ask the Father anything in My name, He will
give it to you."

Asking in His name means asking for love of Him, since the name
represents the person bearing it. We ask for what we need to love
Him. Even if we do not use these words, what we really mean is this:
"O Lord, please give me what I need to please You, and if what I
am asking for does not really please You, then do not give it to me.
Give me instead what would really please You, even if it is a cross."
Such a prayer, God has guaranteed to answer.

480. Why do we not always obtain what we pray for?

We do not always obtain what we pray for, either
because we have not prayed properly or because God
sees that what we are asking would not be for our
good.

Many people do not pray in the name of Christ, as explained in
the preceding answer, but pray in this way instead: "O Lord, please
give me what I want." And they often do not think whether or not
it will help them to love God more, and sometimes they do not even
care. God has never guaranteed to answer a prayer such as this,
as it is not really a prayer but selfishness.

481. Are distractions in our prayers always displeasing to God?

Distractions in our prayers are not displeasing to
God, unless they are willful.

DISTRACTIONS

SINFUL

HARMLESS

Distractions are the wanderings of our imagination.

If we deliberately let it wander and do not even try to pray, that is a sin.

But if it wanders when we do not want it to, then this does no harm to our prayer It is still very good and very pleasing to God.

If you notice a distraction, gently turn your mind back to some thought of God. Meanwhile, your heart is praying all the time.

482. How many kinds of prayer are there?

There are two kinds of prayer: mental prayer and vocal prayer.

483. What is mental prayer?

Mental prayer is that prayer by which we unite our hearts with God while thinking of His holy truths.

Mental prayer usually begins with meditation, which means thinking about God to move our hearts to love Him. Our hearts then speak to Him in our own words or even without words. Then we listen to Him in silence, not only of lips, but of heart. This is the highest form of private prayer.

It is not hard to do. Think about God's goodness, about the way Christ suffered for you, about Our Lady or one of the saints. Think for a while, then let your heart speak and listen. Take five, ten, fifteen minutes or more. As long as you want to pray and don't deliberately do or think about something else, your heart is praying, even if nothing seems to be happening. It is time well spent and very profitable for your soul.

484. What is vocal prayer?

Vocal prayer is that prayer which comes from the mind and heart and is spoken by the lips.

485. May we use our own words in praying to God?

We may use our own words in praying to God, and it is well to do so often.

486. What are the prayers that every Catholic should know by heart?

The prayers that every Catholic should know by heart are: the Our Father, the Hail Mary, the Apostles' Creed, the Confiteor, the Glory be to the Father, and the acts of faith, hope, charity, and contrition.

487. How do we usually begin and end our prayers?

We usually begin and end our prayers with the sign of the cross.

488. Why do we make the sign of the cross?

We make the sign of the cross to express two important mysteries of the Christian religion, the Blessed Trinity and the Redemption.

489. How are these mysteries expressed by the sign of the cross?

When we say "In the name," we express the truth that there is only one God; when we say "of the Father, and of the Son, and of the Holy Spirit," we express the truth that there are three distinct Persons in God; and when we make the form of the cross on ourselves, we express the truth that the Son of God, made man, redeemed us by His death on the cross.

DISCUSSION QUESTIONS:

1. What promise has Our Lord attached to prayer?
2. What does asking in the name of Christ mean?
3. If we ask God to let our team win just because we want to win, is this asking for love of God or selfishness?
4. What are distractions in prayer?
5. What should we do about distractions in prayer?
6. What is meditation?
7. What should we think about when we want to meditate?
8. How would you go about making mental prayer?
9. Give an example of vocal prayer.
10. Explain the Sign of the Cross.

CHOOSE THE BEST ANSWER:

1. God grants what we ask when: (a) we ask with feeling (b) we have no sin on our soul (c) it is good for us (d) we are holy. ☐

2. Prayer is asking God for things because: (a) we want them (b) we need them (c) we think they are good (d) they help us to love Him more. ☐

3. Distractions in prayer are sinful if: (a) we want them (b) we don't notice them (c) they stay a long time (d) they bother us. ☐

4. Distractions that we do not want: (a) make our prayer displeasing to God (b) make it sinful (c) make it useless (d) do no harm. ☐

5. Time spent trying to pray but with distractions we don't want is: (a) time wasted (b) time well spent (c) sinful (d) useless. ☐

FILL IN THE BLANKS:

1. Prayer is the lifting up of the .... and .... to God.

2. It is also called .... with ....

3. Prayer that uses set words is called .... prayer.

4. By the sign of the Cross we express our belief in the mysteries of .... and ....

5. In prayer we must listen to God with our ....

6. To obtain graces from God, we must have a great .... for them.

7. Prayer of the heart without set words is called ....

8. Besides speaking to God in prayer, we must also ....

9. The wanderings of our imagination are called ....

10. Prayer with .... distractions is displeasing to God.

READ FROM THE BIBLE:

How to pray — Matt. 7, 7-11; 18, 19-20
Christ's example — John 17; Matt. 26, 36-46; Luke 22, 39-46.
Effect of prayer — Acts 12, 1-17.

CLASS PROJECT:

Let everyone in the class look at the crucifix in silence for a few minutes. Then write on paper how you imagine Our Lord must have felt, His sufferings, what He heard and saw, how He must have acted. Then write out the thoughts or desires of the heart with which this meditation inspires you.

Try to take out one minute during the course of each day to look at the crucifix in silence and think about it.

PRAYER:

Direct we beseech You, O Lord, our actions by Your holy inspirations and carry them on by Your gracious help, that every prayer and work of ours may begin always from You, and by You be happily ended. Through Christ Our Lord. Amen.

(Missal: Prayers before Mass)

LESSON 38 — The Our Father

"Father, I have made known to them Thy name, and will make it known, in order that the love with which Thou hast loved Me may be in them, and I in them" (John 17, 26).

490. Why is the Our Father the best of all prayers?

The Our Father is the best of all prayers because it is the Lord's Prayer, taught us by Jesus Christ Himself, and because it is a prayer of perfect and unselfish love.

491. Why is the Our Father a prayer of perfect and unselfish love?

The Our Father is a prayer of perfect and unselfish love because in saying it we offer ourselves entirely to God and ask from Him the best things, not only for ourselves but also for our neighbor.

1. GOD'S GLORY
2. UNION WITH GOD
3. PERFECT LOVE
4. NEEDS OF SOUL AND BODY
5. FORGIVENESS OF SIN
6. PROTECTION IN TEMPTATION
7. FREEDOM FROM ALL HARM

There are seven petitions in the Our Father. We cannot really desire what these petitions express unless we love unselfishly, for they are arranged in the order of love. We must, for example, be more desirous that God's will should be done (No. 3) than that we should escape our own troubles (No. 7).

Most people begin by desiring the last petitions of the Our Father and only gradually grow in love to the point where they desire chiefly what is expressed in the first petitions.

- 231 -

All prayer should be made in the spirit of the Our Father, really desiring what its petitions express.

492. Why do we address God as "Our Father who art in heaven"?

We address God as "Our Father who art in heaven" because we belong to Him, our loving Father, who created us and watches over us, who adopts us through sanctifying grace as His children, and who destines us to live forever with Him in heaven, our true home.

The word "our" is important. It is in the plural. Christ has highly recommended prayer in common in which we as God's children who love one another unite to ask our loving Father for what we need. The official prayer of the whole Church as a body is called the *liturgy*. This public prayer of the Church is of far more value than private prayer, even though this too is necessary and highly important.

493. For what do we pray when we say "hallowed be Thy name"?

When we say "hallowed be Thy name," we pray that God may be known and honored by all men.

The name represents the person. God's name represents God Himself. The first desire of love is that God should be known, loved, and honored by all. *Hallowed* means "acknowledged as holy and all-perfect." The four Hebrew letters spell "Jahweh," meaning "I am who am" (Ex. 3, 13-14).

יהוה
GOD

"This is My name forever" (Ex. 3, 15).

494. For what do we pray when we say "Thy kingdom come"?

When we say "Thy kingdom come," we pray that the kingdom of God's grace may be spread throughout the world, that all men may come to know and to enter the true Church and to live as worthy members of it, and that, finally, we all may be admitted to the kingdom of God's glory.

True love desires that God's kingdom, the Church, should spread on earth until the day when Christ will come again to take us all, body and soul, to heaven.

"Then comes the end, when He delivers the kingdom to God the Father" (1 Cor. 15, 24).

495. For what do we pray when we say "Thy will be done on earth as it is in heaven"?

When we say "Thy will be done on earth as it is in heaven," we pray that all men may obey God on earth as willingly as the saints and angels obey Him in heaven.

Here we ask that our love grow to perfection. Love seeks to do God's will and to please Him perfectly. We ask that our love will grow till we love Him as much as He is loved in heaven where all love is perfect. We are asking Him to make us saints.

"Not My will but Thine be done" (Luke 22, 42).

496. For what do we pray when we say "Give us this day our daily bread"?

When we say "Give us this day our daily bread," we pray that God will give us each day all that is necessary to support the material life of our bodies and the spiritual life of our souls.

For example, our soul needs grace, the virtues, the gifts of the Holy Spirit and their increase. It also needs crosses, trials and troubles, which many people forget and are surprised when God sends them.

Our body ordinarily needs food, clothing, shelter and other material things. However, at times God has to withhold some of these things for the good of the soul.

"Your Father knows that you need all these things (food, drink, clothing). But seek first the kingdom of God and His justice, and all these things shall be given you besides" (Matthew 6, 32-33).

497. For what do we pray when we say "and forgive us our trespasses as we forgive those who trespass against us"?

When we say "and forgive us our trespasses as we forgive those who trespass against us," we pray that God will pardon the sins by which we have offended Him, and we tell Him that we pardon our fellow men who have offended us.

Here Our Lord reminds us that if we want God's merciful love to forgive us the horrible offense of sin, we must love others enough to forgive them their offenses against us.

"Father, forgive them, for they do not know what they are doing" (Luke 23, 34).

498. For what do we pray when we say "and lead us not into temptation"?

When we say "and lead us not into temptation," we pray that God will always give us the grace to overcome the temptations to sin which come to us from the world, the flesh, and the devil.

It is no sin to be tempted. Our Lord Himself was tempted. And we also must be tempted if we are to acquire any virtue. But we pray that when temptation comes, as it must often come, that we may not be overcome by it.

"And when the devil had tried every temptation, he departed from Him for a while" (Luke 4, 13).

499. For what do we pray when we say "but deliver us from evil"?

When we say "but deliver us from evil," we pray that God will always protect us from harm, and especially from harm to our souls.

We ask, too, that bodily evils, sickness, suffering, poverty, etc., will never become so severe that we cannot bear them with the grace of God.

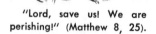

"Lord, save us! We are perishing!" (Matthew 8, 25).

DISCUSSION QUESTIONS:

1. Why do we say "Our Father" instead of "My Father"?
2. What does God do for us to show His fatherly love?
3. Why do we pray for needs of our body?
4. Why does God sometimes refrain from giving us some of the things we need for our body?
5. Why does someone who holds a grudge find it impossible to really pray the Our Father?

CHOOSE THE BEST ANSWER:

1. The petitions of the Our Father are arranged: (a) in no special order (b) in the order we should desire them (c) in reverse order. ☐

2. In asking for our daily bread, we pray for: (a) food (b) our bodily needs (c) all our needs of soul and body. ☐

3. In saying "Thy kingdom come," we pray for: (a) the spread of the Church (b) Catholics to conquer the world by force (c) the power of all earthly rulers to cease. ☐

4. When we say "Thy will be done," we pray for grace to: (a) put up with (b) give in to (c) love God's Holy Will. ☐

5. In the Our Father we pray that we may never: (a) be tempted (b) be overcome by temptation (c) have great temptations. ☐

FILL IN THE BLANKS:

1. The Our Father was taught us by ....

2. The official prayer of the whole Mystical Body of Christ is called ....

3. In saying "Thy will be done on earth as it is in heaven," we are praying for perfect ....

4. God's name represents ....

5. We want God to be acknowledged as holy and all-perfect when we use the word ....

READ FROM THE BIBLE:

Matt. 6, 5-17; 7, 1-11; Luke 11, 1-13.

CLASS PROJECT:

Let the class read carefully the passages in Sacred Scripture given in the illustrations of this lesson. Then groups could be assigned to give a five-to-ten minute dramatization of each of the seven incidents in the Bible. A fuller treatment of the second petition will be found in Matt. 25, 31-46.

PRAYER:

The Our Father, page 5.

APPENDIX — WHY I AM A CATHOLIC

The reason why I *am* a Catholic should for most of us be different from the reason why I *became* a Catholic.

Most of us can say that the reason why I *became* a Catholic was that when I was too small to know what was going on, my parents had me taken to church and baptized as a Catholic.

But we should be able to say that the reason why I *am* a Catholic is that I have studied the Catholic religion well and am thoroughly convinced of its truth.

Our Catholic Faith should not be a blind unreasoning thing, but something based on a firm foundation of reason. This lesson shows us this foundation. It gives us a brief outline of the steps we can use to prove to ourselves the reasonableness of believing in everything that the Church teaches, whether we can understand it or not. Then it shows how certain are the facts from which we derive these reasons.

It is important to note, however, that these are steps which can be taken by a Catholic who already has the faith to demonstrate to himself how reasonable that faith is. But it is not the procedure to follow in convincing non-Catholics of the truth of our faith.

The best way to win non-Catholics was given us by Christ when He said, "By this will all men know that you are My disciples, if you have love for one another" (John 13, 35). If non-Catholics see Catholics who are truly kind to one another and are interested in all men, even those outside the Church, even their enemies, even those they do not like, this is bound to make an impression and to encourage them to examine the Catholic Church more carefully.

If Catholics live like pagans, are kind to their friends, and unkind to those they do not like, then no amount of fine reasons will ever convince non-Catholics that the Catholic Church is really the true Church of Christ.

THIS	NOT THIS

A. THE STEPS OF THE PROOF

I. How does our reason point out the truth of the Catholic religion?

Our reason points out the truth of the Catholic religion by these principles:

first, there is a God;

second, the soul of man is immortal;

third, all men are obliged to practice religion;

fourth, the religion God has revealed through Christ is worthy of belief;

fifth, Christ established a Church which all are obliged to join;

sixth, the only true Church of Christ is the Catholic Church.

B. EACH STEP EXPLAINED

II. How can we prove that there is a God?

We can prove that there is a God because this vast universe could not have come into existence, nor be so beautiful and orderly, except by the almighty power and the wisdom of an eternal and intelligent Being.

III. How can we prove that the soul of man is immortal?

We can prove that the soul of man is immortal because man's acts of intelligence are spiritual; therefore, his soul must be a spiritual being, not dependent on matter, and hence not subject to decay or death.

IV. How we prove that all men are obliged to practice religion?

We can prove that all men are obliged to practice religion because all men are entirely dependent on God and must recognize that dependence by honoring Him and praying to Him.

V. How can we prove that the religion God has revealed through Christ is worthy of belief?

We can prove that the religion God has revealed through Christ is worthy of belief, because:

> *first,* Jesus Christ, announcing Himself as the ambassador and the true Son of God, whose coming was foretold by the prophets, preached doctrines which He said all must believe;

> *second,* Christ worked wonderful miracles, which show that the God of truth approved His teachings.

1. "The Father . . . has given all judgment to the Son, that all men may honor the Son even as they honor the Father. He who does not honor the Son, does not honor the Father who sent Him" (John 5, 23).

"If you believed Moses you would believe Me also, for he wrote of Me" (John 5, 46).

"He who does not believe is already judged, because he does not believe in the name of the only-begotten Son of God" (John 3, 18).

2. "The works which the Father has given Me to accomplish, these very works that I do, bear witness to Me, that the Father has sent Me" (John 5, 36).

(The New Testament uses the word "work" to mean "miracle.")

VI. How we prove that Christ established a Church which all are obliged to join?

We can prove that Christ established a Church which all are obliged to join, because:

   first, He gathered about Him a group of disciples, and called it His Church;

   second, He promised that this Church would last until the end of time;

   third, He declared that all men must believe and be baptized, that is, join His Church, in order to be saved.

1. "Thou art Peter, and upon this rock I will build My Church" (Matt. 16, 18).

2. "Behold, I am with you all days, even unto the consummation of the world" (Matt. 28, 20).

3. "He who believes and is baptized shall be saved, but he who does not believe shall be condemned" (Mark 16, 16).

VII. How can we prove that the only true Church of Christ is the Catholic Church?

We can prove that the only true Church of Christ is the Catholic Church because:

   first, only the Catholic Church possesses the marks of the Church established by Christ, that is, unity, holiness, catholicity, and apostolicity;

   second, the history of the Catholic Church gives evidence of miraculous strength, permanence, and unchangeableness, thus showing the world that it is under the special protection of God.

For us who know the Church it is easy to see that the four marks, or identification tags, are found only in the Catholic Church. (See pages 77-78.)

The list of popes extends from Peter to the present day. No kingdom or civil government in the history of the world has ever lasted that long. Only divine power could keep the succession of popes going on despite the efforts of the enemies of the Church to destroy the papacy. And only divine power too could sustain the Church in the many persecutions and inner troubles it has had to face through the centuries. The Church has an inner power of life by which it can heal its own wounds.

C. THE SOURCES OF OUR FACTS

VIII. Whence do we chiefly derive our historical knowledge of Jesus Christ, His life and teachings, and of the Church He established?

We derive our historical knowledge of Jesus Christ, His life and teachings, and of the Church He established chiefly from the books of the Bible, which can be proved to be reliable historical records.

IX. What else are the books of the Bible besides being reliable historical records?

Besides being reliable historical records, the books of the Bible are the inspired word of God, that is, written by men with such direct assistance of the Holy Ghost as to make God their true Author.

X. How is the Bible divided?

The Bible is divided into the Old Testament and the New Testament; the Old Testament being the inspired books written before the time of Jesus Christ, and the New Testament the inspired books written after His coming.

XI. Are all the truths revealed for us by God found in the Bible?

Not all the truths revealed for us by God are found in the Bible; some are found only in Divine Tradition.

XII. What is meant by Divine Tradition?

By Divine Tradition is meant the revealed truths taught by Christ and His apostles, which were given to the Church only by word of mouth and not through the Bible, though they were put in writing, principally by the Fathers of the Church.

XIII. Why must Divine Tradition be believed as firmly as the Bible?

Divine Tradition must be believed as firmly as the Bible because it also contains the word of God.

XIV. How can we know the true meaning of the doctrines contained in the Bible and in Divine Tradition?

We can know the true meaning of the doctrines contained in the Bible and in Divine Tradition from the Catholic Church, which has been authorized by Jesus Christ to explain His doctrines, and which is preserved from error in its teachings by the special assistance of the Holy Ghost.

"When the Advocate has come, whom I will send you from the Father, the Spirit of truth who proceeds from the Father, He will bear witness concerning Me. . . . But when He, the Spirit of truth, has come, He will teach you all the truth" (John 15, 26; 16, 13.)

Since many things in the Bible are difficult to understand, Christ has given His Church the work of explaining them. That is why we have catechisms written in language that even little children can understand. *See Question 23F.*

D. LIVING AND SPREADING OUR FAITH

XV. How can we best show our gratitude to God for making us members of the only true Church of Jesus Christ?

We can best show our gratitude to God for making us members of the only true Church of Jesus Christ by often thanking God for this great favor, by leading edifying and practical Catholic lives, by trying to lead others to the true faith, and by helping the missions.

PRAYER	EXAMPLE	ENCOURAGEMENT	HELPING THE MISSIONS

1. Every day we should thank God for bringing us into His Church.

2. To edify others means to give them good example. This does not mean merely putting on a show for others to see. It means acting the way we know Christ would like us to, whether others are watching or not. Others often see us when we are not aware of it.

3. A word of encouragement or invitation is often the beginning of a conversion.

4. We should all be mission-conscious and desire to spread the faith all over the world.

XVI. How can we help the missions?

We can help the missions:

first, by praying for the missions, home and foreign, and for missionaries that they may fulfill the command of Christ: "Go, therefore, and make disciples of all nations";

second, by knowing the missions and making them known to others;

third, by making sacrifices for the missions, that is, by helping to support them and by personal service;

fourth, by fostering vocations of self-sacrificing young men and women for every need of the missions.

QUESTIONS:

1. Sum up in your own words the reasons why you are a Catholic.

2. What is the best way to win non-Catholics to the Church?

3. What should the difference be in the reasons why we became Catholics and the reasons why we are Catholics?

4. Why is it that many non-Catholics turn against the Church when they see the kind of life that many Catholics lead?

5. What should we do to edify others?

6. How do we know that Jesus Christ really lived?

7. Where do we find the facts about His life?

8. Why should we examine the reasons for our beliefs?

9. How do we know what the Bible really means?

10. What is wrong with saying one religion is as good as another?

CHOOSE THE BEST ANSWER:

1. Our faith is something we: (a) hope (b) think (c) can never be sure (d) know for certain is true.   ☐

2. The chief purpose of studying the foundations of our faith is: (a) to win converts (b) to see how reasonable they are (c) to be able to sound intelligent (d) to win arguments.   ☐

3. The best way to win converts is by: (a) knowing your faith (b) reason (c) love (d) good arguments.   ☐

4. The Bible is: (a) easy (b) difficult (c) impossible to understand.   ☐

5. We accept something as a truth of faith: (a) when we can understand it (b) when we find it in the Bible (c) when the Church teaches it (d) when it is reasonable.   ☐

Give a quotation from Sacred Scripture for each of the following statements:

1. Christ is the Son of God.
2. He is the ambassador of the Father.
3. He was foretold by the prophets.
4. Men must believe the teachings of Christ.
5. The miracles of Christ prove that God approved His teachings.
6. Christ established a Church.
7. He promised that it would last till the end of time.
8. He declared that all men must join His Church in order to be saved.
9. He wanted His Church to teach nothing but truth.
10. Love is the best way to show men we are true followers of Christ.

READ FROM THE BIBLE:

John, Chapters 7—11.

CLASS PROJECT:

Each class should actually carry on a permanent project to help the missions in some way, such as collecting stamps, collecting holy pictures, writing to missionaries, etc. Perhaps Sister can get the names of some missionary priests, Brothers and Sisters. They often have needs that even grammar school boys and girls can help to fill.

PRAYER:

O Jesus, Author of our faith, preserve it pure within us; keep us safe in the bark of Peter, faithful and obedient to his successor and Your Vicar here on earth, that so the unity of the holy Church may be maintained, holiness fostered, the Holy See protected in freedom, and the Church universal extended to the benefit of souls.

(The Raccolta, No. 649)

DICTIONARY AND INDEX

ab so lu′ tion (ăb-sō-lū′shàn), the freeing from sin by God through the priest. 379, 381, 433.

ab solve′, to free from sin, to forgive. 381.

ab stain′, to keep from doing, or from eating something, as flesh meat. 284, 290.

ab′ sti nence (ăb′stà-nĕns), not doing or eating something. 288, 289, 291, 292, Appendix V.

a buse′, misuse.

ac′ tion, anything we do. 64.

ac′ tu al sin, any sin that we commit ourselves. 63-76.

Ad′ am, the first man God created. 51-61, 77.

ad min′ is ter, to give. 449.

a dore′, to praise and worship God as our Creator. 41, 200.

a dul′ter y (à-dŭl′tēr-ĭ), giving to another love that belongs to husband or wife. 195.

Ad′ vent, the time of preparation for Christmas. 302.

all- ho′ly, possessing all goodness and virtue. 21.

all- just′, possessing full justice or fairness. 21.

all- mer′ ci ful, possessing complete forgiveness. 21.

all- pow′ er ful, possessing the power to do all things. 123.

ıll- wise′, possessing all knowledge of what is best in any circumstances. 21.

al might′ y, possessing power to do all things. 7.

alms′ giv ing, helping the poor with either money or goods. 425.

al′ tar, a place or table where sacrifice is offered. 356.

an′ gel, a spirit without a body, possessing understanding and free will. 36-46.

An′ gel Ga′ bri el, the angel who who told the Virgin Mary that she was to become the Mother of God. 87.

an′ ger, a strong feeling of displeasure, often resulting in a loss of temper, one of the seven capital sins. 12.

An nun ci a′ tion (à-nŭn-sĭ-ā′shàn), God's message to Mary through an angel: that He wished her to become the Mother of His Son (March 25). 87.

a noint′, to rub or spread with oil. 332.

a pos′ ta sy (à-pŏs′tà-sĭ), rejection of one's faith. 205.

A pos′ tles, the men selected by Christ to preach the Gospel to the world. 6.

Ap os tol′ ic (ăp-às-tŏl′ĭk), relating to Christ's Apostles and their times. 159.

ap pear′ an ces (of bread and wine), what we know through the senses, such as color, weight, taste, smell. 343 351.

As cen′ sion (à-sĕn′shàn), Christ's going up into heaven forty days after Easter. 101.

ash′ es, the remains of burned palms, from the last Palm Sunday, placed on the forehead on Ash Wednesday. 473.

As sump′ tion (à-sŭmp′ shàn), the taking up into heaven of the body and soul of the Blessed Virgin Mary (August 15). 178.

a tone′ ment (à-tōn′mĕnt), the doing of penance for sins committed. 420.

at′ tri bute (ăt′rĭ-būt), a quality belonging to a person or thing. 161-165.

au thor′ i ty, one of the three chief attributes of the Church: the power given by Christ to teach, to sanctify, and to govern in spiritual matters. 162.

bap′ tism, the sacrament which takes away original and actual sin and gives the life of Christ, sanctifying grace, to the soul. 305, 310, 313-327 Appendix VI.

bear false wit′ ness, to lie about one's neighbor. 195.

be at′ i tudes (bē-ăt′ĭ-tūdz), the standards or conditions for perfect happiness given by Our Lord. Beatitude means "perfect happiness." 127-129.

be lieve′, to accept truth on the word of another. 7.

Ben e dic′ tion (of the Blessed Sacrament), the service in which Jesus Christ is adored in the consecrated Host exposed on the altar, and in which the priest blesses the faithful with the Sacred Host. 378.

be nig′ ni ty (bē-nĭg′nà-tĭ), kindness, one of the fruits of the Holy Ghost. 128.

Bi′ ble (Sacred Scripture), the book written under God's inspiration. 23-23H, Appendix VIII-XIV.

bish′ op, the head of a diocese, who possesses the power to confirm, ordain, and consecrate; a successor to the Apostles who were the first bishops. 136, 145, 146, 149, 151, 331-334, 336, 451, 456, 472.

blas′ phe my (blǎs′fà-mĭ), the use of insulting words in reference to God and His Church. 233.

Bless′ ed Sac′ ra ment, the consecrated Host in which Christ dwells in the tabernacle of the altar. 371, 378.

Bless′ ed Trin′ i ty, the three divine Persons (Father, Son and Holy Ghost) in one God. 25-33, 82, 105, 488.

Bless′ ed Vir′ gin Mar′ y, the Mother of Jesus. 62, 81, 86-89, 178, 285, 439, 440.

bless′ ings, see sacramentals.

bribes, money, goods, or favors sinfully offered for the concealment of truth or for the relaxation of duty. 261.

cal′ um ny (kăl′ám-nĭ), false statements that injure the reputation of another, also called slander. 269, 271.

cap' i tal sins, the seven causes of all sin: pride, covetousness, lust, anger, gluttony, envy, sloth. 74, 75.

cath' o lic, 1. universal affecting all mankind at all times; 2. (with capital C) a member of the Roman Catholic Church. 158.

Cath' o lic Ac' tion, work of the laity in helping the Church bring souls to Christ. 151.

Cath' o lic Church, see Church.

cer' e mo ny, a set form of religious acts for a special occasion. 302.

char' ac ter, all the moral qualities of an individual; reputation; see also sacramental character. 267, 314, 317, 337, 339, 453.

char' i ty, love, the theological virtue which enables us to love God above all things, and to love our neighbor for the love of God. 121, 124, 203, 210, 447.

chas' ti ty,́ the virtue of purity in thought, word and act. 128, 135, 197, 257, 258, 276.

Christ, Messiah, the One anointed or sent by God to redeem the world. 78-104, 137, 138, 144-148, 330, 343-356, 359, 360, 362, 364A, 365, Appendix, V-VIII.

Chris' tian (krĭs'chàn), one who accepts the teachings of Christ. 164.

Christ' mas, the day on which Christ, our Savior, was born (December 25). 89.

Church, the Mystical Body of Christ, founded by Christ and governed by the successors of the Apostles chosen by Christ to do His work. 5-7, 136-169, 297-302, Appendix VI-VIII, XII, XIV.

Cir cum ci' sion (sër-kàm-sĭzh'àn), the ceremony performed when Jesus was eight days old, at which He was given the name Jesus (January 1). 283.

com mand' ment, a law of God. 54, 55, 195-302.

com mem o ra' tion (kà-mĕm-ō-rā'shàn), a remembrance, a celebration. 356.

com mit', to do. 63.

com mun' ion, a union with, a joining with, a sharing; see also Holy Communion. 136.

com mun' ion of saints, the sharing of grace among all members of Christ's Church, whether on earth, in purgatory, or in heaven. 7, 170-174.

con ceived' by the Ho' ly Ghost (kàn-sēvd'), given life through the workings of God, the Holy Ghost. 7.

con fes' sion, the telling of our sins to an authorized priest in the Sacrament of Penance. 70, 293, 294, 408-434.

con fes' sion al (kàn-fĕsh'àn-àl), the enclosure or box where the priest hears confessions. 426.

Con fir ma' tion, the sacrament, administered by the bishop, in which a baptized person receives added strength from the Holy Ghost, enabling him to be strong in his Faith and its defense. 305, 311, 313, 314, 330-342

Con fit' e or (kàn-fĭt'ē-ôr), a prayer of sorrow for sin, beginning, "I confess to Almighty God." 486.

con' science (kŏn'shàns), the judgment of our reason as to whether an act is good or bad. 426.

Con se cra' tion (kŏn-sē-krā'shàn), that part of the Mass in which the priest, using the words of Our Lord, changes bread and wine into the Body and Blood of Christ. 355.

con sent' (of the will), agreement, permission, acceptance. 69.

con' ti nen cy (kŏn'tà-nàn-sĭ), control over impure desires and acts. 128.

con tri' tion (kàn-trĭsh'àn), sorrow for sin with the intention of not committing the sin again. 373, 384, 388-407, 426, 433.

con vic' tion (kàn-vĭk'shàn), belief beyond doubt. 471.

cor' po ral works of mer'cy (kôr'pō-ràl), acts of love to care for the physical needs of our neighbor, such as feeding the hungry. 191, 193, 194.

coun' sel (koun'sàl), advice, especially that gift of the Holy Ghost through which we receive His light to guide us in practical matters. 125, 192.

cov' e nant (kŭv'à-nànt), an agreement or promise, as the covenant between God and His people. 346.

cov' e tous ness (kŭv'à-tàs-nĕs), a strong desire for possessions, especially those of another; one of the seven capital sins. 74.

Cre a' tor, God, the Maker of all things. 1-3, 7, 35, 36, 48, Appendix 11.

crea' tures, all things, living and non-living, that God has made. 8, 35, 36, 48.

Creed, a set of beliefs, as the Apostles' Creed, containing the chief truths taught by Christ to the Apostles. 6, 7, 187, 486.

cru' ci fy, to put to death by fastening to a cross. 7, 91.

curs' ing (kĕr'sĭng), wishing evil upon a person or thing. 232.

death, the separation of the soul from the body. 56, 91-94, 173.

Dec' a logue (dĕk'à-lŏg) (the Ten Commandments), the ten chief laws given by God to man. 195.

de spair' (dē-spăr'), deliberate refusal to trust in God, a sin against hope. 207, 209.

de trac' tion, hurting a person's reputation by revealing his faults without necessity. 266, 268, 271.

dev' il, a fallen angel, especially Satan, the chief of the bad angels. 44.

de vo' tion, an act of our will (often one we do not feel) by which we give ourselves readily to the service of God.

de vo' tions, prayers or thoughts about God or a saint which arouse devotion. 378.

dig' ni ty, high rank, degree or position; elevation and nobility of character. 461.

di' o cese (dī'ō-sēs), the territory, comprising many parishes, over which a bishop rules. 297.

dis charge' (of duty), the fulfilling of obligations.

dis hon' es ty, lying, cheating, stealing, lack of truth. 261.

dis o be' di ence (dĭs-ō-bē'dĭ-àns), not fulfilling the commands of God or lawful superiors. 55-61, 250.

dis pen sa' tion (dĭs-pĕn-sā'shàn), a special exception or exempting from a law granted by one in authority. 287, 289, 301.

dis po si' tions (dĭs-pō-zĭsh'ànz), attitude of mind and heart (when receiving the sacraments). 309.

dis re spect' (dĭs-rē-spĕkt'), failure to show honor, esteem, or courtesy. 250.

dis trac' tions (dĭs-tràk'shànz), anything that turns our attention away from what we are doing. 481.

Di vine′ na′ ture, God's essence, what He is. 32, 80, 85.

doc′ trine (dŏk′trĭn), dogma or teaching, as, Christian **doctrine** means the teachings of Christ's Church. 163.

East′ er, the day on which Christ rose from the dead. 98, 295, 296, 376.

ed′ i fy ing (ĕd′à-fĭ-ĭng), uplifting morally and spiritually by good example. Appendix, XV.

en′ vy, willful discontent, or even resentment consented to, at another's good fortune; one of the seven capital sins. 74, 278.

E piph′ a ny (ē-pĭf′à-nĭ), the revelation of Christ as God, made to the Magi, made at His Baptism by John in the Jordan, and at His first miracle during the wedding feast at Cana (January 6.)

e ter′ nal, lasting forever. 13, 104, 382, 421, 422.

e ter′ ni ty, endless duration. 103.

E van gel′ i cal Coun′ sels (ē-văn-jĕl′à-kàl koun′sàlz), recommendations of Our Lord for those seeking perfection in the spiritual life: voluntary poverty, perpetual chastity, and perfect obedience. 197.

Eve, the first woman God created. 51-61, 77.

ev er last′ ing, without end, forever. 3.

e′ vil, bad, the oppposite of good. 71.

ex am i na′ tion of con′ science, the calling to mind of all sins committed since the last confession, so that they may be confessed, repented of, and forgiven. 384-387, 426.

ex com mun′ i cate (ĕks-kŏm-ū′nà-kāt), to punish by cutting off from the sacraments and communion with the Church; an excommunicated person loses his rights but not his obligations. 169F.

ex′ or cisms (ĕk′sôr-sĭzmz), the driving away of devils by the power of Christ. 472.

Ex treme′ Unc′ tion (ĕks-trēm′ ŭngk′shàn), the last sacrament, or the sacrament of the sick who are in danger of death, which gives strength to the soul, and often to the body, through prayers and anointing with oil. 305, 311, 443-450.

faith, the theological virtue by which we believe all that God has revealed; also, the body of truths which we believe. 121, 122, 156, 164, 169A, 169C, 169D, 200, 201, 204-206; 373; 447, 486.

faith′ ful, all those who are practicing members of the Church. 143.

fast, to take no food or liquid within a prescribed period of time. 286, 287, 290, 292, 370-372, Appendix V.

fear of the Lord, great awe and reverence for Our Lord, which keeps us from offending Him by sin. 125.

fer′ vent, having great devotion. 72.

fi del′ i ty (fĭ-dĕl′à-tĭ), loyalty, faithfulness to duty and to pledges.

for give′, to pardon, to let someone off without making him pay for a wrong deed. 175.

for′ ti tude (fôr′tà-tūd), 1. a cardinal virtue wrich disposes us to do what is good in spite of any difficulty; 2. a gift of the Holy Ghost which gives us a Christlike courage to love God in the face of all obstacles, even death. 125, 132, 134.

fos′ ter fa′ ther (fôs′tēr fä′thēr), one who takes the place of a father and assumes his duties. 88.

fos′ ter ing, encouraging, promoting. (Appendix XVI).

free will, the power to make a choice between two opposites. 9, 114.

Ga′ bri el, the angel who announced to Mary that she was chosen to be Mother of God. 87.

Gar′ den of Par′ a dise, a symbol of the state of happiness in which our first parents were created. 53-56.

glo′ ry, honor and praise to one who is worthy or deserving; often indicates heavenly bliss or even heaven itself. 100, 177, 486.

glut′ ton y (glŭt′àn-ĭ), overeating, or overdrinking; eating greedily; one of the seven capital sins. 74.

God. our Creator, Maker of all things. 1-3, 8-23, 25, 26, 27, 28, 35, 36, 48, 78-128, Appendix 11.

god′ par ents, the man (godfather) and woman (godmother) who present the child (or adult) for baptism; they become responsible for the Catholic upbringing of the child, if the parents fail in this duty. ′326, 328, 329.

Gol′ go tha (gŏl′gō-thà), Calvary, the place where Christ died. 93.

good′ ness, all the qualities and virtues which make us what God wants us to be. 128.

good works, actions performed for love of God or our neighbor. 173-174.

grace, any gift of God, especially His great gift of sanctifying grace, the divine life of our soul. 52, 53, 56, 57, 108-119, 304, 308; 311, 315, 337-341, 368, 369, 375, 382, 464, 471.

grat′ i tude (grăt′à-tūd), thankfulness, appreciation for benefits received. 378.

griev′ ous (grēv′às), serious, severe. 66.

Guard′ i an An′gel (gär′dĭ-àn), the special angel assigned by God to each of us to keep us from harm and to guide and inspire us on the way to heaven. 42, 43.

hal′ lowed (hăl′ōd), blessed, honored, esteemed. 493.

hap′ pi ness, a state of bliss, joy, peace, and comfort. 4.

ha′ tred, extreme dislike and ill will, the opposite of love. 253.

heav′ en, the place and state of eternal happiness. 4, 68, 77, 90, 101, 171, 172, 178, 183, 186.

hell, the place and state of eternal punishment of the fallen angels and those who die in mortal sin. 7, 44, 95, 183, 185.

her′ e sy (hĕr′à-sĭ), the denial of a truth of the Catholic Faith. 169B, 169C, 205.

ho′ li ness, closeness to God, in the state of sanctifying grace. 38.

ho′ ly chrism (hō′lĭ krĭzm), consecrated oil used in the sacraments of Baptism, Confirmation, and Holy Orders. 334.

Ho′ ly Com mun′ ion, the receiving of the Body and Blood of Christ. 281, 343, 356, 364, 366-377.

ho′ ly day (hō′lĭ-dā), a special day set aside by the Church for worshipping God or honoring the Blessed Mother or the saints, when we are obliged to attend Mass and to refrain from unnecessary servile work. 282-285.

Ho′ ly Eu′ cha rist (hō′lĭ ū′kà-rĭst), the sacrament in which we receive Our Lord's Body and Blood under the appearances of bread and wine. 118, 305, 311, 343-356, 366, 378.

Ho' ly Ghost, the third Person of the Blessed Trinity; God. 7, 25, 28, 86, 105-128, 139-143, 163, 330, 332, Appendix IX, XIV.

Ho' ly Or' ders, the sacrament through which men become priests by receiving from the bishop the power to offer sacrifice and to forgive sins. 305, 311, 313, 314, 451-456.

Ho' ly See, the seat of authority for the whole Church in Rome, under the leadership of the Pope. 297.

Ho' ly Spir' it, God the Holy Ghost, the third Person of the Blessed Trinity. 320, 380.

ho' ly wa' ter, water blessed by a priest to drive away the power of the devils and to obtain graces for us. 473.

hon' or, to praise or show respect and courtesy for someone. 135, 214-218.

hope, the theological virtue which enables us to trust firmly in God and His promise of eternal life to those who love and obey Him. 121, 123, 200, 202, 207, 373, 447, 486.

host, the bread which is changed into the Body and Blood of Christ at Mass.

hu' man, relating or belonging to man. 51, 81, 85.

hu mil' i ty (hū-mĭl-à-tĭ), freedom from pride or pretension; a quality enabling a person to see himself as he is and to acknowledge his limitations. 135.

i dol' a try (ī-dŏl'à-trĭ), the giving of worship to any creature or thing instead of to God.

ig' no rance (ĭg'nō-ràns), lack of knowledge, or imperfect knowledge, about something. 60.

im' age (ĭm'ĭj) (of God), the likeness of man to God. 48-50.

im' ag es (sacred), pictures or statues representing Our Lord, the Blessed Virgin, or the saints. 221-223, 473.

Im mac' u late Con cep' tion (ĭm-măk'ū-lĭt kàn-sĕp'shàn), the special privileges granted by God to the Blessed Virgin Mary whereby she was free from original sin from the first moment of life; the feast is on December 8th. 62.

im mod' es ty (ĭm-mŏd'ĕs-tĭ), unbecoming dress or conduct. 256.

im mor' tal (ĭm-môr'tàl), never dying, lasting forever. 50, 98, Appendix I, III.

im ped' i ment (ĭm-pĕd'à-mànt) (to marriage), any reason or fact that would make impossible a valid marriage under the laws of God and the Church; an obstacle to marriage.

im per' fect (ĭm-pēr'fĕkt), having a defect, incomplete. 400.

im print' (ĭm-prĭnt'), to place a mark on, to fix indelibly. 314.

im pu' ri ty (ĭm-pū'rà-tĭ), uncleanness, lack of chastity in thought, word, or act. 256, 274-276.

In car na' tion (ĭn-kär-nā'shàn), the taking of a human nature by God the Son, when He became Man and was born of the Virgin Mary. 77-89.

in cli na' tion (ĭn-klà-nā' shàn), a tendency, bent, or leaning toward something. 56.

in de fect i bil' i ty (ĭn-dē-fĕk-tà-bĭl'à-tĭ), one of the three chief attributes of the Church: that it will last until the end of time. 161-165.

in del' i ble (ĭn-dĕl'à-bàl), lasting, cannot be removed or blotted out. 339.

in dif' fer ent ism (ĭn-dĭf'-ēr-ànt-ĭzm), lack of interest or zeal as to what is true or false in regard to religion. 205.

in dis sol' u ble (ĭn-dĭ-sŏl'ū-bàl), cannot be broken, separated, disunited, or annulled. 459.

in dul' gence (ĭn-dŭl'jàns), the taking away by the Church of some or all the temporal punishment that one must suffer, in this life or in purgatory, for sins committed. 435-442.

in fal li bil' i ty (ĭn-făl-à-bĭl'à-tĭ), a guarantee of truth which excludes error, given by Christ to His Church; it is one of the three chief attributes of the Church. 161, 163, 164.

in' fi del (ĭn'fà-dĕl), a disbeliever; one who does not accept Christianity. 205.

in' fi nite (ĭn'fà-nĭt), without limit or end.

in' no cence (ĭn'ō-sàns) (original), freedom from sin; the state of Adam and Eve before they disobeyed God's command.

in spire' (ĭn-spīr'), to influence the soul directly to act. 470.

in spi ra' tion (ĭn-spà-rā'shàn) (of the Bible), a divine influence which moved the Sacred Writers to write what God wanted them to write. 23-23L, Appendix IX, XIV.

in tel' li gence (ĭn-tĕl'à-jĕns), the power of knowing, understanding, and reasoning; the mind in operation. 51A, Appendix III.

in ten' tion, the application of ten merits of Holy Mass, prayers, and the sacraments to a particular person or purpose.

in ter ces' sion (ĭn-tēr-sĕsh'àn), a prayer of petition on behalf of another; for example, we often obtain blessings from God through the intercession of a saint to whom we have prayed. 469.

in te' ri or (ĭn-tēr'ĭ-ēr), inside, within, spiritual. 391.

in vol' un tar y (ĭn-vŏl'àn-tēr-ĭ), not willed.

ir rev' er ence (ĭ-rĕv'ēr-àns), lack of due. honor and respect for someone or something sacred. 312.

Je ru' sa lem, city in Palestine which was the religious center in the time of Christ and the site of His suffering and death. 93.

Je' sus Christ, the Son of God, the second Person of the Blessed Trinity, who became Man and suffered and died on the Cross to redeem us. 7, 78-104, 137, 138, 144-148, 330, 343-356, 359, 360, 362, 365, 377, 380, Appendix V-VIII.

Jo' seph, the spouse of Mary and the foster father of Jesus Christ. 88.

judg' ment, the time when we shall receive from God the reward or punishment earned by our life on earth. 104, 180-182.

jus' tice, 1. holiness, especially the holiness of God; 2. that cardinal virtue which disposes us to give to everyone what belongs to him. 61, 129, 132-134, 182, 361.

know, to understand, to recognize, to distinguish; as to **know** right from wrong. 4, 5, 22, 23.

knowl' edge, a gift of the Holy Ghost which enables us to see God reflected in all creatures and to praise Him in them, but yet to see the nothingness of creatures in themselves so that we will desire God alone.

la' i ty (lā'-à-tĭ), all the members of the Church aside from the clergy and religious. 150-151B.

Last Sup' per, the meal the night before Christ died, at which He took bread and wine and changed them into His Body and Blood, and gave to the Apostles to eat and to drink, telling them to do the same in remembrance of Him. 344, 354.

law (of God), a command of God, the violation of which demands punishment. 64, 66, 70, 188-197, 279-281.

Lent, the forty-day period of prayer and fasting between Ash Wednesday and Easter Sunday. 296, 302.

lie, a statement which one knows to be untrue when he makes it. 266.

lim' bo, the place of rest where the souls of all the just remained until heaven was re-opened after the death of Christ; the place where unbaptized infants go. 95, 97.

love, to will good to another and to want to do only what is good for another; as, we **love** our neighbor by helping him and wishing him well. 4, 5, 124, 189, 190, 399.

lust, the desire for unlawful bodily pleasure: one of the seven capital sins. 74.

mar' riage (măr'ĭj); see Matrimony.

mar' tyr dom (mär'tēr-dàm), the giving up of one's life for the Faith or in defense of virtue. 322.

Mass, the continuation of the Sacrifice of the Cross under the ceremonies given us by Our Lord at the Last Supper, chiefly the changing of bread and wine into His Body and Blood. 173, 302, 303, 343, 357-365, 454, 468.

Mat' ri mo ny (măt'rà-mō-nĭ), the sacrament which a baptized man and woman bind themselves in marriage for life. 298-303, 305, 311, 457-468.

men' tal prayer (mĕn'tàl prăr) (meditation), uniting our hearts with God and thinking about Him and the truths of our religion in order to increase our love of God. 483.

mer' cy, clemency, a relaxation of the strict dictates of justice. 129, 191-194.

mer' it (mĕr'ĭt), the right to a reward for good actions done for love of God or neighbor. 68.

Mes si' as (mà-sī'às), the promised Redeemer, Jesus Christ.

min' is try (mĭn'ĭs-trĭ), the name given to the entire body of the clergy belonging to the Church; also, the act of ministering to another. 353.

mir' a cle (mĭr'à-kàl), an external event beyond the power of a creature to perform, brought about by the direct action of God. Appendix V.

mod' es ty (mŏd'ĕs-tĭ), purity or chastity in one's words and actions, and also in regard to dress and sex. 128, 255.

mor' al (mŏr'àl), conforming to God's laws about what is right and good; also, a teaching, a maxim. 130-135, 163.

mor' tal, fatal, deadly, destructive to life. 65-69, 282, 312, 325, 368, 403-405.

mo' tive, any emotion or desire which spurs a person to action. 392.

mys' ter y (mĭs'tēr-ĭ) (supernatural), a truth of our Faith which we cannot fully understand but which we accept as true because God has revealed it. 33, 34, 285, 488.

Mys' ti cal Bod' y of Christ (mĭs'tĭ-kàl), the

Church; so-called because the bond of union existing between Christ as the Head and the faithful as members resembles the bond of union in a human body. 145, 166-169F, 174.

Na tiv' i ty (nà-tĭv'à-tĭ), the birthday of Jesus Christ, Christmas (December 25). 89.

nat' u ral rea' son, the power of man to know, understand, and form judgments, unaided by the light of God's revelation. 22, 23.

na' ture, the essence of a thing; what it is. 80-85.

New Law, the law of loving one another as Our Lord has loved us, and all the laws which flow from that, replacing the Old Law given to Moses, which emphasized fear rather than love. 357.

New Tes' ta ment (nu tĕs'tà-mànt), the second part of the Bible, written after the coming of Christ to earth. 23D, 23H, Appendix X.

non- Cath' o lic, one who is not a member of the Catholic Church.

nup' tial (nŭp'shàl), relating to marriage or the wedding ceremony. 302, 303, 468.

oath, asking God to witness the truth of a statement or promise. 226, 227.

o be' di ence, the keeping of God's commandments; also following the orders of parents and lawful superiors. 55, 135, 197, 242-247.

ob li ga' tion (ŏb-lĭ-gā'shàn), duty imposed by the laws of God or of man. 281.

ob serve', to fulfill the law or obey the rules; to celebrate, as to **observe** a feast. 281.

oc ca' sion of sin (à-kā'zhàn), any person, place, or thing which may lead us into sin. 73, 406.

of' fer, to give; also, to want to give. 356, 357-359, 362.

Old Tes' ta ment (ōld tĕs'tà-mànt), the first part of the Bible telling the story of the Jewish people before the coming of Christ. 23D, Appendix X.

or dained' (ôr-dānd'), having received the Sacrament of Holy Orders. 305, 311, 313, 314, 359, 451-456.

o rig' i nal sin (ō-rĭj'à-nàl), our inherited condition from the sin of Adam and Eve by which we are born without grace and inclined to love ourselves more than God. 58-63, 316.

Our Fa' ther, the prayer given to us by Christ Himself, also called the Lord's Prayer. 486, 490-499.

Our Lord, Jesus Christ, the Son of God, the second Person of the Blessed Trinity. 7.

par' don, to forgive, to remit the penalty for an offense. 70.

par' ish, a division of a diocese with a priest at its head, designated by the bishop as its pastor or administrator. 149.

par' tial (pär'shàl), incomplete, affecting only part. 438.

pas' sion, 1. (with capital P) the sufferings of Christ from the Last Supper until His Death on the Cross; 2. lust, a strong desire for bodily pleasure, also any of the emotions. 91, 275.

pa' tron saint, a special advocate before God selected by a person, a country, a town, a diocese or any special group; for example, the **patron saint** of our country is Our Lady under her title of the Immaculate Conception.

pen′ ance, 1. (with capital P) the sacrament in which all sins committed after Baptism are forgiven through the power received by the priest from Christ; 2. the prayers or good works assigned by the priest after one has confessed his sins; 3. self-denial, making our body do what it does not like to do to teach it to obey our soul. 305, 310, 379-434.

Pen′ te cost (pĕn′tà-kôst), the day on which the Holy Ghost descended upon the Apostles, fifty days after Easter; also called Whitsunday. 140.

per′ fect, without defect or fault. 2, 8, 11-21.

per′ ju ry (pĕr′jĕr-ĭ), calling on God to witness the truth of a lie; lying under oath. 228.

per pet′ u al (pĕr-pĕt′chū-àl), continuous, lasting forever. 197.

per se cu′ tion (pĕr-sē-kū′shàn), harm, suffering, and even death, inflicted upon a person because of his religious beliefs. 129.

per se ver′ ance (pĕr-sà-vēr′àns), continuous performance of a good act despite great difficulty. 477.

per′ son, a being having intellect and free will. 25-33, 82.

Pe′ ter, the Apostle chosen by Christ to be the head, or first Pope, of the Church He founded. 147, 148, 280.

pi′ e ty (pī′à-tĭ), 1. one of the seven gifts of the Holy Ghost by which we are attracted to reverence God as our Father and all others as His children, our brethren; 2. special love and devotion to God and His saints; 3. zeal in prayer and worship; also, 4. affection and gratefulness to parents, country, etc. 125, 135.

ple′ na ry (plē′nà-rĭ), complete, entire. 437.

Pon′ tius Pi′ late (pŏn′shàs pī′làt), the Roman governor of Judea during the time of Christ's suffering and death, who sentenced Jesus to death even though he himself believed Him innocent. 7.

pope, Christ's representative on earth as the lawful successor of St. Peter and visible head of the Church. 136, 147, 148, 164, 280.

pov′ er ty, 1. the vow by which religious give up the right to personal property; 2. the Christian ideal of a sufficient amount (but no more) of this world's goods to live decently; 3. lack of the necessities of life. 197.

prayer, the lifting up of the mind and heart to God; conversation with God. 73, 117, 173, 217, 258, 457, 475-499.

pre′ cepts of the Church (prē′sĕpts), the commandments of the Church; see also commandment, law. 281.

pre sump′ tion (prē-zŭmp′shàn), the belief that one can save himself without God's help, or that God's help alone will save without the efforts of the individual. 208.

pride, esteeming ourselves as more than we are and desiring to be treated as more than we are; one of the seven capital sins. 74.

priest, a mediator between God and man, especially one who has received Holy Orders and takes the place of Christ, the High Priest, 149, 318, 353-355, 357-360, 364, 364A, 379-381, 408-410, 419, 420, 448-455, 465.

prin′ ci ple, a basic law, a fundamental truth or doctrine. Appendix 1.

proph′ et (prŏf′ĕt), 1. a messenger sent by God; 2. one who foretells the future. Appendix V.

Prov′ i dence (prŏv′à-dàns), God in His love and care for us; Divine guidance. 19.

pru′ dence (prōō′dàns), a cardinal virtue which helps us to make practical judgments on what to do and what not to do. 132-134.

pur′ ga to ry (pĕr′gà-tō-rĭ), the place of temporary punishment where the souls of those who die in the state of grace must be cleansed before entrance into heaven, if their love for God is not yet perfect. 72, 170, 171, 173, 183, 184.

pu′ ri ty, the moral virtue which controls our inclinations toward sinful pleasures of the body. 135, 255, 273.

rash judg′ ment, a deliberate judgment concerning a fault of another without sufficient evidence. 266, 267.

rea′ son (the use of), the age (usually of seven, often before) when a child knows the difference between right and wrong and is therefore responsible for his acts. 22, 116, Appendix I.

Re deem′ er, the One who saved us, Jesus Christ, who offered His sufferings and death to God the Father as an infinite satisfaction for our sins, and thus reopened heaven to us. 90.

Re demp′ tion (rē-dĕmp′shàn), Christ's satisfaction (His suffering and death) for the sins of mankind, which freed man from the bondage of sin and restored Him to friendship with God. 90-103, 488.

re li′ a ble (rē-lī′à-bàl), trustworthy, dependable. Appendix VIII.

rel′ ic (rĕl′ĭk), the body, or part of the body, of a saint, or anything, such as clothing, associated with the saint which the Church venerates because of the sanctity of the person while on earth. 216, 219, 222, 223.

re li′ gion, the relationship between God and man; all the teachings and practices of the Church by which we join ourselves to God. Appendix I, IV, V.

re li′ gious, a person who is a member of a congregation or religious order, dedicated to serving God through the voluntary vows of poverty, chastity, and obedience. 150, 452C.

re mis′ sion of sin (rē-mĭsh′àn), the forgiveness of sins, accomplished chiefly through the Sacraments of Baptism and Penance. 375, 382.

rep a ra′ tion (rĕp-à-rā′shàn), the making of amends for wrong or injury done; the repairing of harm done to another or damage to another's property. 263, 281.

re pent′ (rē-pĕnt′), to have sorrow for one's sins and a firm intention of not committing the sins again. 175.

re solve′, to decide, to make up one's mind. 406.

re spect′ (rē-spĕkt′), esteem, honor, high regard, consideration. 135, 221, 242, 243, 247, 260.

re spon si bil′ i ty (rē-spŏn-sà-bĭl′à-tĭ), a duty for which one is held accountable. 244.

res ti tu′ tion (rĕs-tĭ-tū′shàn), the return of found or stolen property to its rightful owner; payment for injury to a person or property damage. 262, 263.

res ur rec′ tion (rĕz-à-rĕk′shàn), 1. the rising of the body to be united with the soul at the end of the world; 2. (with capital R) the day on which Our Lord rose from the dead after His suffering and death on the Cross (Easter Sunday). 7, 98-100, 176-179.

re tain' (rē-tān'), to withhold forgiveness, to re fuse absolution; the priest does this when the conditions are not present for a valid reception of the Sacrament of Penance. 380.

Rev e la' tion (rĕv-à-lā'shàn), Sacred Scripture (the Bible) and Tradition (what has been handed down from age to age) which contain the sum of revealed doctrine. 23-23L, Appendix V, IX-XIV.

re venge' (rē-vĕnj'), to inflict harm or injury in return for a wrong. 253.

'rev' er ence (rĕv'ēr-àns), honor and respect given to creatures such as the saints, the clergy and religious, great men, parents, sacred places, etc. 225, 230.

right, that to which a person has a just claim; what is in accord with the laws of God. 52, 56, 61.

rite, the words and actions used in a religious ceremony.

ro'sa ry, 1. a string of beads consisting of five sets each of ten small beads separated by one single bead, with the addition of a crucifix and 5 more beads; 2. the special prayers to the Blessed Virgin which are said with the use of these beads, consisting of the Apostles' Creed, the Our Father, the Hail Mary, and the Glory Be to the Father. 473.

sac' ra ment, an outward sign instituted by Christ to give grace. 73, 136, 304-468.

sac ra men' tal char' ac ter (săc-rà-mĕn'tàl kăr'-àk-tēr), the imprint on the soul of a lasting spiritual mark by the sacraments of Baptism, Confirmation, and Holy Orders which, for this reason, can be received only once. 314, 317, 337, 339, 453.

sac ra men' tal con fes' sion, the telling of one's sins to an authorized priest in the Sacrament of Penance. 70.

sac ra men' tals (săk-rà-mĕn'tàlz), special prayers, actions or objects, the use of which obtains spiritual benefits through the prayers of the Church to God. 469-474.

Sa' cred Scrip' ture (sā'krĕd skrĭp'tchēr), the revealed word of God as recorded in the Old and New Testaments of the Bible. 23-23H, Appendix VIII-XI, XIV.

sac' ri fice, the offering of a gift (victim) to God by a priest on behalf of all the people, to adore Him, to satisfy for sin, to thank Him, and to ask His blessings. God's acceptance of the sacrifice symbolizes His acceptance of the heart of the giver. 136, 357-365.

sac' ri lege (săk'rà-lĭj), irreverent treatment, or mistreatment, of sacred persons, places, or things; also, the reception of any of the sacraments unworthily. 211, 213, 312, 368, 417.

saint, a very holy person, one who loves God perfectly and is now in heaven, especially one who died with perfect love and did not have to pass through purgatory. The Bible at times calls all the faithful saints, since Baptism gives the beginning of holiness. 170-173, 214-218, 327.

sal va' tion, the attainment of God in heaven

through the freeing of the soul from sin and its punishment. 166-168.

sanc' ti fy (săngk'tà-fī), to make holy. 108, 143.

sanc' ti fy ing grace, Divine life in the soul. 110, 112, 115, 119, 307, 375, 382, 445, 453, 466.

Sav' ior, Jesus Christ who died to save all men. 77, 78.

scan' dal, any word or deed that may be the occasion of sin to our neighbor; malicious gossip; harming the good name or reputation of another. 210.

scap' u lar (skăp'ū-lēr), two small squares of cloth joined by strings so that they can be worn over the shoulders, one to the back and one to the front; indulgences are attached to the wearing of a scapular. 473.

schism (sĭzm), a separation from the Church by refusal to recognize the authority of the Pope in 'Rome. 169B, 169E.

scourg' ing (skēr'jĭng), a lashing or whipping; the sufferings of Our Lord as He was tied to a pillar and beaten until covered with wounds. 41.

self- ex ist' ing, being independent of any other being, or cause. 8.

sep' ul chre (sĕp'àl-kēr), a tomb. 97.

serve, to keep the commandments of God. 5.

ser' vile work (sēr'vĭl), any work requiring bodily rather than mental effort. 238-240, 284.

Sign of the Cross, a sacramental consisting of the movement of the right hand from the forehead to the breast, then from the left to the right shoulders. 487-489.

sin, breaking God's law. 45, 47, 55-76, 282, 312, 325, 368, 403-405, 420-425.

sin cere', genuine, real, free from deception. 412.

slan' der (slăn'dēr), harming another person's reputation by telling lies about him or by distorting the truth. 269.

sloth (slōth), one of the seven capital sins; laziness that causes neglect of duty. 74.

sor' row, contrition, grief, regret, penitence; see also contrition. 384, 386, 388, 390, 406, 407, 426.

soul, the spiritual part of man, the source of his life. 48-50, 67, 111, 119, 149, 151, 176-179, 209, 314, 315, 317, 337; 443; Appendix III.

Sov' er eign Pon' tiff (sŏv'ēr-ĭn pŏn'tĭf), the Pope, the Vicar of Christ on earth, the visible head of the Church. 136.

spir' it, 1. a being without a body; 2. (with capital S) God the Holy Ghost, the third Person of the Blessed Trinity. 8, 9, 37, 320.

spir' it ists (spĭr'ĭt-ĭsts), those who believe that one can communicate with the dead. 212.

spir' it u al (spĭr'ĭt-chū-àl), relating to the soul, to angels, or to God. 162, 314.

spir' it u al works of mer'cy, acts of love to care for the spiritual needs of our neighbor, such as comforting the sorrowful. 192-194.

state of grace, the presence of sanctifying grace (God's special gift) in one's soul; freedom from mortal sin. 118, 186, 294, 340, 403.

Sta' tions of the Cross, fourteen representations of events during the Passion and Death of Christ, which appear on the walls of the church.

steal, to take as our own something which does not lawfully belong to us; an offense against the seventh commandment of God. 259-261.

sub' stance, that which makes a thing what it is; the essence, the material of which a thing is made. 347, 348, 350.

su' i cide (sū'á-sīd), the taking of one's own life. 253.

Sun' day, the day of rest, when we are commanded by the laws of the Church to assist at the Holy Sacrifice of the Mass and to refrain from all unnecessary servile work. 235-240, 281, 282, 284.

su' per a bun' dant (sū'pēr-á-bŭn'dánt), more than enough, overflowing, excessive. 439, 440.

su' per nat'u ral (su'pēr-năt'chēr-ál), above nature, beyond the natural order of things. 23, 33, 34, 67, 109, 113, 115, 119, 169, 174, 310, 390, 392, 454.

su' per sti' tion (sū'pēr-stĭsh'án), any belief or act that gives to a creature the honor which belongs to God alone; also the giving of false honor to God. 211, 212.

Su preme' Be' ing (sū-prēm'), God, the perfect and highest Being. 2, 8-23.

swear, to call on God to witness the truth of what we say or the promises we make; also, to curse. 227.

tem' per ance (těm'pēr-áns), one of the cardinal virtues which enables us to control the desires of the senses and to use them according to the designs of God. 132, 134.

tem' ple, 1. a place of worship; 2. (with capital T) the place of worship and sacrifice of the Jews, located in Jerusalem until its destruction in 70 A.D. 73.

tem' po ral pun' ish ment (těm'pō-rál), the medicine of suffering given either here or in purgatory to heal the effects of sins already forgiven. 184, 382, 420-425, 435, 437-439.

temp ta' tion, a strong inclination to sin which may come from the devil, from something outside us, or from man's tendency toward evil as a result of Adam's fall. 45-47.

Ten Com mand' ments, the ten chief laws given by God to Moses. 195.

thanks giv' ing, a prayer expressing gratitude to God for all His gifts. 374, 476.

the o log' i cal (thē-ō-lŏj'ĭ-kál), relating to God. 119, 120-124.

tithes (tīthz), our contribution to the support of the Church; formerly, one-tenth of one's yearly income, given to the Church. 5.

Tra di' tion (trá-dĭsh'án), the handing down by word of mouth from century to century of the teachings of Christ through the Apostles; the source of revealed truth in addition to the Bible. 23, 23A, 23I-23L, Appendix XI-XIV.

tran sub stan ti a' tion (trăn-sŭb-stăn-shĭ-ā'shán), the change of the entire substance of the bread and wine into the Body and Blood of Christ at the Consecration of the Mass. 347-350.

tres' pass es (trěs'pás-ĕz), sins or offenses against God. 497.

Trin' i ty (trĭn'á-tĭ), the three distinct Persons in one God: the Father, the Son, and the Holy Ghost, all having the same Divine nature. 25-33.

Trin' i ty Sun' day, the first Sunday after Pen-

tecost, when the Church honors the mystery of the three Persons in one God. 296.

truth, the conformity of what we say or do with the actual facts and with our conscience. 135, 169C, 226, 227, 265.

un chaste' (ŭn-chāst'), impure in thought or act, immodest. 275.

un der stand' ing, the gift of the Holy Spirit which gives us an insight into the mysteries of faith so that we may live by them. 9, 37, 50, 125.

u' ni ty of God (ū'ná-tĭ), the state of being one: God is one even though there are three divine Persons in the one God. 24, 31-33.

u ni ver' sal (ū-ná-vēr'sál), referring to the whole world, to all men of all time. 155, 158, 280.

u' su ry (ū'zhōō-rĭ), the lending of money at an excessive interest rate; unjust gain made from the loan of money.

ven' er ate (vĕn'ēr-āt), to honor, to regard with respect and admiration. 222.

ven' geance (vĕn'jáns), unrestrained revenge, the infliction of punishment on another in return for an injury. 253.

ve' ni al sin (vē'nĭ-ál), an offense against the laws of God which is not so grievous as mortal sin; it does not deprive the soul completely of sanctifying grace, but lessens God's grace in the soul. 65, 70-72, 231, 397, 407, 411.

Vi at' i cum (vī-ăt'ĭ-kám), Holy Communion given to those in danger of death.

Vic' ar of Christ (vĭk'ēr), the Pope who is visible head of the Church and the representative of Christ on earth. 148.

vic' tim, an offering to God in sacrifice, usually something alive or something that sustains life. 358, 360, 364A.

vig' il, the day before certain feasts, such as the day before Christmas.

vir' tue, the habit of doing good and avoiding evil. 119-124. 130-135, 215, 257-258.

vol' un tar y (vŏl'án-tēr-ĭ), of one's own free will or choice. 197.

vow, a promise made to God to perform some act pleasing to Him and better than its opposite; for example, to enter religious life is better than to get married. 197, 225, 229.

wel' fare, state of well-being, of living in health, safety, and freedom from evil. 244-246, 248, 249.

will, the power of the soul by which man seeks what the intellect presents to it as good or seemingly good. 37, 50, 114.

will' ful, intentional. 64.

wis' dom, the gift of the Holy Spirit which enables us to judge correctly concerning the things of God. God is love and the Holy Spirit gives the wisdom of love to appreciate divine things, even crosses and tribulations, and really relish them, even though at times they may be repulsive to human nature. 38, 125.

womb, that place in a woman's body where her child is nourished and developed until it is ready to be born. 86.

wor' ship, the adoration and honor which we give to God alone. 199, 200, 205, 206, 220.

wor' thy, meriting, deserving, having fulfilled all requirements. 375.

wrong, all that is not in accord with the laws of God; the opposite of right. 69, 71, 253.

THE STATIONS OF THE CROSS

I N the Stations of the Cross, or Way of the Cross, we follow the footsteps of Our Blessed Lord from the palace of Pilate to Calvary. We think of His sufferings to impress on our minds and hearts how much He has loved us to suffer so much for us. When we see how much He loves us, our hearts are moved to want to love Him in return, to keep away from sin which hurts Him and to do even hard things to please Him.

It is very easy to make the Stations of the Cross. Just do these two things: 1. Visit each Station. 2. Think of Our Lord's sufferings.

For this you can gain a plenary indulgence. Take five, ten, fifteen minutes, or whatever time you can spare. No set prayers are required. The following thoughts are suggested to help you make the Stations. But they are only suggestions. It is best to follow whatever thoughts come to your own mind.

Although it is not required, it is best to begin with an Act of Contrition. At each Station, this prayer may be said: "Holy Mother, pierce me through, In my heart each wound renew of my Savior crucified."

1. Jesus is Condemned to Death

Our Lord accepted His death in obedience to His Father because He loved us so much. He even obeyed Pilate. Dear Lord, I will always obey everyone the Father wants me to obey.

2. Jesus Accepts His Cross

Our Lord did not like the Cross, but He accepted it willingly from His Father. Dear Lord, teach me to do willingly each day the things the Father wants that I do not feel like doing.

3. Jesus Falls Under the Cross

It hurt Our Lord so much to fall with the Cross on top of Him. Dear Lord, I am willing to follow You no matter how much it hurts. I am so weak, but give me Your strength.

4. Jesus Meets His Mother

How it hurt His Sacred Heart to see His Mother's sorrow! Dear Lord, help me never to cause my mother needless sorrow. And if my leaving home some day does cause her sorrow, You console her heart for me.

5. Simon Helps Jesus with the Cross

Our Lord did not need Simon's help but gave Simon the privilege of helping Him. Dear Lord, let me help you with the Cross by helping others, whether I like them or not.

6. Veronica Wipes the Face of Jesus

Our Lord is always so grateful for any kindness done to Him. Dear Lord, help me always to show my gratitude for everything that is done for me.

7. Jesus Falls Again

They laughed at Our Lord when He fell. Dear Lord, help me never to be afraid to do what pleases You even if others may laugh at me.

8. Jesus Speaks to the Holy Women

Our Lord was so pleased when the women gave Him their sympathy. Dear Lord, I will try to console You too by thinking every day on Your Passion.

9. Jesus Falls a Third Time

Every time Our Lord fell, He kept getting up, even though it hurt so much. Dear Lord, help me to get up every time I fall too.

10. Jesus is Stripped of His Clothes

The soldiers took Our Lord's clothes because they wanted them. Dear Lord, teach me never to be selfish with what belongs to me.

11. Jesus is Nailed to the Cross

The nails went right through Our Lord's hands and feet and held Him fast to the Cross. Dear Lord, help me to use my hands and feet to please You and never to nail You to the Cross again.

12. Jesus Dies on the Cross

Our Lord loved us so much He gave His life for us. Dear Lord, I give my life to You to live only to please You and to die willingly whenever You call me to Yourself.

13. Our Lady Receives the Body of Jesus

Our Lady had willingly given her Son to the Father for us, but how deep was the pain in her Immaculate Heart. Dear Mother, show me how to make up for all the sins I have committed.

14. Our Lady Watches Her Son Being Buried

Our Lady was so sad because men had put her Son out of their lives. Dear Mother, never let me drive Him out of my life by sin, but let me die to myself that I may live for Him.

THE HOLY ROSARY

THE Rosary is Our Lady's special prayer. It is not hard to say. On the big beads we say an **Our Father** and on each small bead a **Hail Mary.** Usually we say a **Glory be to the Father** at the end of each ten **Hail Mary's,** though this is not strictly necessary. At the very end we may say the **Hail Holy Queen.**

While we say the prayers of the Rosary, we try to think of Our Blessed Lord. We try to look at Him through Our Lady's eyes and to understand Him with her heart. While we say each group of ten **Hail Mary's** — which is called a decade — we think of one of the mysteries of His Birth, Passion and Glory. If we notice our mind wandering, we bring it back to the mystery. As long as we are doing our best, our Rosary is well said, even though we have distractions. The following suggestions will help us to think about each mystery.

Say your Rosary every day. Families which say it together will be specially blessed by God.

The FIVE JOYFUL MYSTERIES

Said on Mondays and Thursdays

1. The Annunciation

The angel told Mary that God wanted her to be the Mother of His Son. Mary said, "Yes." She always said "Yes" to God.

2. The Visitation

Mary went right away to help her cousin, St. Elizabeth. She always helped those in need.

3. The Nativity

Jesus was born in a poor stable. He wanted to be one of us in poverty and need.

4. The Presentation

In the Temple, Mary offered Jesus to the Father. She would raise Him to be offered later on the Cross.

5. The Finding in the Temple

Mary and Joseph found Jesus after He had been lost for three days. He was beginning the work His Father had sent Him to do.

THE FIVE SORROWFUL MYSTERIES

*Said on
Tuesdays
and Fridays*

1. The Agony in the Garden
Our Lord prayed for strength to drink the cup of suffering, to suffer, die and rise for us.

2. The Scourging
Our Lord was cruelly scourged. He accepted pain so we would never have to suffer too much.

3. The Crowning with Thorns
Jesus accepted being crowned with thorns so we would not be afraid to be laughed at.

4. The Way of the Cross
Jesus carried His Cross willingly to make it easier for us to carry our crosses.

5. The Crucifixion
Our Lord died on the Cross for us. This is how much He loved us.

THE FIVE GLORIOUS MYSTERIES

*Said on Sundays,
Wednesdays
and Saturdays*

1. The Resurrection
Our Lord rose to a new and changed life, all for His Father. He rose that we may rise too.

2. The Ascension
Our Lord went home to heaven to prepare a place for us. Our hearts should be there already.

3. Descent of the Holy Spirit
Jesus sent His Holy Spirit to His newborn Church. The Holy Spirit makes us strong in love.

4. The Assumption
Jesus took Mary's body and soul into heaven, so we will not be afraid to die and go there.

5. The Coronation
Our Lord crowned Mary Queen of Angels and Saints to rule hearts and attract them to His Father.

THE HOLY LAND

Matson Photo Service

THE RIVER JORDAN — The most important river in Palestine measures 135 miles in a straight line, but because of its numerous windings covers a distance of about 250 miles. Its width varies from 80 to 180 feet and its depth from 5 to 12 feet. Here Jesus was baptized by John the Baptist.

"Jesus came from Galilee to John, at the Jordan, to be baptized by him" — Mt 3, 13.

Matson Photo Service

MOUNT OF TEMPTATION — According to a tradition dating back to the fourth century this is the mountain on which Christ was tempted by the devil. It rises 1600 feet above the Jordan Valley, less than 3 miles from Jericho. A Greek Orthodox Monastery is seen in the foreground.

"The devil took Him to a very high mountain. and showed Him all the kingdoms" — Mt 4 8

MOUNT OF OLIVES — Showing the Church built in the Garden of Gethsemani (foreground), the Russian Church (above and to the right, the Church of the Agony) and on the summit (center) the tower of the Church of the Ascension.

"After reciting a hymn, they went out to the Mount of Olives . . . " — Mk 14, 26.

GARDEN OF GETHSEMANI — Close-up of the Garden of Christ's Agony, showing part of the Basilica of all Nations on the left and the city wall with the Golden Gate on the hill beyond.

"Jesus came with them to a country place called Gethsemani . . . And He took with Him Peter and the two sons of Zebedee, and He began to be saddened and exceedingly troubled" — Mt 26, 36-37.

ANCIENT TOMB — Ancient tomb west of Jerusalem. The stone in front is rolled into a groove cut into the wall. To seal the tomb the stone was rolled in front of it. Jesus was laid in a similar tomb.

"Joseph, taking the body (of Jesus), wrapped it in a clean linen cloth, and laid it in his new tomb, which he had hewn out in the rock. Then he rolled a large stone to the entrance" — Mt 27, 59-60.

MOUNT OF THE ASCENSION — An overall view of the Mount of Olives and surroundings where Jesus led His disciples before His Ascension. The Church of the Ascension rises in the background.

"He led them out towards Bethany, and He lifted up His hands and blessed them. And it came to pass as He blessed them, that He parted from them and was carried up into heaven" — Lk 24. 50-51.

THE HOLY MASS

The Mass is our Gift of love to the Father.

The ordained priest takes the place of Christ, our High Priest, and takes our place, too.

The Father is pleased with this Gift and invites us to eat at His table in Holy Communion.

The Liturgy of the Word of God

The priest comes to the foot of the altar and begins the prayers of preparation for Mass. The people may sing a hymn at this time.

Entrance Rite

GLORY be to the Father and to the Son and to the Holy Ghost.

The Mass—Christ's Gift and ours

AT THE KYRIE

Priest: Lord, have mercy. People: Lord, have mercy.
Priest: Lord, have mercy. People: Christ, have mercy.
Priest: Christ, have mercy. People: Christ, have mercy.
Priest: Lord, have mercy. People: Lord, have mercy.
Priest: Lord, have mercy.

AT THE GLORIA

Priest: Glory to God in the highest.

People: **And on earth peace to men of good will. * We praise You. We bless You. We worship You. We glorify You. * We give You thanks for Your great glory. * Lord God, heavenly King, God the Father almighty. * Lord Jesus Christ, the Only-begotten Son. * Lord God, Lamb of God, Son of the Father. * You, Who take away the sins of the world, * have mercy on us. * You, Who take away the sins of the world, * receive our prayer. * You, Who sit at the right hand of the Father, * have mercy on us. * For You alone are holy. * You alone are Lord. * You alone, O Jesus Christ, are most high, * With the Holy Spirit, in the glory of God the Father. Amen.**

— AT THE PRAYER (COLLECT) —

Priest: The Lord be with you. People: **And with your spirit.**

Priest: Let us pray . . . forever and ever. People: **Amen.**

The Word of God

AT THE END OF THE EPISTLE

Server (at low Mass) concludes: Thanks be to God.

AT THE GOSPEL

At the GOSPEL

Deacon (or Priest): The Lord be with you.

People: And with your spirit.

Deacon (or Priest): ✠ A reading from the holy Gospel according to N. . .

People: Glory to You, O Lord.

O GOD, I stand out of respect for the words of Your Son, Whom You have sent to teach us. Give me the grace to imitate Him.

We listen to the word of God

AT THE END OF THE GOSPEL

Server (at low Mass) concludes: Praise to you, O Christ.

AT THE NICENE CREED

Priest: I believe in one God.

People: **The Father almighty, Maker of heaven and earth, * and of all things visible and invisible. * And I believe in one Lord, Jesus Christ, * the Only-begotten Son of God. * Born of the Father before all ages. * God of God, Light of Light, true God of true God. * Begotten, not made, * of one substance with the Father. * By Whom all things were made. * Who for us men and for our salvation came down from heaven. * And He became Flesh by the Holy Spirit of the Virgin Mary: * AND WAS MADE MAN. * He was also crucified for us, * suffered under Pontius Pilate, and was buried. * And on the third day He rose again, according to the Scriptures. * He ascended into heaven and sits at the right hand of the Father. * He will come again in glory to judge the living and the dead. * And of His kingdom there will be no end. ***

And I believe in the Holy Spirit, the Lord and Giver of life, * Who proceeds from the Father and the Son. * Who together with the Father and the Son is adored and glorified, * and Who spoke through the Prophets. * And One Holy, Catholic, and Apostolic Church. * I confess one Baptism for the forgiveness of sins. * And I await the resurrection of the dead. * And the life of the world to come. Amen.

The Liturgy of the Eucharist

The Preparation of the Gifts

— AT THE OFFERTORY —

At the
OFFERTORY

We offer
Bread and
Wine

Priest: The Lord be with you.
People: And with your spirit.
Priest: Let us pray.

PRAYER OVER THE GIFTS (SECRET)

WE offer You, O Heavenly Father, our gifts of bread and wine as a sign of our love and our desire to give ourselves and all our actions to please You. We beg You to accept our offering. Come, Holy Spirit, and bless this sacrifice we offer to You in remembrance of the Passion, Resurrection and Ascension of Jesus Christ, our Lord. Priest: . . . forever and ever.

People: Amen.

The Eucharistic Prayer

At the
PREFACE

We give
thanks

AT THE PREFACE

Priest. The Lord be with you.

People: And with your spirit.

Priest: Lift up your hearts.

People: We have lifted them up to the Lord.

Priest: Let us give thanks to the Lord our God.

People: It is right and just.

YOU deserve, O God, that at all times and in all places we should give thanks to You through Christ our Lord. Let us sing Your praises in union with the Angels.

At the
SANCTUS

Our hymn
of praise

AT THE SANCTUS

People: **Holy, Holy, Holy Lord God of Hosts.** * **Heaven and earth are filled with Your Glory.** * **Hosanna in the highest.** *

Blessed is He Who comes in the name of the Lord. * **Hosanna in the highest.**

At the CONSECRATION

Look at the Host and say: "My Lord and my God!"

Adore the Precious Blood with the Priest.

THE CANON OF THE MASS

CONSECRATION OF THE BREAD

WHO, the day before He suffered, took bread into His holy and venerable hands, and having raised His eyes to heaven, to You, O God, His Almighty Father, giving thanks to You, He blessed it, ✠ broke it, and gave it to His disciples, saying: All of you take and eat of this:

FOR THIS IS MY BODY

CONSECRATION OF THE WINE

IN like manner, when the supper was done, taking also this goodly chalice into His holy and venerable hands, again giving thanks to You, He blessed ✠ it, and gave it to His disciples, saying: All of you take and drink of this:

FOR THIS IS THE CHALICE OF MY BLOOD OF THE NEW AND ETERNAL COVENANT: THE MYSTERY OF FAITH: WHICH SHALL BE SHED FOR YOU AND FOR MANY UNTO THE FORGIVENESS OF SINS.

As often as you shall do these things, in memory of Me shall you do them.

OFFERING OF THE VICTIM TO GOD

MINDFUL, therefore, O Lord, not only of the blessed passion of the same Christ, Your Son, our Lord, but also of His resurrection from the dead, and finally His glorious ascension into heaven, we Your ministers, as also Your holy people, offer to Your supreme Majesty, of the gifts bestowed upon us, the pure ✠ Victim, the holy ✠ Victim, the all-perfect ✠ Victim: the holy ✠ Bread of life eternal and the Chalice ✠ of unending salvation.

THE MINOR ELEVATION

THROUGH Him and with Him and in Him is to You God the Father Almighty all honor and glory.

AT THE CONCLUSION OF CANON

Priest: Per omnia saecula saeculorum. People: **Amen.**

(World without end.)

**At the
OUR FATHER**

We ask bread
for the body
and the soul

**At the
AGNUS DEI**

We prepare to
receive Jesus

**At the
COMMUNION
of the PRIEST**

The priest
receives Jesus

The Eucharistic Banquet

AT THE LORD'S PRAYER

Priest: Let us pray: Taught by our Savior's command and formed by the word of God, we dare to say:

People: **Our Father, Who art in heaven, * hallowed be Thy name; * Thy kingdom come; * Thy will be done on earth as it is in heaven. * Give us this day our daily bread; * and forgive us our trespasses * as we forgive those who trespass against us; * and lead us not into temptation, * but deliver us from evil. * Amen.**

AT THE PRAYER FOR PEACE

Priest: . . . . forever and ever.

People: **Amen.**

Priest: May the peace of the Lord be always with you.

People: **And with your spirit.**

AT THE AGNUS DEI

People: **Lamb of God, Who take away the sins of the world, * have mercy on us. ***

  Lamb of God, Who take away the sins of the world, * have mercy on us. *

  Lamb of God, Who take away the sins of the world, * grant us peace.

(*In Requiem Masses*: . . . grant them rest . . . grant them rest . . . grant them eternal rest.)

AT THE COMMUNION OF THE PRIEST

I will take the Bread of heaven, and call upon the name of the Lord.

Lord, I am not worthy that You should come under my roof. Speak but the word and my soul will be healed. (3 times).

May the Body of our Lord Jesus Christ preserve my soul to life everlasting. Amen.

May the Blood of our Lord Jesus Christ preserve my soul to life everlasting. Amen.

At the
COMMUNION
of the PEOPLE

We receive
Jesus

At the
LAST
BLESSING

The priest
blesses us

AT THE COMMUNION OF THE FAITHFUL

Priest: Behold the Lamb of God,* behold Him Who takes away the sins of the world.

People (three times): Lord, I am not worthy that You should come under my roof.* Speak but the word and my soul will be healed.

The Priest gives Holy Communion to each saying:

Priest: The Body of Christ.
Communicant: Amen.

(Thank Our Lord in your own words for coming into your heart and listen to Him in silence for a while.)

AT THE POSTCOMMUNION PRAYER

Priest: The Lord be with you.

People: And with your spirit.

Priest: Let us pray . . . forever and ever.

People: Amen.

AT THE DISMISSAL

Priest: The Lord be with you.
People: And with your spirit.
Deacon (or Priest): The Mass is ended. Go in peace.
People: Thanks be to God.

(In Requiem Masses: May they rest in peace.
People: Amen.

AT THE BLESSING

Priest: May almighty God bless you, the Father, and the Son, ✠ and the Holy Spirit.
People: Amen.